THE ECONOMICS OF R & D POLICY

THE ECONOMICS OF R & D POLICY

Edited by

George S. Tolley
James H. Hodge
James F. Oehmke

PRAEGER

PRAEGER SPECIAL STUDIES • PRAEGER SCIENTIFIC

New York • Philadelphia • Eastbourne, UK
Toronto • Hong Kong • Tokyo • Sydney

Library of Congress Cataloging in Publication Data
Main entry under title:

The Economics of R&D policy.

Bibliography: p.
Includes indexes.
1. Research—Economic aspects—United States.
2. Research, Industrial—Economic aspects—
United States. I. Tolley, George S., 1925—
II. Hodge, James H. III. Oehmke, James F. IV. Title:
Economics of R and D policy.
HC110.R4E28 1985 338'.06 85-6318
ISBN 0-03-000892-1 (alk. paper)

Published in 1985 by Praeger Publishers
CBS Educational and Professional Publishing, a Division of CBS Inc.
521 Fifth Avenue, New York, NY 10175 U.S.A.

56789 052 987654321

Printed in the United States of America on acid-free paper.

INTERNATIONAL OFFICES

Orders from outside the United States should be sent to the appropriate address listed below. Orders from areas not listed below should be placed through CBS International Publishing, 383 Madison Ave., New York, NY 10175 USA

Australia, New Zealand
Holt Saunders, Pty, Ltd., 9 Waltham St., Artarmon, N.S.W. 2064, Sidney, Australia

Canada
Holt, Rinehart & Winston of Canada, 55 Horner Ave., Toronto, Ontario, Canada M8Z 4X6

Europe, the Middle East, & Africa
Holt Saunders, Ltd., 1 St. Anne's Road, Eastbourne, East Sussex, England BN21 3UN

Japan
Holt Saunders, Ltd., Ichibancho Central Building, 22-1 Ichibancho, 3rd Floor, Chiyodaku, Tokyo, Japan

Hong Kong, Southeast Asia
Holt-Saunders Asia, Ltd., 10 Fl, Intercontinental Plaza, 94 Granville Road, Tsim Sha Tsui East, Kowloon, Hong Kong

Manuscript submissions should be sent to the Editorial Director, Praeger Publishers, 521 Fifth Avenue, New York, NY 10175 USA

List of Contributors

George S. Tolley
University of Chicago

James H. Hodge
IBM Corporation

Walter N. Thurman
North Carolina State University

James F. Oehmke
University of Chicago and
Michigan State University

Brian D. Wright
Yale University

Carole Kitti
U.S. Office of Management and Budget (OMB)

Ronald L. Engel
Chicago, IL

Joseph G. Asbury
Argonne National Laboratory

Stuart B. Townsend
BETASOFT
Chicago, IL

William Schulze
University of Colorado

Ronald G. Cummings
University of New Mexico

Stephen Barrager
Decision Focus, Inc.
Los Altos, CA

Oliver Gildersleeve
Electric Power Research Institute
Palo Alto, CA

Mark A. Grenchik
University of Chicago

Preface

Research and development (R & D) is more than ever a top national concern. Much interest in R & D stems from its widespread importance—extending from its role in finding better ways to cope with dwindling energy resources, to strategic competition with Eastern countries in arms and space technology, to concern over stagnant economic growth, to international competition in industrial technology and the decline in U.S. labor productivity.

Expenditures on R & D are large, and the economic returns are complicated and diverse, yet there has been much less attention to economic considerations for R & D than for other expenditures involving lesser amounts. As a result, the formulation of R & D policies has suffered from lack of in-depth knowledge.

The present volume attempts to bring the tools of economics more fully to bear on policy issues surrounding R & D. The book grapples with the unique characteristics of R & D: it takes place in a setting different from that of other expenditures. It involves greater than usual uncertainties, and the economic issues are more closely intertwined with other disciplines. This book contributes to the forging of links between the disciplines of economics, law, and the physical sciences—all of which must be included for adequate understanding.

Part 1 provides a fundamental framework. Part 2 is concerned with private and public R & D, bringing in technical, legal, and political considerations. Part 3 develops methods of benefit-cost analysis to improve funding decisions for R & D. Part 4 makes policy recommendations.

THE INTRODUCTION

Part 1 consists of an introductory chapter providing a framework for the evaluation of R & D policies. It draws on recent advances in the literature and develops new quantifiable models of economic incentives affecting private and public returns to R & D. The economics necessary to understand the profit incentives for R & D are presented in terms accessible to the informed reader. The groundwork is laid for later chapters on the effects of R & D policies and benefit-cost analysis.

PROVIDING FOR PRIVATE AND PUBLIC R & D

Part 2 examines how patents, trade secret laws, and other regulations affect decisions to invest in R & D and the social benefits derived from the research.

In Chapter 2, Brian D. Wright, associate professor of economics at Yale University, extends his previous work published in major academic journals. He demonstrates how patents, trade secret laws, and prizes and rewards to inventors affect the profit incentives for R & D. The limited effectiveness of the patent system in inducing an optimal number of inventions is brought out. This system is compared with others for giving rewards to inventors.

In Chapter 3, Carole Kitti of the U.S. Office of Management and Budget (OMB) discusses how different incentive systems affect the optimal timing of innovations. This chapter contains her seminal work in the area, showing how it is possible to determine the optimal date to start a new process and the reasons why this date might not be achieved. The current system contains many incentives to delay the innovation.

Chapter 4 concerns the practical effectiveness of patent laws. Ronald L. Engel, formerly of Kirkland and Ellis, shows that the court system is unduly slow to try patent cases, effectively limiting the redress inventors can seek if someone copies their invention. The long delays create substantial expenses in the form of losses in production and sales, high legal fees, and court costs.

Chapter 5 contains a discussion of an important type of government research institution: the national laboratory. Joseph G. Asbury, a physicist, economist, and high official at the Argonne National Laboratory, explains the role of national laboratories in R & D. He discusses which projects are suited for government investment, and which of these can be handled at a national laboratory. Asbury concludes that these institutions have a definite place in public R & D work, but are not always used as fully or effectively as they might be.

Each of the chapters in Part 2 suggests that the current system, with its strong dependency on patent laws, may be unable to provide adequate incentives to induce private corporations to invest in R & D. Although patents provide the successful researcher with a means of capturing part of the economic benefits from innovation, the share going to the innovator is often too small to cover the costs and risks of R & D. Moreover, the patent system provides no reward for innovations aiding society in areas such as foreign policy and space exploration that have no direct economic benefits. Wright suggests that the first problem can be alleviated by varying patent lives for different types of innovations. Asbury proposes that an increased R & D role for national laboratories can alleviate the latter problem.

R & D PROJECT EVALUATION

Part 3 focuses on the decision to undertake a particular R & D project. General considerations such as profitability and costs are examined, and specific examples demonstrate how to use the concepts.

Chapter 6 applies the principles of benefit-cost analysis to the evaluation of R & D projects. George S. Tolley, professor of economics at the University of Chicago, and Stuart B. Townsend of Betasoft, present a complete and widely applicable theoretical analysis, discussing what types of economic costs and benefits are involved and how market forces affect the size of the benefits. These authors develop a unique computer simulation model applicable to many R & D projects, as well as empirical results on energy storage R & D.

In Chapter 7, two of the nation's leading natural resource economists, William Schulze, professor of economics at the University of Colorado, and Ronald G. Cummings, professor of economics at the University of New Mexico, examine R & D funding decisions from two perspectives: the decision to develop a particular technology and the decision that a particular method of developing that technology is best. This division of the R & D process allows for continual monitoring of the project and the introduction of technical, engineering, institutional, and political considerations into an economic decision process. Solar heating systems are used as an example of the decision process and illustrate the need for this type of interdisciplinary approach.

In Chapter 8, Stephen Barrager of Decision Focus, Inc. and Oliver Gildersleeve of Electric Power Research Institute suggest solutions to several problems that arise from the uncertainty inherent in R & D projects, such as sensitivity analysis and participant review to select those variables that are to be treated probabilistically. An empirically applicable model is developed and used to examine the economic costs and benefits of various types of public utility technologies.

POLICY IMPLICATIONS

Chapter 9 examines the implications of the previous chapters. Important insights into the problem of R & D are summarized and used to bring new perspectives to current problems. George S. Tolley, James H. Hodge, and Mark A. Grenchik detail how the different disciplines involved in R & D projects affect each other and policy considerations. Recommendations are made on how overall government policies can increase the effectiveness of private and public R & D, and how the operation of particular R & D projects can be improved.

Most R & D activity is devoted to increasing the output of goods and services by lowering the cost of production. Hence, the benefits of R & D are readily approximated by the cost savings per good multiplied by the number of goods sold. Noneconomic benefits may be somewhat more difficult to quantify. Even so, serious estimates of nondollar effects can and should be developed so that better decisions can be made by objectively weighing consequences. Thus, it is possible to objectively determine how much R & D should be undertaken.

The immediate question becomes: Are we currently undertaking the right amount of R & D? The answer depends on the effectiveness of current government R & D policies. Whereas almost certainly there are highly significant distortions in the kinds of R & D being undertaken, it is difficult at this time to say whether there is too much or too little R & D as a whole. However, in some instances, it is reasonably clear that more R & D would be advantageous. Cases in which a general patent system does not adequately promote certain types of R & D occur when, despite patent protection, an inventor is not adequately rewarded for an invention that produces benefits in the national interest that exceed those reflected in market incentives. Weapons development provides an example. In basic research preeminently, and in certain applied areas such as health and foreign energy dependence, a case can be made that there can be gains from promoting more and different R & D than would occur under private incentives as fostered by patents. Because of the national security and foreign policy implications of dependence on foreign oil, government sponsorship of R & D resulting in less oil use appears called for, over and above that decline brought about by the fluctuations in oil prices of the last decade.

If more R & D is needed, what policies should be pursued? The earlier chapters of this book suggest several promising policy recommendations. These include varying the length of the patent term and passage of legislation which strengthens and clarifies protection against patent infringement as well as a greater commitment in the funding of the Patent and Trademark Office, the agency which is responsible for carrying out such legislation. Policy instruments such as fuel tariffs, R & D tax incentives, prizes, and direct funding by the government are other possibilities. It is recommended that those government activities and policies be avoided which discourage private inventive activity. This book provides a comprehensive analysis of government research policies and their effects on incentives for public and private R & D.

Much of the work for this book was done under a grant from Exxon to the Resource Analysis Group of the Committee on Public Studies of the University of Chicago. Members of the Resource Analysis Group made valuable contributions in framing topics and commenting on results. These and other individuals who contributed thinking to the volume include Joseph Asbury, Stephen Berry, Joel Gibbons, Mark Grenchik, Michael Knoll, Brent Kroetsch, Ronald Krumm, Victor Levy, Thomas Long, Theodore Schultz, Larry Sjaastad, Siddarth Tiwari and Stuart Townsend. The art work was done by Betsy Brooks. Special acknowledgment should be given to Mark Grenchik for his editorial assistance.

Contents

PREFACE vii

PART 1. INTRODUCTION 1

1. A Framework for Evaluation of R & D Policies 3
George S. Tolley, James H. Hodge, Walter N. Thurman, and James F. Oehmke

PART 2. PROBLEMS IN PROVIDING FOR PUBLIC AND PRIVATE R & D 39

2. The Resource Allocation Problem in R & D 41
Brian D. Wright

3. Patent Life and the Optimal Timing of Innovations 70
Carole Kitti

4. Patent Enforcement: The Uncertainties of Patent Litigation 95
Ronald L. Engel

5. The Role of National Laboratories in R & D 102
Joseph G. Asbury

PART 3. R & D PROJECT EVALUATION 123

6. Project Evaluation Approach to R & D 125
George S. Tolley and Stuart B. Townsend

7. Economic Analysis of a Technology at the Early Stages of Its Development 138
Ronald G. Cummings and William Schulze

8. A Methodology to Incorporate Uncertainty into R & D Cost and Performance Data 149
Stephen Barrager and Oliver Gildersleeve

PART 4. POLICY IMPLICATIONS 171

9. Toward Improved R & D Policy 173
George S. Tolley, James H. Hodge, and Mark A. Grenchik

INDEX 189

I
Introduction

1

A Framework for Evaluation of R & D Policies

George S. Tolley, James H. Hodge, Walter N. Thurman, and James F. Oehmke

The problem of devising a framework for evaluating research and development (R & D) policies and projects raises a number of issues, which have been explored in various degrees of depth. The issues include those produced by differences between private and public incentives to undertake R & D, such as appropriability of gains and timing of the activity, the effect of different market structures on R & D efforts, measurement of social and private returns to R & D, the effects of patents, licensing, trade secret laws, tax laws, government sponsorship of research, and other policies on actual and optimal R & D activities, as well as the evaluation of particular R & D projects.

A major challenge is to consider these diverse subjects in a coherent fashion that will provide a formulation for policy. Quantitative insights are required in devising wise R & D policies. With this challenge in mind, the present chapter attempts to integrate and put into perspective major strands of investigation of R & D. It provides a framework for bringing together and contributing to the growing amount of economic analysis concerned with R & D, setting the stage for the remainder of the book. Major previous work is critiqued. Of most importance, a set of unified analytical models containing key parameters is developed. One of the contributions of the modeling in this chapter is to bring out considerations bearing on the magnitude of various effects that have previously been considered, if at all, only in qualitative terms.

Following this introductory section, the next section of the chapter considers the relation between social goals and the incentives to undertake R & D. A first topic considered is how the inability to appropriate all the returns from R & D activity causes the amount of such activity undertaken to be less than socially optimal. The next subject is the contrary incentive given by a patent system to engage in too much R & D activity because of the fear of not being the first to patent an innovation. Then, consideration is given to the recent literature on the mixed incentives of imperfect competition and other industrial organization effects on R & D. Later in the chapter, the model developed earlier is extended to show the extent to which externalities in the markets for goods produced with innovations can cause the amount and timing of R & D to deviate from a socially optimal course. Results are considered for energy and agriculture.

The third section of this chapter deals with how to estimate the returns to R & D investment, reviewing methods that have been used and commenting on procedures needed in working with applied and basic research. The two most commonly used means of estimating benefits are direct estimation of benefits and costs associated with a particular project and regression analysis for a firm or industry. The applicability of the former to ex ante analyses of applied research projects is discussed, with particular attention given to data requirements and availability. Regression analysis is more frequently used to estimate the profitability and marginal rates of return of investment in research. The role of such ex post information in making decisions about levels of funding is examined and compared with its role in determining which particular projects should be funded.

The fourth section is concerned with policies affecting R & D activity. Analytical models are developed, showing the effects of patents on incentives and the determination of the socially optimal life of a patent. Attention is then turned to the relations between patents and licensing and to the effects that patent enforcement and regulation have on incentives to undertake R & D. Reasons why the trade secret approach is sometimes followed in preference to patents are considered next. The analytical model is then extended to analyze the effects of tax incentives on R & D.

Government-sponsored R & D is also considered. Topics include the extent to which government and private R & D are competing or complementary, the reward structure for government-sponsored R & D, policy for national laboratories, and the development of ex ante evaluation procedures for choosing among potential R & D projects.

Finally, directions for the improvement of R & D policies suggested by the analysis are indicated.

INVENTIVE ACTIVITY AND ITS RELATION TO SOCIAL GOALS

The Private and Social Rewards from R & D

Following Arrow (1962), Demsetz (1969), Scherer (1972), and others, let an innovation be represented by shifting the supply curve down from S to S' in Figure 1.1.

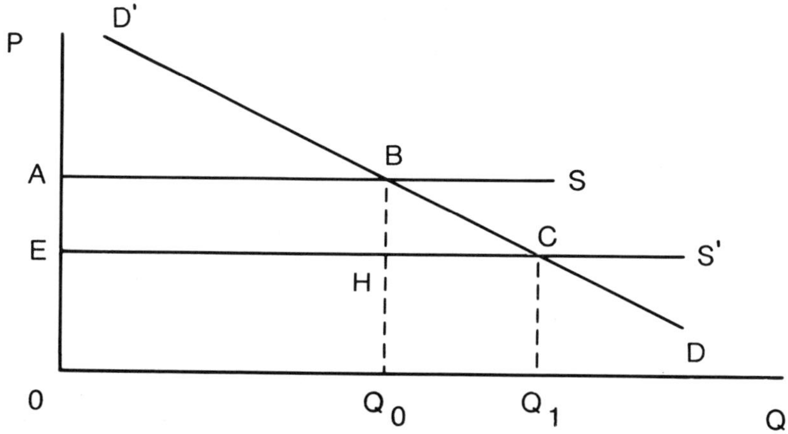

FIGURE 1.1

For the moment, assume the market is competitive and that property rights over the innovation cannot be enforced; i.e., it can be freely copied. The innovation may then be adopted by everyone in the market, and the supply curve will shift down from S to S'. The social benefits generated by such a process are the increase in the area between the demand and supply curve. This is equal to the trapezoid $ABCE$. The rectangle $ABHE$ represents the benefits associated with the reduction in price of each good already sold. The area in triangle BCH represents the worth to society of the new goods sold minus the costs of producing them.

Another situation is the case of a company in a competitive industry that produces an innovation. If the company can capture the property rights to the innovation, say, through a patent, it can act as a monopolist within certain bounds. Assume that the company lowers its costs of production from S to S'. It will now face a demand curve given by ABC. That is, beyond B, it is the only firm that can produce the good at the price demanded. In this region, it acts like a classical monopolist, but for outputs lower than B, it cannot set its price above the old market because of competition from other firms. Thus, it will face the demand and supply situation shown in Figure 1.2. The old demand curve the industry faced before the innovation is D'. The demand curve the innovating firm now confronts is ABC. It faces an associated marginal revenue curve given by $ABFG$. The drop in marginal revenue is given by the kink in the demand curve at B. Acting as a monopolist, the firm will produce where its marginal cost curve (represented by S') intersects the marginal revenue curve. For any reductions in cost less than $B - F$, the monopolist will produce the same quantity that the industry produced before the innovation, since the marginal cost curve will intersect only the discontinuous section of the marginal revenue curve associated with the kink in demand at Q_0. In this situation, the

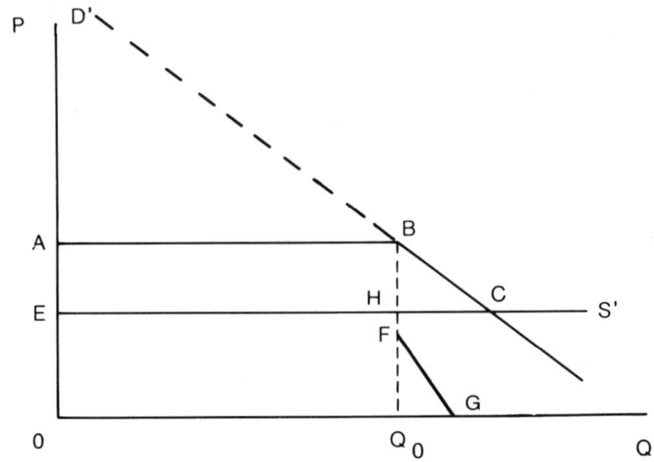

FIGURE 1.2

price remains the same, the quantity produced remains the same, but the profits associated with production rise and are represented by the area *ABHE*. This area represents the social benefits associated with production. If there is a large fall in production costs, then the new marginal cost curve may intersect the *FG* portion of the marginal revenue curve. In this case, production will increase, and the price at which the good is sold will fall. Again, the social benefits earned are measured by the increase in the area between the demand and supply schedules.

Identical results will be obtained if an innovator separate from the industry licenses the innovation to maximize the rental stream from it. A more complex discussion of patents and licensing is given by Brian D. Wright in Chapter 2. He includes a discussion of which industries are most likely to patent, and comments on the possible effects of such patents on market structure.

An innovator has incentive to allocate resources to producing more innovation as long as the returns exceed the costs of doing so.

In Figure 1.3, there is an initial supply curve *S* and a research effort equal to *Q′*, which will produce an innovation shifting the cost curve to *S′* and, assuming production is socially optimal, will lead to benefits *ABCE*. This addition to national welfare is represented by the area of the shaded trapezoid in the graph on the right. The marginal cost curve for producing innovations is *MC*.

Innovations should be produced to the point where *MB* and *MC* intersect to obtain maximum social benefits. In the situation in which the innovation is produced privately by an institution that can capture the associated property rights, the innovator will not receive all the benefits from the innovation. Thus, the private marginal benefit curve will lie below the social marginal benefit curve. This happens because the social benefit, given by area *ABCE*, is greater than the private benefit, given by area *ABHE*. These marginal benefit and marginal cost curves can be aggregated to obtain the analogous curves for all possible innovations.

Even if persons can capture the immediate benefits from an innovation, it is not clear whether they can earn these same benefits period after period. As the innovation becomes well known, people will tend to copy it and compete away the benefits the inventor enjoys over time. Thus, in a completely free market, the innovator is faced with, at worst, not being able to capture any benefits of the innovation or, at best, watching the size of the stream of benefits dwindle over time.

However, if innovators can capture some or all of the benefits of their innovation for a time, possibly through patents, trade secrets, or time lags in the copying of the innovation, then they will earn excess profits *ABHE* for that time. Levin (1978), Dasgupta and Stiglitz (1980), and others show that when R & D is an ongoing process and the first successful innovation provides an advantage in developing further innovations, then the innovator can perpetuate an excess profit situation. The advantage in developing newer innovations is a decrease in the cost of future R & D for the successful innovator relative to the unsuccessful researchers. A closer look at Levin's model is worthwhile. Two possible explanations for the reduction in the future cost of R & D are considered: cumulative advances in knowledge and ease in obtaining funds. If successful innovators gain insight from solving their R & D problem, and this advance in knowledge enables them to solve similar problems more quickly or more easily, then further research is less

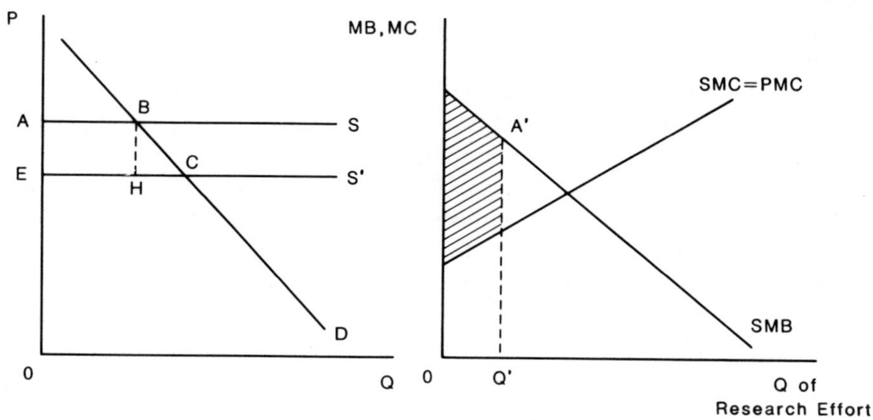

FIGURE 1.3

costly for them. The nature of this specialized knowledge is extremely influential in determining whether or not a firm can maintain an advantage. If the insights affect only the researchers' human capital, then they can be hired away by other firms and the advantage is lost. If the insight is firm specific but not worker specific, then hiring away the researchers will not help and the innovating firm will maintain its advantage until other firms can copy it, which may involve a time lag. Most likely, the advance in knowledge will be somewhat firm specific, but will also affect the researchers' human capital. For example, as part of an R & D project, a firm may redesign a laboratory to implement a new procedure, and the new laboratory setup may be vastly superior to the old. Workers in the laboratory will know the new setup and can be hired away by competing firms, but there may be a significant time lag before the competing firms can use this knowledge to rearrange laboratories. Thus, the original firm enjoys an advantage for what could be a considerable length of time.

Additional advantages may be enjoyed by successful innovators if they are able to receive better terms on the financing of future R & D projects (Kamien and Schwarz, 1980). This advantage occurs because many R & D projects are perceived as risky by investors, and thus firms must pay a large premium to finance them. Successful innovation may alter these perceptions, so that a firm that has been successful in the past pays a lower premium than do unsuccessful firms. (Note that a competing firm hiring away the head of a successful R & D division may also obtain this advantage.) Moreover, if the firm's perception of the riskiness of future R & D differs from market perception, then it can finance projects from its excess profits at a comparative advantage to other firms, since they have no internal funding (assuming they are competitive and operating so that price equals average cost).

Four important points about these types of advantages should be mentioned. First, it will be shown below that the crucial assumption is that the innovating firm has a cost advantage in pursuing further R & D. Numerous reasons can be given for why these advantages come about (Kamien and Schwarz, 1982), but it does not matter if it is because of accumulated knowledge, better financing, or better exploitation of market information (Nelson, 1959), so long as there is an advantage. Second, the existence of a cost advantage is assumed to imply a greater amount of R & D undertaken (see Figure 1.5). But if R & D shows some form of diminishing returns to scale, it may be that the benefits from further R & D are less for the successful innovator than for other firms, so that in the future relatively less R & D is undertaken by the innovator. Third, this description assumes that a firm is some well-defined, easily recognizable entity. It is not possible to summarize the theory of the firm literature in this chapter, but it should be noted that there is little agreement on the essence of a firm, so it is not clear how to interpret the loss of

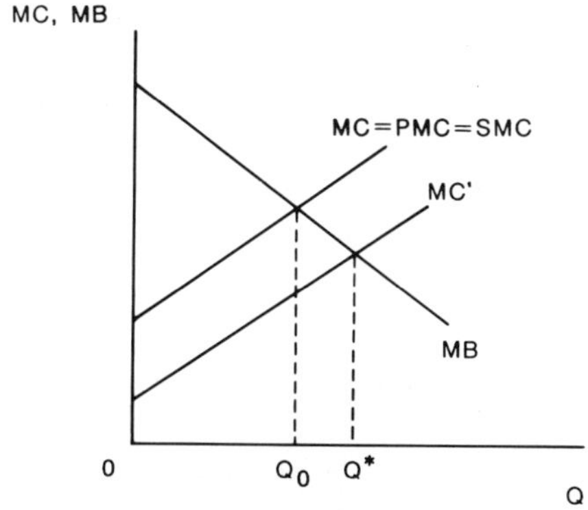

FIGURE 1.4

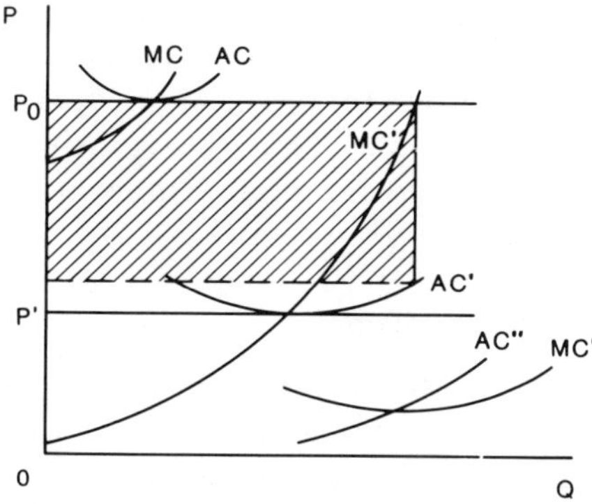

FIGURE 1.5

a research scientist or an entire R & D division to a competing firm [for a summary of literature on the nature of the firm, see Williamson (1981), see also Schumpeter (1934), Knight (1921), and Coase (1927)]. This muddies the concept of a firm's comparative advantage and causes difficulties in empirical testing. Fourth, the above discussion does not show that the firm can maintain an advantage from a single innovation, but indicates that the firm must continually innovate. This ongoing change is the reason that Levin is able to construct a model in which a successful innovator can perpetuate an excess profit situation.

In Levin's model, the perpetuation of excess profits is a direct result of the perpetuation of a comparative cost advantage. The cost advantage is represented diagramatically by a shift of the marginal and average cost curves from MC and AC to MC' and AC' for the successful innovator, while the curve remains at MC for competing firms. The shaded area represents the excess profits captured by the innovator until the industry discovers and implements the new technology.

For reasons discussed above, the innovating firm enjoys an advantage in undertaking future R & D, so that its cost of research curve shifts down and to the right. This implies that the innovator will undertake a quantity Q^* of R & D greater than the quantity Q_0 undertaken by competing firms. Assuming this increased R & D expenditure causes earlier innovation, the original innovator will be able to perpetuate this technological advantage and consistently earn excess profits. As a simple illustration, suppose that the first innovation occurs at time 0 and shifts the cost curves to MC' and AC'. By the time other firms duplicate the invention, the original innovator has further reduced costs so that he or she faces MC'' and AC'', again earning excess profits.

The above example clearly indicates that although the successful innovator can maintain an excess profit situation for a (perhaps long) period of time, eventually these profits must go to zero. Although the evidence from empirical studies is far from conclusive, it does seem to indicate that firms can maintain excess profits for a time but not perpetually [for a summary see Kamien and Schwarz (1982)]. Thus, the scenario in which innovators watch their stream of benefits from one or more innovations dwindle over time is perhaps the most likely one.

Analytical Model

The above points can be represented in a simple algebraic form, which will be useful for later developments of the chapter. In any period, the present value of the social benefits of any innovation may be represented by V_s. Assuming that demand and cost conditions stay the same over time, V_s is equal to $\int_0^\infty V_0 e^{-rt} dt$ or $V_s = V_0/r$, where V_0 is the per period social benefit.

Let the fraction of social benefits captured by the innovator in the initial period be B, and assume that these benefits will be eroded away over time at a rate of γ. Then V_p, the present value of the private benefits, is $\int_0^\infty BV_0 e^{-(r+\gamma)t} dt$ or $V_p = BV_0/(\gamma + r)$.

If Levin's model is correct, then the above expression must be modified slightly. Suppose that in addition to the immediate private benefits V_p, the firm experiences cost reductions in future R & D projects. If the firm undertakes these projects, then society also experiences the cost reduction. As a first approximation, the per period societal benefits from the cost reduction can be represented as the area between the two marginal cost curves MC and MC', the marginal benefits curve MB, and the vertical axis (Figure 1.4). Let V_0' denote the amount of these benefits. Assume that the innovator captures a fraction B' of these benefits and that his or her share is eroded away over time at rate γ' (which may be a function of future R & D expenditures). The equation for the present value of the private benefits then becomes

$$V_p' = \int_0^\infty BV_0 e^{-(r+\gamma)t} dt + \int_0^\infty B'V_0' e^{-(r+\gamma')t} dt'$$

or

$$V_p' = \frac{BV_0}{\gamma + r} + \frac{B'V_0'}{\gamma' + r}.$$

In the special case when $B' = B$ and $\gamma' = \gamma$, the simpler expression $V_p = BV_0/(\gamma + r)$ holds so long as V_0 and V_p are interpreted to include not only benefits of the immediate decline in production costs but also the impact of the innovation on future R & D costs. Note that in any case where $B < 1$ or $B' < 1$, there will be underinvestment in R & D.

The Problem of Timing of Innovations

The preceding analysis dealt with the traditional idea that copiability leads to incentives to underinvest in R & D. The concomitant existence of incentives to overinvest was apparently first the object of a study by Arrow (1962) and of later work by Barzel (1968), Kitti (1973), Loury (1979), Dasgupta and Stiglitz (1980a,b), Dasgupta (1981), Kamien and Schwarz (1976, 1982), and others.

Figure 1.6 shows the net present value of the social benefits of an innovation as a function of the time it is introduced. As will be brought out below, more resources devoted to an innovation will bring it on line sooner. However, increasing costs make it nonoptimal to produce the innovation instantaneously. The production of knowledge needed for applied research leading to the innovation may also affect the timing of the research. Changes in factor prices and in the demand for products over time could affect optimal timing.

Barzel's major point is that private innovators have incentives to produce the innovation at a time earlier than the socially optimal time because they are afraid that others will produce it first and capture all the benefits. The incentives lead to having the innovation come on line as soon as the present value becomes positive, which, as can be seen from Figure 1.6, is prior to the socially optimal value.

Analytical Model

The following model is developed to illustrate Barzel's point more fully. In Chapter 3, Carole Kitti provides a detailed analysis of the optimal timing

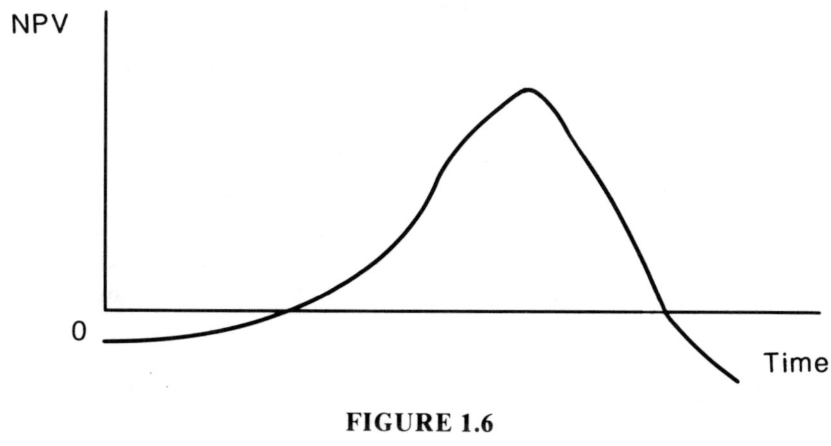

FIGURE 1.6

question. The model she develops is general enough and shows that patents increase the incentives to innovate prematurely.

Let the present value of resources devoted to producing an innovation be R, and consider the production function

$$R = R(t),$$

where t is the time the innovation is introduced. This relation indicates the amount of resources required to introduce the innovation at any given time. The resources required decrease as the time becomes more distant for two reasons. First, the present value of costs is less the further in the future they occur. Second, it is more expensive to produce an innovation immediately than it is to conduct the research over time.

For simplicity, assume $R(t)$ can be written as

$$R(t) = Ce^{-at},$$

where C is the cost of producing the innovation in the present time period. In this function, a is the percentage increase in resources required to produce the innovation one year earlier.

The problem is to maximize the social gain from the innovation, which is

$$G = V_s e^{-rt} - R(t),$$

where V_s, as in the preceding section, is the present value of social benefits at the time the innovation is introduced. The marginal rule that gives the optimal time to introduce an innovation is

$$\frac{\partial G}{\partial t}(t_s) = 0 = -rV_s e^{-rt_s} + aCe^{-at_s},$$

where t_s is the socially optimal time. Rearrangement of this expression yields the following optimal time:

$$t_s = \frac{1}{a - r} \ln \frac{Ca}{rV_s} \, .$$

The cases of interest are those in which the percentage increase in resources required to produce the innovation one year earlier is greater than the interest rate ($a > r$), since otherwise the innovation should be produced immediately.

How does this socially optimal time of innovation compare with time brought about by private decision makers? Private entrepreneurs, afraid of losing the returns of an innovation to a competitor, will produce the innovation over a time period that drives profits to zero, making average returns equal to average costs, instead of at the point where the marginal returns equal marginal costs. Thus, the time t_p brought about by private decisions is such that

$$V_p e^{-rt_p} = R(t) = Ce^{-at_p}$$

where V_p is the present value of the returns available to the innovator at the time of introduction. Solving this equation for the time t_p yields

$$t_p = \frac{1}{a - r} \ln \frac{C}{V_p}$$

As long as V_p is greater than $(r/a)V_s$, t_p will be less than t_s. Substituting in the values for V_s and V_p from the first section of the chapter, this condition becomes

$$Ba > r + \gamma.$$

The inequality may not hold if B, which is the percentage of the total benefits in any period that the innovator captures, is small or if γ, the rate at which the benefits are dissipated, is high.

In Figure 1.7, the Ce^{-at} curve shows how the costs of the innovation decrease the longer the innovation is delayed. The $V_s e^{-rt}$ and $V_p e^{-rt}$ curves show how the present value of the social and private benefits decay the longer

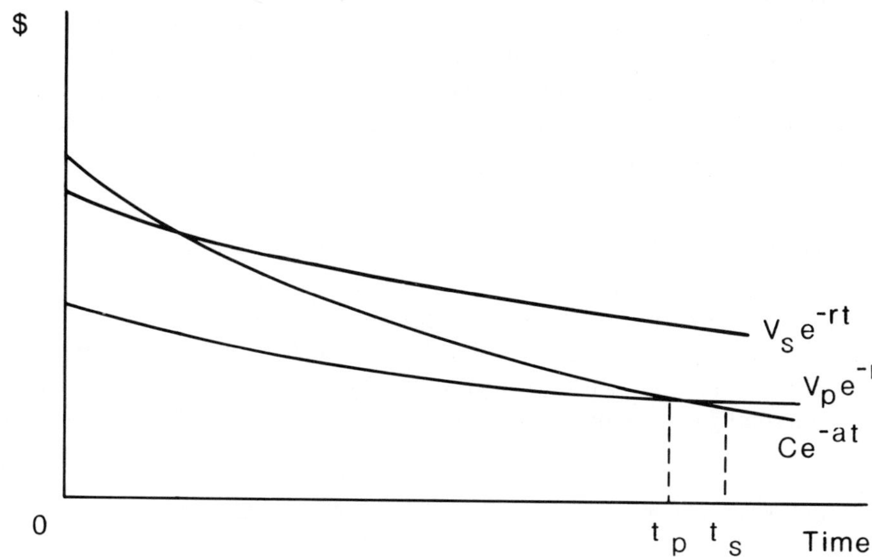

FIGURE 1.7

the innovation is delayed. As discussed in the preceding section, the social return is likely to be greater than the private return.

The actual time of introduction t_p is the earliest time at which the innovation can be brought on line without making negative profits, given by the point where the private return curve $V_p e^{-rt}$ cuts the curve Ce^{-at} from below. The time t_p may be earlier than the socially optimal time t_s for maximizing the distance from the social benefit curve $V_s e^{-rt}$ to the cost curve Ce^{-at}.

Thus, there are distortions acting in opposite directions. The first is that there is an incentive to underinvest in R & D and, once developed, to delay the production of an innovation because the inventor cannot appropriate all the benefits associated with it. A tendency for the firm to overinvest in R & D is imparted by the fact that if it can capture excess profits for a time, it may be able to perpetuate this advantage. An industry with a competitive market structure tends to overinvest in R & D because the large number of firms in the industry means that they will duplicate each other's research efforts. A tendency for the firm to innovate before it is socially optimal is conveyed by the fact that the innovator has an incentive to introduce an innovation too early to make sure he or she does not lose the benefits from it to a competitor. As indicated by the inequality $Ba > r + \gamma$, the innovation will be introduced too soon if the proportion of the benefits B captured by the inventor multiplied by the percentage increase in resources required to advance the discovery by a year a is greater than the sum of the rate of interest r plus the rate of decay of benefits γ. The innovation will be introduced too late if the condition is reversed. This condition provides a basis for gaining quantitative insights, as well as suggesting magnitudes in need of estimation. If the inventor receives half the benefits ($B =$ 0.5), the resources parameter is 0.4, the rate of interest is 0.1, and the rate of decay is 0.1, the actual and optimal times will coincide. It seems quite possible that, depending on the type of R & D, there are cases in which there is too much investment in R & D and others in which there is too little.

Imperfect Competition

Thus far, innovation has been assumed to occur in a market that, at least at the start, is perfectly competitive. Recently, however, economists have focused attention on technical progress in noncompetitive markets and the effects of industrial organization on the innovative process. Much of this work is an attempt to explicitly model Schumpeter's statement (1954):

> A system—any system, economic or other—that at *every* given point of time, fully utilizes its possibilities to the best advantage may yet in the long run be inferior to a system that does so at *no* given point of time, because the latter's failure to do so may be a condition for the level or speed of long-run performance.

Static analysis clearly shows that competitive equilibrium is economically optimal; the classic treatise is Debreu's *Theory of Value* (1959). However, it has already been pointed out that competition leads to the suboptimal timing of innovation in a Barzelian world, bearing out Schumpeter's statement that a form of industrial structure that is not optimal at any given point of time may be the most efficient in a dynamic sense. Much of the recent literature on R & D uses an industrial organization-type approach to show that certain noncompetitive markets could lead to more efficient investment in R & D. Good surveys of this work are provided by Dasgupta (1981) and Kamien and Schwarz (1982). Here, the industrial organization argument will be developed and related to the model developed above.

To determine the points of time at which a system should diverge from static efficiency to achieve dynamic efficiency, it is necessary to specify a relationship between industrial structure, the intensity (or sometimes level) of investment in R & D, and the timing of innovation. Following Dasgupta and Stiglitz (1980), consider an oligopolistic industry with free entry. Assume that the unit cost facing firm i depends on the amount of R & D undertaken by that firm; i.e., $c_i = c(x_i)$, where c is unit cost, x is the amount of R & D, and i is a subscript indexing the firm. Assume that the functional form of the unit cost function is independent of the firm, and for simplicity assume that $c(0) = \infty$. In a Cournot game, firm i maximizes profit by solving

$$\max_{x_i,\, Q_i} [p(Q_i + \hat{Q}_i)Q_i - c(x_i)Q_i - x_i],$$

where

$$\hat{Q}_i = \sum_{j \neq i} Q_j .$$

Assuming that the functions are well behaved, this yields the first-order conditions

$$c(x_i) = p(Q)\left(1 + \frac{EQ_i}{Q}\right)$$

$$1 = -Q_i c'(x_i)$$

where Q is the total output of the industry and E is the elasticity of demand for the product. In a symmetric Cournot equilibrium, let n^* be the number of firms in the market, Q^* be the equilibrium industry output, and x^* the R & D expenditure of any firm. The first-order condition on Q_i becomes

$$c(x^*) = p(Q^*)\left(1 + \frac{E}{n^*}\right) \cdot$$

A free-entry condition is the zero-profit equation

$$n^*x^* = [p(Q^*) - c(x^*)]Q^*.$$

Combining the last two equations yields

$$\frac{1}{n^*} = \frac{z^*}{-E},$$

where $z^* = n^*x^*/pQ^*$. Since the markets are in symmetric equilibrium, the usual concentration ratios are not helpful in making intermarket comparisons, but $1/n^*$ can be interpreted as an index of the degree of concentration. z^* is the percentage of gross revenue spent on R & D and thus is interpreted as an index of research intensity. Clearly then, the determinants of the industrial structure also affect the level of R & D.

Since different industrial structures are associated with different intensities of R & D effort, it will usually be the case that only one industrial structure is associated with the socially optimal level of R & D. Moreover, the relationship between n^* and z^* expressed above indicates that competition is likely to be associated with highly intense R & D, quite possibly leading to an excessive amount of resources invested in it. Dasgupta and Stiglitz show that this is indeed the case by comparing the Cournot game to a socially planned economy, and conclude that some form of oligopoly is optimal.

Industrial structure is related not only to the intensity of R & D effort, but also to the timing of innovation. It is intuitively plausible to expect a positive correlation between R & D expenditure and speed of innovation. Thus, the qualitative relationship between industrial structure and time until innovation should be the same as that between industrial structure and intensity of R & D effort. In a more formal manner, Dasgupta and Stiglitz do obtain the Barzelian result that competition leads to innovations too quickly.

Although this result depends on the assumptions that firms behave in a Cournot manner and that equilibrium is symmetric, other authors have found similar results with slightly different assumptions (e.g., Loury, 1979; Kamien and Schwarz, 1980; Reinganum, 1980; Fethke and Birch, 1982). A particularly interesting model is developed by Telser (1984), and shows that firms will sometimes merge to increase the profits from innovation. This increase in profits can occur not only from the greater market share, but also from the availability of the patented information to both firms and hence possible cost reductions. The important point in these models is that market structure affects the returns to successful innovations.

Analytical Model

The model developed above is easily modified to include the effects of market structure on the private benefits to an innovator. Note that earlier the fraction of the social benefits accruing to a private innovator was denoted by *B*, but no explanation was given concerning the determinants of this variable. As a first approximation, *B* can be said to depend on the initial market structure. Since the amount of R & D expenditures depends on *B*, this is a simple way to incorporate the relationship between market structure and R & D into the Barzelian framework. In a more realistic approach, the percentage of the social benefits that the private innovator can capture should be jointly determined with the market structure at the time of innovation and after and with the amount of R & D expenditures. However, the existing literature has not adequately explored this problem. Determination of an equilibrium and other considerations force authors to make simplifying assumptions: Dasgupta and Stiglitz assume the equilibrium is symmetric; Telser (1982) assumes that the firm can keep its innovation secret and in the absence of externalities will capture all the benefits. The empirical evidence does not yield clear answers: Schmookler finds that concentration increases R & D intensity, whereas Griliches et al. (1984) have evidence to the contrary. For the present purposes, however, the contribution of the industrial organizations literature to the general framework is adequately summarized by having *B* vary with the type of market structure.

Externalities: The Energy Example

There may be significant divergences between the social and the private benefits, apart from the fixation of benefits accruing to the inventor. An example is provided by energy and the threat of oil embargo. This topic has been a matter of concern to several economists including Tolley and Wilman (1977). The demand and supply situation in the United States is shown in Figure 1.8. At the world price W_p, the United States produces Q_0 amount of oil and consumes Q_1 amount of oil. In the absence of an embargo threat, an innovation that lowers the domestic supply curve to *S′* will result in a gain per period to society measured by the area *ABCH*.

A consequence of the possibility of oil embargo by foreign producers is that there are externalities associated with consuming foreign oil, stemming from unemployment and foreign policy cost resulting from oil supply disruption. The social price of purchasing world oil is the actual per unit price of oil on the world market plus *T*, the associated per unit external cost associated with the purchase of the oil. Thus, the social price is higher than the world price, as shown in Figure 1.8.

Since the private price is W_p, Q_0 of domestic oil is produced and *I* is imported. The resource costs of this consumption are given by *OABEFQ*. An innovation that lowers the supply curve from *S* to *S′* results in two types of gains. The first is analogous to the gains generated in the absence of the externality represented by area *ABCH*. The second is the extra gain associated

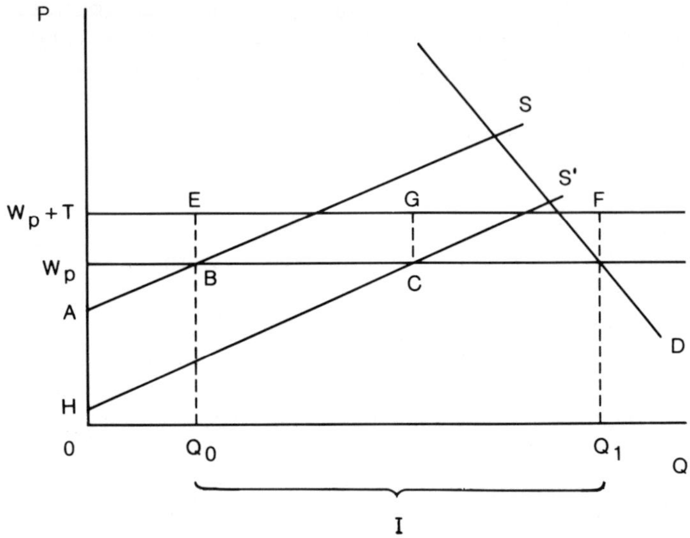

FIGURE 1.8

with reduction of the external costs as represented by the area *EGCB*. Thus, the social gains associated with the innovation have been increased.

Analytical Model

The effect of such an externality can be represented explicitly in the model developed above. Previously, the social benefits generated in any period were defined as V_0. With the oil externality, the social benefits will be αV_0, where $\alpha > 1$ will be determined below. Employing the demand and supply setup, it is known that the private gain associated with a reduction in the cost of producing oil is represented by the gain in the producer's surplus.

To derive an expression for α, assume that there is a linear supply curve of domestic oil in the form

$$P = A + bQ_s \text{ or } Q_s = \frac{P - A}{b} .$$

Substituting this expression into producer surplus $\int_A^{W_p} Q_s(P)dP$ yields a value of producer surplus S equal to

$$\frac{W_p^2}{2b} - \frac{AW_p}{b} + \frac{A^2}{2b} .$$

This is a measure of the V_0 generated by an innovation. The extra social benefit associated with the externality rectangle in Figure 1.8 is equal to the externality cost multiplied by the change in the quantity of domestic oil produced as a result of an innovation, represented by a change in A. Noting that $dQ = -dA/b$, one obtains the external benefit as $W_p\tau(-dA/b)$, where τ is the percentage difference between the private and social world price. Tolley and Wilman (1977) give a numerical example where τ is 14 percent. Thus, the size of the extra social gain relative to V_0 equals

$$\frac{-0.14\ W_p dA/b}{-(W_p - A)dA/b}$$

or

$$\frac{0.14}{1 - A/W_p}\ .$$

The value of A/W_p is closer to 1 the flatter the supply curve is. For example, assume that A is one-tenth of W_p. This implies that the extra welfare gain not taken into account by private individuals is $0.16V_0$. In this case, the α in the expression for social benefits, αV_0, is 1.16. That is, in this instance, the actual gain to an innovation is 1.16 times the size of the generated just employing market data.

Since t_s, the optimal time of the introduction of an innovation, is $1/(a-r) \cdot \ln aC/r\alpha V_0$, where αV_0 has been substituted for V_s, it can be seen that the size of α may have substantial effects on t_s. In the above example, a value for α of 1.16 substantially lowers the time over which an innovation should be produced and then introduced to the market.

Subtracting the value of t_s with the externality from t_s without the externality gives the decrease in time imparted by the existence of the externality as

$$\frac{1}{a-r}\ln \alpha.$$

Combining the value of α of 1.16 with $a = 0.12$ and $r = 0.1$ gives a decrease in the optimal time due to the externality of 1.48 years. Using the expression for resources required, $R = Ce^{-at}$, implies $\ln R_l/R_0 = a(t_1 - t_0)$ or 0.2(1.48) and gives a change in the optimal amount of resources devoted to innovation of approximately 35 percent.

The discussion to this point has considered the effects of the introduction of an externality on the amount of resources devoted to innovation. In the case of energy, there has also been a quadrupling of the price of oil, which increases the returns V_s and V_p and does not represent an externality. Using the expressions for t_s and t_p given earlier, the actual and optimal times are both decreased by $1/(a-r) \ln V_1/V_2$, or in the example with $a = 0.2$, $r = 0.1$, and $V_l/V_0 = 4$, a decrease in time of 13.8 years, which, using the formula $R = Ce^{-at}$ gives approximately a fourfold increase in resources devoted to R & D. This increase would take place on private account without any government incentives, whereas the 30 percent increase considered previously would not be reflected in market incentives and would require a government policy to bring it about.

The examples in this section, while at best suggestive, lead to the conjecture that the energy events of the 1970s were an impetus for increased private R & D in energy and a case for increased policies to encourage even more than is occurring on private account, but that the extra encouragement needed is small relative to that to be expected on private account.

Research and Innovation: An Example from Agriculture

Agricultural research in the United States has faced many of the problems discussed in this chapter. Numerous innovations have been developed in the public sector by the system of U.S. Department of Agriculture research programs and land grant universities, often working in conjunction with private research institutions and industry. Ruttan (1982) describes three reasons for such an extensive research system: (1) The private sector lacks research incentives. (2) There is a strong complementarity between education and agricultural research. (3) Public research maintains a competitive structure in the agricultural sector. Ruttan's analysis of agricultural research will be used here to illustrate the theoretical results discussed earlier.

The lack of private sector incentives stems from the very problem discussed earlier: Private firms can capture only a small fraction of the social benefits of research. For example, seed companies rarely capture all the benefits from the development of a new crop variety. Although patent laws cover some types of seed development, the protection provided is often inadequate. To make it difficult for competitors to copy a particular hybrid, a company will often inbreed a patented strain not available to competitors and develop the desired variety from this strain. But such inbreeding often reduces the productivity of the variety, causing a reduction in social benefits. The benefits from basic research such as genetic research are even harder to acquire. Ruttan finds that "even in corn breeding, in which economic incentives have been the strongest, the private-sector companies continue to make only limited investments in the supporting sciences, such as genetics, plant pathology, plant physiology, and related areas." The willingness of the public sector to undertake these types of research could be part of the reason why the private sector does not. Yet even in the complete absence of public funds, it seems clear that the innovators will capture only a small fraction of the benefits and hence investment will be suboptimal.

The second reason for public funding of agricultural research, its complementarity with education, can be analyzed using the concept of a positive externality associated directly with "consumption" of research. It has long been recognized that the quality of universities and other educational institutions is enhanced by research activity. Much of the agricultural research performed at these institutions leads directly to improvements in agricultural techniques and inputs. However, a private corporation undertaking research to improve the same input—that is, consuming research—will be unable to capture its educational benefits. Figure 1.9 depicts the problem in the market for research. The demand for research by agricultural business firms and other corporations benefiting directly from the research is given by the demand schedule *D*. The level *R* of private research activity is determined by the

THE MARKET FOR RESEARCH

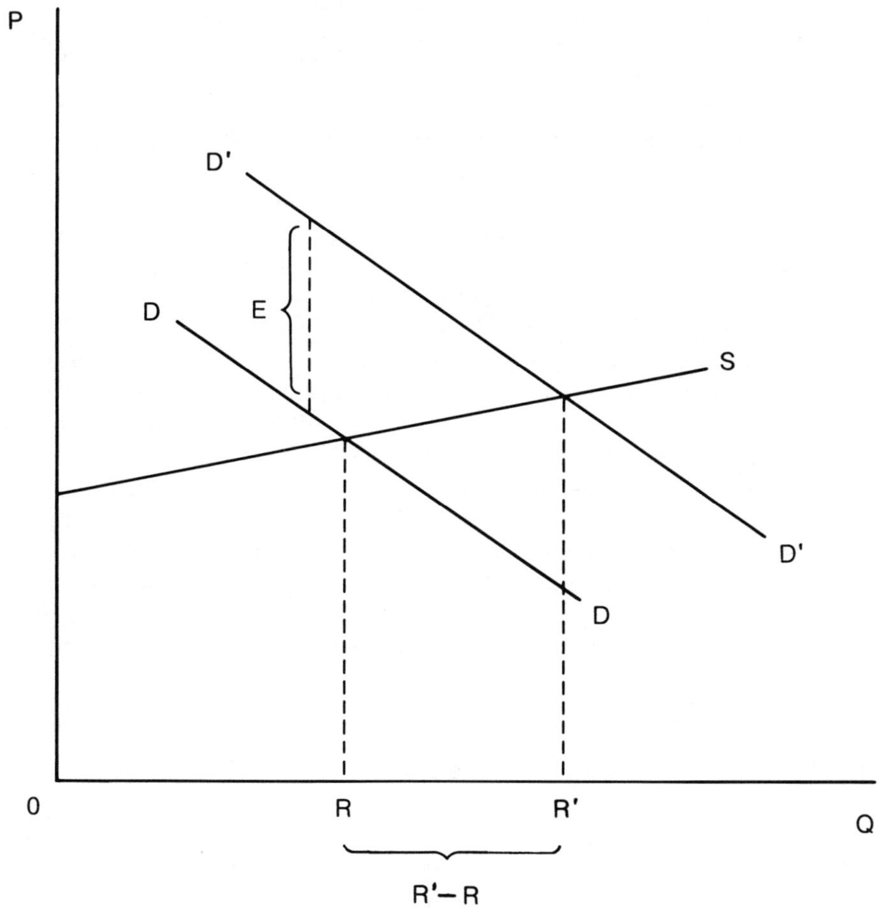

FIGURE 1.9

intersection of the supply of research S and the demand D. The positive externality associated with the complementarity between education and agricultural research increases the social value of research by an amount E, leading to a social demand curve D'. The socially optimal amount of research is thus R', determined by the intersection of D' and S. The public sector should thus undertake an amount $R' - R$ of research to achieve the optimal level.

An important caveat to this analysis is the existence of "crowding out." If the public sector undertakes an amount $R' - R$ of research, this might reduce the level of private research by a substantial amount, perhaps by as much as $R' - R$. Thus, the public sector investment has crowded out the private investment, and the social optimum is not achieved. Crowding out usually occurs when the government performs the same research as the private sector, e.g., if the government engages in the same type of hybridization programs as do private firms. In this case, it is cheaper for the firms to let the government do the work, so private firms will not invest in the research. Mansfield (1984) has estimated that each \$1.00 of government R & D expenditure crowds out up to \$0.20 of private expenditure in the same area, but stimulates up to \$0.25 of R & D in new areas. Two important but difficult questions have been raised: (1) How much research should the public sector undertake? (2) Is it possible to undertake this research in a way that minimizes crowding out yet is socially beneficial, say, by sponsoring programs undertaken at land grant universities? The first question and many related ones are discussed in Part 2 and the second question in Part 3 of this book.

The third reason for public funding of agricultural research is that it induces competition in the private sector. For example, if a state experiment station develops a new seed strain for use as a parent line but not as a productive hybrid variety, then private firms will compete to see who can develop the most productive high-yielding variety first. Of course, this is an example of the optimal timing problem raised previously. Each firm has incentives to introduce its new variety at the earliest possible time and capture as much of the market as possible before other firms introduce their hybrids. However, an early introduction reduces the number of cross-breeding attempts, and hence the variety may not be as productive as one introduced after additional research. The complexities of the relationship between competition, research, and optimal timing are discussed in detail by Kitti in Chapter 3.

ESTIMATING THE RETURNS FROM R & D

There are two main approachs to calculating the rate of return to R & D. The first is the direct estimation of the cost and benefit flows attached to a certain R & D project and the calculation of a rate of return from those flows.

This might be termed the "direct approach" and is the method employed by Griliches (1958) in his study of the returns to hybridizing corn and also by Mansfield et al. (1977) in their recent study of industrial innovation.

The second approach, the "indirect approach," estimates the return to R & D by the use of regression analysis. The general methodology is as follows: A sample of firms' profit rates is regressed on various determinants of profitability, among those R & D expenditure. The estimated coefficient of R & D is then construed to be a rate of return measure. This technique is often used in agricultural studies, and estimates of the rate of return to agricultural R & D are consistently above 30 percent (see Evenson et al., 1979). The method is indirect in that specific projects are not analyzed. Rather, an effect on net returns is inferred from the average behavior of firms—income in response to different levels of R & D expenditure. The two approaches are outlined more fully below.

Rate of Return Approach

In their study, Mansfield et al. (1977) collected data on 17 specific industrial innovations marketed in the last 20 years and estimated the cash flows generated by their R & D projects. The estimation relied primarily on questionnaire data from the firms producing the innovation. While the cost flows were fairly easy to identify from accounting records, and while the private returns similarly showed up as income numbers, the flows of social returns required a model characterizing the markets that employed the innovations.

They divided their sample of innovations into three categories: product innovations used by firms, product innovations used by households, and process innovations. In each category, the innovation was regarded as an input that reduced production costs for a final good or service. This approach allowed them to estimate the social benefits as the shaded area in Figure 1.10. In this figure, the innovation reduces the production costs of a perfectly competitive constant cost industry by $P_1 - P_3$. The innovator is assumed to charge a royalty of $P_2 - P_3$ (plus costs of invention) for the use of the invention. Since P_2 is now the unit cost of production to the industry, competition ensures that the new equilibrium price equals average cost, and the new equilibrium output is Q_2.

The shaded area of net social benefit is composed of two parts. The upper shaded area represents the addition to consumer surplus arising from the cost-reducing innovation. Its source is the price reduction in the final product. The lower shaded area, equal to the profits of the innovator (net of R & D and marketing costs to the innovator), may at first glance appear to be a simple wealth transfer and not a net social gain. However, the new average cost of

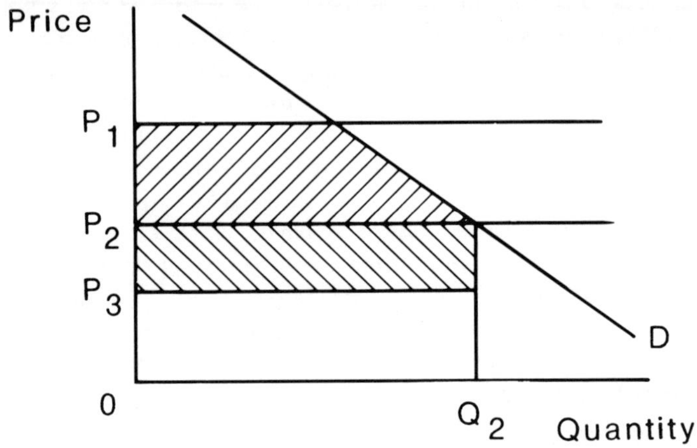

FIGURE 1.10

production in the industry, net of royalties, is P_3, and although the difference between P_2 and P_3 is collected as royalties by the innovator, it also represents the value of productive inputs released to other industries in the economy. It is a true efficiency gain. The net social gain, then, is the sum of the two shaded areas.

A final stage in the estimation of annual flows in the direct approach is to take account of expenditures on uncommercialized R & D projects, or failures. The rate of return finally calculated must include on the cash outflow side those expenditures that did not lead to marketable innovations. One practical way to include these is to adjust the expenses for each firm by a factor based on the firm's past success rate in R & D. If a firm has typically spent $1.50 on uncommercialized projects for each $1.00 it has spent on successful ones, and if the innovation considered cost $1 million, then the adjusted cost of the project is $2.5 million. Finally, if, when the innovation was produced, competitors were working on similar projects, their costs must be added to the costs of the successful project.

To this point, a procedure has been outlined to estimate the benefit and cost flows that are inputs into the rate of return calculation. The next step is the capitalization of those flows.

Mansfield et al. (1977) accomplished this task using an internal rate of return (IRR) approach. Although the IRR approach has substantial theoretical drawbacks, it does provide a consistent measure over relatively short periods with standard cash flow patterns [for a discussion of various measures, see Hirshleifer (1970)]. They obtain IRRs in excess of those available from other investments, implying that not enough research is being carried out in the areas they examined.

The IRR is the solution to the following equation:

$$B_t + \frac{B_{t+1}}{1+i} + \frac{B_{t+2}}{(1+i)^2} + \cdots + \frac{B_{t+N}}{(1+i)^N} = 0,$$

where B_t is the net cash flow in period t and N is the number of periods in which the project generates cash flows.

For the 17 innovations studied by Mansfield et al., the median private IRR (as measured by expenditures and revenues) was 25 percent. The median social IRR (calculated as in Figure 1.10) was over twice that rate, 56 percent. They also found wide variances about those medians. For six innovations, the private rate of return (pretax) was below 10 percent, whereas for five, it was in excess of 40 percent.

There are many criticisms of the IRR approach. Two particularly relevant ones are that (1) there is not a unique solution to the internal rate equation if the net cash flows change sign more than once, and (2) implicit in the IRR calculation is the assumption that all intermediate cash inflows can be reinvested at the internal rate, and hence the opportunity cost of intermediate expenditures is that rate. The second of these problems can become important as the length of the evaluated project increases.

In his study, Griliches experimented with different cost structures while retaining the perfect competition assumption (appropriate for the agricultural producers he studied) to estimate the rate of return on hybrid corn. By varying the supply elasticity from infinity (the constant returns to scale case) to zero, he found that the net social benefit continuously increased. He noted, however, that the ratio of benefits under the perfectly inelastic assumption to those under the perfectly elastic assumption was only 1.07. In his final calculations, he opted for the conservative infinite elasticity assumption. Griliches performed his study by estimating a benefit-cost ratio. First he discounted forward and backward all cash flows to a common time period. He brought forward in time all research expenditures on hybrid corn and all estimated benefits (as previously explained in Figure 1.10) to the base year 1955 at a compound rate of 10 percent. He then converted all flows to equivalent perpetuities (the perpetual annual flows that could be generated at a 10 percent interest rate from the 1955 capitalized values). To these perpetual flows he added a projected flow of net benefits that would accrue to the investment indefinitely. By dividing the perpetuity equivalent benefits by the perpetuity equivalent expenses, Griliches estimated an annual rate of return of $7.00 for every $1.00 invested in hybrid corn development. This perpetual return is perhaps more easily visualized as a benefit-cost ratio that has been converted to an equivalent infinite flow. By comparing all past and future benefits and costs in terms of 1955 equivalent dollars, the estimated benefit-cost ratio is close to 70. Multiplying the benefit-cost ratio by a 10 percent interest rate yields a perpetual return figure of $7.00

for each \$1.00 invested for hybrid corn. This indicates the underinvestment taking place in R & D activities associated with hybrid corn.

Regression Approach

The second major approach to the rate of return calculation is the indirect approach, in which firm profits are regressed on (among other things) R & D expenditures. The partial regression coefficients from such cross-section analyses are taken to be indicators of the profitability of research investments. The methodology is straightforward and will not be described in detail here. A few pertinent points should be made, however.

This approach is certainly to be preferred from data collection considerations, as no estimation of supply and demand curves or areas under them is necessary. It is deficient in that the validity of the estimated returns depends critically on the specification of the other variables determining profits. Are there barriers to entry in the industry, and do they enhance profits? Such questions must be dealt with in a correctly specified model. Another limitation to the indirect approach is that it yields only estimates of private returns to firms. The methodology alone cannot approach the question of social rates of return.

Recently, several authors have noted that many of the regression analyses of firms' profit rates have been flawed in their treatment of R & D expenditures. It is argued that R & D is more properly viewed as a capital stock of know-how that depreciates over time through obsolescence and general technical advance and that is augmented through investments in R & D.

Grabowski and Mueller (1978) argue that profit rates are usually incorrectly defined as

$$\pi_t = \frac{S_t - VC_t - \lambda_k K_t - r_t}{K_t}$$

where π_t is the firm's profit rate in period t, S_t is sales, VC_t is variable costs, λ_k is the depreciation rate of physical capital, K_t is the physical capital stock, and r_t is R & D expenditures.

If R & D is viewed as a capital stock, the correct representation of profit rates is

$$\pi_t = \frac{S_t - VC_t - \lambda_k K_t - \lambda_R R_t}{K_t + R_t},$$

where R_t is the capital stock of technical knowledge and λ_R is the depreciation (obsolescence) rate of technical knowledge.

Ayanian (1975) notes that if the depreciation rate is less than 100 percent, the result of regressing this first equation on an R & D flow variable is to bias upward the estimated rate of return on R & D investments.

Grabowski and Mueller, using a definition of profit rate similar to that used in the second equation, found an after-tax rate of return to R & D of 15 to 20 percent in their 86-firm cross-sectional sample. This estimate is within the bounds of the returns estimated by Mansfield et al. in their industrial innovation survey. Methodologically, Grabowski and Mueller note that the approach to profitability embodied in the second equation reduced the estimated variance of profit rates by approximately one-half.

The studies considered above do not exhaust the issues related to estimating returns to R & D. In general, in considering benefits to be expected from R & D activities, if the benefits from an innovation will require further R & D to be realized, the costs of this additional work should be subtracted from the ultimate benefits in calculating the benefits of the original innovation.

This methodology is relatively straightforward for applied research, where there are clear goals in terms of performance and cost characteristics. However, in the case of basic research—research not being undertaken to achieve a particular objective—the benefits are more difficult to foresee. Over time, the results of the basic research will be used in several areas in combination with directly applied research efforts. Nonetheless, attempts can be made to calculate the benefits from basic research only by following the foregoing tenet of starting with gross benefits from all the related projects and then subtracting the costs of the applied research.

This procedure should also be adhered to when discussing the benefits of past projects. Often one hears discussions of whether the benefits of hybrid corn should be attributed to scientists' efforts on this venture or to Mendel's genetics work. If one is interested in the benefits due to hybrid corn, one should calculate only the benefits associated with the research specific to this goal. If one is interested in the benefits of Mendel's work, one should calculate the entire benefit of the basic work, in all applications making sure to subtract the costs of any R & D required for application.

POLICIES

Effects of Patents on Private Incentives

The patent system, since its inception in the late fifteenth century, has developed into a system that ensures innovators that they will receive at least part of the benefits of any innovation they might develop. Being of only finite life, it prevents innovators from capturing the entire stream of benefits generated from their invention. Not all types of innovations are patentable. For example, in the United States, patents are given only for innovations that appear to be immediately marketable and not to pure ideas. Moreover, it is often possible for an imitator to generate a similar yet different concept from the public disclosure of the innovation when it is patented.

Analytical Model

Recall the model presented earlier in which the innovator sees returns decay at rate γ, so that the present value of the stream of returns is

$$PV = \int_0^\infty BV_0 e^{-(r+\gamma)t} dt$$

or

$$PV = \frac{BV_0}{r+\gamma}.$$

Suppose that the patent offers only limited protection; i.e., it reduces the rate of decay to $\gamma_1 < \gamma$ for the life of the patent, L years. After L years, the rate of decay returns to its original value γ. The present value of returns under the patent system is given by the expression

$$PV_p = \int_0^L BV_0 e^{-(r+\gamma_1)t} dt + e^{-(r+\gamma_1)L} \int_L^\infty BV_0 e^{-(r+\gamma)t} dt.$$

The assumption that $\gamma_1 < \gamma$ implies that the rate at which the benefits from innovation are dissipated because of copying is lower under the patent system. Thus, everything else held equal, including the length of life of the patent, a patent law does increase the rewards to the inventor, and thus encourages innovation. This can be represented algebraically. Since $\gamma_1 < \gamma$, it follows that

$$\int_0^L BV_0 e^{-(r+\gamma_1)t} dt > \int_0^L BV_0 e^{-(r+\gamma)t} dt$$

so that

$$PV_p = \int_0^L BV_0 e^{-(r+\gamma_1)t} dt + e^{-(r+\gamma_1)L} \int_L^\infty BV_0 e^{-(r+\gamma)t} dt$$

$$> \int_0^L BV_0 e^{-(r+\gamma)t} dt + e^{-(r+\gamma)L} \int_L^\infty BV_0 e^{-(r+\gamma)t} dt = PV.$$

As a special case, assume that at the expiration of the patent, the innovation becomes public knowledge and the innovator no longer receives any benefits from it. The equation for the present value under the patent system then becomes

$$PV'_p = \int_0^L BV_0 e^{-(r+\gamma_1)t} dt$$

or

$$PV'_p = \frac{BV_0}{r+\gamma_1} [1 - e^{-(r+\gamma_1)L}].$$

A special case often analyzed in the literature (e.g., Loury, 1979; Dasgupta, 1981; Kamien and Schwarz, 1982), is when the patent gives perfect protection.

If the returns decay at rate γ after the expiration of the patent, then the present value is given by

$$PV_p'' = \int_0^L BV_0 e^{-rt} dt + e^{-rL} \int_L^\infty BV_0 e^{-(r+\gamma)t} dt$$

$$= \frac{BV_0}{r}(1 - e^{-rL}) + \frac{e^{-rL} BV_0}{r+\gamma} e^{-(r+\gamma)L}.$$

If the innovator receives no benefits after the patent expires, then

$$PV_p''' = \frac{BV_0}{r}(l - e^{-rL}).$$

In each of these cases, the patent increases rewards to the inventor.

However, the limited life of the patent tends to decrease the social value of the innovation, since it gives the innovator some degree of monopoly power, which permits nonoptimal pricing of output. The net effect of the patent on social welfare will depend on the relative magnitudes of the coefficients.

For the special case in which the innovator receives no benefits after the expiration of the patent, the change in the values of the benefits generated by reducing the rate of decay through patent laws can be represented as

$$\frac{\partial PV_p'}{\partial \gamma} = \frac{BV_0}{(r+\gamma)^2}\left\{[(r+\gamma)L + 1]e^{-(r+\gamma)L} - 1\right\}.$$

With a value for $r + \gamma$ of 0.2 and a patent life length of 17 years, the expression becomes $\partial PV_p'/\partial\partial > = -21.33 BV_0$. Multiply this expression by γ and divide it by BV_0 to obtain an elasticity of the size of the benefit with respect to γ. The size of this elasticity, employing the posited values of the parameter and an estimated γ value of 0.12, is

$$E_{PV_{p'},\gamma} = -2.56.$$

That is, a 1 percent decrease in the value of γ will increase the value of the gain by −2.56 percent. For example, say that with the advent of a patent law, the rate of decay falls from 10 percent to 5 percent (assuming the length of time the benefits can be captured stays the same). This is a 50 percent drop and will increase the net benefit by 127.5 percent. If the patent law has no restrictions on the amount of time over which the patent can be employed, the expression reduces to

$$\frac{\partial VP}{\partial \gamma} = -\frac{BV_0}{(\gamma + r_0)^2},$$

which yields an elasticity of $E_{vp,\gamma}$ – 3.0. Thus, it can be seen under varying conditions of patent length, changes in the law that significantly affect γ have substantial effects on benefits and thus the incentive to invent.

Although many studies conclude that the patent laws significantly lower the rate of decay, people's opinions concerning the level of decay are much more diverse. The arguments run from those contending that the laws are necessary to views that patent laws do not prevent imitation and/or that persons can afford themselves almost as much right to their innovations in the absence of patent laws as they can in their presence. [For a good review of this literature, see Cheung (1977).]

Optimal Life of Patent

The determination of the appropriate length of a patent has received much attention in the last two decades. For every period that the innovator is protected by the patent laws, there is a welfare loss because output is overpriced. However, as discussed above, the patent laws provide an incentive to produce innovations. The longer the patent law is in effect, the greater the incentive is. Thus, there is a trade-off between encouraging more innovative activity and the increased welfare loss associated with the lengthening of patent life. The problem of maximizing social gains in view of this trade-off has been studied by Nordhaus (1969) and Scherer (1972). Scherer concludes: (1) "The larger is the arc elasticity of demand in the neighborhood of the preinvention and postinvention competitive equilibrium, the shorter is the socially optimal patent life." (2) "The 'easier' it is to achieve a given cost reduction...the shorter the socially optimal patent life." (3) "The optimal patent life is shorter, the sharper the curvature of the invention possibility function [production function] in the neighborhood of the optimal R & D expenditure."

Analytical Model

The logic of determining an optimal patent life can be illustrated by extending the above analytic model. For simplicity, consider the case in which patents offer complete protection and the benefits to the innovator disappear when the patent ends. As shown above, the private benefits are given by

$$PV_p''' = \int_0^L BV_0 e^{-rt} dt$$

$$= \frac{BV_0}{r} (1 - e^{-rt}).$$

For notational ease, let the value of the private return PV_p''' now be abbreviated by V_p.

The social return to the innovation includes the return during the life of the patent plus the return after it expires. If it is assumed for simplicity that the innovator is able to capture all the returns during the life of the patent, i.e., if $B = 1$, then social returns are

$$V_s = V_p + \int_L^\infty V_0 e^{-rt} dt$$

$$= V_p + \frac{V_0 e^{-rL}}{r}.$$

The social return net of the costs of discovery is

$$V_s \cdot \exp(-rt_p) - R(t_p),$$

where $R(t_p)$ is the present value cost of discovery and where the gross social return V_s and the time of discovery t_p as determined by innovative behavior both depend on the life of the patent. In a market, innovators equate average returns and average costs, so that t_p satisfies

$$V_p \cdot \exp(-rt_p) = R(t_p).$$

Letting $R(t_p) = C \cdot \exp(-at_p)$ and solving for t_p gives

$$t_p = \frac{1}{a-r} \ln \frac{C}{V_p},$$

where the private return V_p as given above is a function of patent life L. Substituting for t_p in the expression for net social returns gives

$$V_s \cdot \exp\left[-r\left(\frac{1}{a-r}\right) \mathrm{Ln}\left(\frac{C}{V_p}\right)\right] - C \exp\left[-a\left(\frac{1}{a-r}\right) \mathrm{Ln}\left(\frac{C}{V_p}\right)\right].$$

To determine optimal patent life, set the partial derivative of net social return with respect to L equal to zero. Using the general expression for net return gives

$$\frac{\partial V_s}{\partial L} \cdot \exp(-rt_p) - rV_s \cdot \exp(-rt_p)\frac{\partial t_p}{\partial L} - R'(t_p)\frac{\partial t_p}{\partial L} = 0.$$

The first term is the decrease in social return due to increasing the life of the patent by one year, for a given time of discovery. The second two terms give the increase in returns due to earlier discovery induced by the increase in patent life. The first of the second two terms is the return from moving the discovery closer in time, which is partially offset by the second of the second two terms giving the increase in costs from bringing about earlier discovery.

The partial derivative $\partial V_s/\partial L$ will be the welfare loss per year from the firm with patent rights acting as monopolist multiplied by the change in the number of years that the patent runs, discounted back to the present. This clearly depends on the demand conditions and industrial organization of the output market. As the above expression for t_p indicates, it is reasonable to assume that the time at which the innovation is introduced depends on C, the cost of instantaneous discovery, and the parameter a determining cost savings from shown discovery. In addition, the fraction of benefits that the innovator can capture will influence the optimal patent life, since it helps determine how much R & D will occur. Perhaps most importantly, the social gain available at any given time, V_0, will be a determining factor. Thus, the optimal life of the patent is clearly different for different types of R & D, since $\partial V_s/\partial L$, C, α, B, and V_0 will depend on the kind of innovation being developed.

Licensing

A firm or individual holding a patent may license out the right to use the innovation to other individuals or firms, a device used by innovators who do not enjoy a comparative advantage of using their patented idea to produce goods. As discussed earlier, innovators sell the rights to the members of an industry in a manner to ensure that they maximize their profits. This is illustrated in Figure 1.1. Assume an inventor produces an innovation that lowers the cost of production from S to S'. Then the innovator will price the innovation so that the marginal revenue to the industry equals marginal cost. That is, he or she will price the innovation in such a manner that the industry's cost curve is S and they sell Q. Royalty fees equal to the area $ABDE$ will be charged. Thus, the innovator forces the industry to behave as if it were monopolistic and captures all the profits of this behavior for himself or herself. Accordingly, licensing behavior involves the same set of issues as do the cases in which patent holders act as monopolists themselves, but also involves other issues surrounding legal requirements and restrictions on the terms of licensing. As a first approximation, these can be thought of as adding transaction costs to the problem, so they do not change the basic ideas in the preceding analysis.

A fuller discussion follows in later chapters. In Chapter 2, Brian Wright discusses why firms would choose licensing instead of patents. In Chapter 3, Carole Kitti shows that the effect of licensing on the timing of innovations is the same as that of patents: It provides incentives to innovate too early. The legal differences between the two systems are discussed by Ronald Engel in Chapter 4. He concludes that the inability to receive redress promptly under the patent system makes other types of protection, including licensing, attractive to many firms.

Trade Secret Laws

Another type of legal structure that innovators can use is the system of trade secret laws. Under the principles of common law, one is protected from the stealing of ideas or innovations. An advantage of relying on this approach is that one does not have to reveal the nature of the innovation. A disadvantage of the laws is that it is very hard to keep a secret idea or innovation from becoming common knowledge, and thus very difficult to prove that someone actually stole the idea behind a concept. Processes that are apt to be kept as trade secrets are those that are difficult to decipher when the final product is distributed, the classic example being the recipe for Coca-Cola. Innovations such as superior designs or plans are usually protected by patents, since it is fairly easy for outsiders to learn the heart of the concept by dismantling the final product. Whether innovators opt to protect their innovation by a patent or by relying on trade secret laws depends on whether they think that the disclosure of the idea with the taking of a patent will make it more susceptible to further innovation or whether it is more likely that the idea can be legally stolen because of the limited protection offered by trade secret laws. In either case, successful innovators are likely to see an erosion of their returns over time, although either form of protection should slow its rate. The trade secret laws can thus be thought of as affecting the value of γ_1, and the above model applies.

Tax Incentives

The major way in which the tax laws give special treatment to R & D is in permitting, beginning in 1954, the expensing of R & D investments. This encourages more R & D relative to other kinds of investment and thus acts to shorten t_p relative to t_s. The issue needs to be explored in the context of a corporate income tax that affects the return on all capital. In a more extended analysis, the interaction of the expensing provision with effects of the corporate income tax on capital of various longevities would need to be explored. The following is a preliminary discussion of the effects of expensing.

Analytical Model

Without expensing, the private return to R & D is $(1 - \mu)V_p$, where μ is the tax rate. The cost, as before, is $R(t)$. The condition that private innovation lends to an equating of average returns and average costs becomes

$$(1 - \mu)V_p e^{-r_p t_p} = Ce^{-at_p},$$

where r_p is the private discount rate affected by taxation. The social rate of return r_s is the total return, whereas the private rate of return r_p is reduced by the tax rate and is $(1 - \mu)r_s$. With R & D investment taxed symmetrically to other investment (no expensing), the capital stock of the economy is allocated optimally between the two—in the absence of other distortions—since the returns to all investments are reduced proportionately by taxes.

Solving the above condition for innovation in the presence of taxation gives as the time of the innovation

$$t_p = \frac{1}{a - r_p} \ln \frac{C}{(1 - \mu)V_p}.$$

If expensing of R & D is allowed, the costs are reduced along with the returns, giving the condition for innovation as

$$(1 - \mu)V_p e^{-r_p t'_p} = (1 - \mu)Ce^{-at'_p},$$

where t'_p is the time of innovation with expensing. The solution for t'_p is

$$t'_p = \frac{1}{a - r_p} \ln \frac{C}{V_p}.$$

The difference between the time of innovation without and with expensing is

$$t_p - t'_p = \frac{-\ln(1 - \mu)}{(a - r_p)}.$$

Using the relation for resources devoted to innovation, $R = Ce^{-at}$, the ratio of resources with and without expensing is

$$\frac{R(t'_p)}{R(t_p)} = (1 - \mu)^{-a/(a - r_p)}.$$

With a tax rate of 50 percent ($\mu = 0.5$), $a = 0.2$, and $r_p = 0.1$, the ratio is 4, indicating that expensing leads to a fourfold increase in the resources devoted to innovation in this example.

Following this approach, one could introduce the nontax reasons for differences between social and private incentives considered earlier and solve for an expensing rate, other than the two rates of 0 and 100 percent considered here, which would make the actual and socially optimal amount of resources devoted to a particular kind of innovation coincide.

Government-Sponsored R & D

In 1975, the federal government either performed or sponsored $17,583 million worth of R & D, representing another means by which attempts can be made to foster optimum R & D. Recent work by Kitch (1979) explores the problems of the effects of government-sponsored research on private research and related policy questions.

Given that the government does sponsor research, the issue of project selection arises. In particular, how should government agencies select a subset of projects to sponsor from the many R & D efforts for which federal monies could be used? This is the topic of Chapter 6, which outlines practical procedures the government can employ to select a set of projects. Asbury in Chapter 5 relates this directly to the energy field by discussing what types of projects should be selected by national laboratories, and why national laboratories should do the projects instead of the private sector.

Steps Needed to Improve Policy

The framework developed in this chapter brings out several issues important in making R & D policy decisions. The first is how to implement a reward structure for successful innovators. This structure should provide incentives for private individuals and corporations to invest in R & D, but not for overinvestment, leading to unnecessary duplication of effort and to premature marketing. Currently, the major incentive policies are patents and trade secret laws. Based on the analysis in Part 2 of the book, some modifications of the existing patent laws, such as variable patent lengths and broader definitions of what is patentable, are suggested by Tolley, Hodge, and Grenchik in the concluding chapter.

A second important issue is how and in what areas to provide public R & D. Public R & D can take many forms, such as direct government research by national laboratories, government hiring of private corporations or institutions, and research contracts and grants. The best combination of these policy instruments depends on the goals of public R & D and the effect each instrument has on private R & D. For example, research grants are useful in stimulating basic research, in which the private sector often underinvests. Tolley, Hodge, and Grenchik (Chapter 9) propose greater use of two often neglected instruments: government purchase of patent rights in certain cases, especially when public knowledge of the patented process would enhance national welfare, and increased use of prizes and special top credits for R & D in specific areas where other incentives have proven inadequate. Examples of such areas are space exploration, health technology, and energy development.

Finally, the relationship between private and public R & D must be examined to establish the proper role of government. In many cases, this role will be determined by the goal of a specific project, such as energy technologies, which must account not only for private returns, but also for national security issues, environmental concerns, and income redistribution effects. Tolley, Hodge, and Grenchik find that there is a need for a careful statement of national policy objectives. This statement could then be used to better determine which policy instruments should be used and in what doses, leading to a comprehensive policy that is more directed and more compatible with private R & D efforts.

REFERENCES

Arrow, K. J., "Economic Welfare and the Allocation of Resources for Inventions," in R. R. Nelson (ed.), *The Rate and Direction of Inventive Activity*, Princeton University Press, Princeton, 1962.

Arrow, K. J., "The Economic Implications of Learning by Doing," Review of Economic Studies.

Barzel, Y., "Optimal Timing of Innovations," *Review of Economics and Statistics*, 50(August, 1968):348–55.

Cheung, S. N. S., "Property Rights and Inventions: An Economic Inquiry," working paper, May, 1977, Univ. of Washington.

Coase, R. H., "The Nature of the Firm," *Economica N. S.*, 4(Nov., 1937):386–405.

Dasgupta, P., "Resource Pricing and Technological Innovations under Oligopoly: A Theoretical Exploration," *Scandinavian Journal of Economics*, 83(2):289–317, 1981.

Dasgupta, P., and J. Stiglitz, "Uncertainty, Industrial Structure, and the Speed of R & D," *Bell Journal of Economics*, 11(1):1–28, 1979.

Dasgupta, P., and J. Stiglitz, "Industrial Structure and the Nature of Innovative Activity," *Economic Journal*, 90:226–93.

Debreu, G., *Theory of Value*, Yale University Press, New Haven, 1959.

Demsetz, H., "Information and Efficiency: Another Viewpoint," *Journal of Law and Economics*, 12(1969):1–22.

Fethke, G., and J. J. Birch, "Rivalry and the Timing of Innovation," *Bell Journal of Economics*, 13(1), Spring, 1982.

Grabowski, H., and D. Mueller, "Industrial Research and Development, Intangible Capital Stocks, and Firm Profit Rates," *Bell Journal of Economics*, 9:328–43.

Griliches, Z., ed., *R & D, Patents and Productivity*, University of Chicago Press, Chicago, 1984.

Hirshleifer, J., *Investment, Interest and Capital*, Prentice-Hall, Englewood Cliffs, N.J., 1970.

Kamien, M., and N. Schwarz, *Market Structure and Innovation*, Cambridge University Press, N.Y., 1982.

Kamien, M., and N. Schwarz, "Market Structure and Innovation: A Survey." *Journal of Economic Literature*, March, 1975, pp. 1–37.

Kitch, E., "Problems in the Management of Federal Support of Research and Development in the Energy Industries," presented at the Conference on Research and Development Policy, Univ. of Chicago, Spring, 1979.

Kitti, C., "Patent Policy and the Optimal Timing of Innovations," Ph.D. Dissertation, University of Chicago, 1973.

Knight, F. H., *Risk, Uncertainty and Profit*, Boston, Houghton-Mifflin, 1921.

Levin, R. C., "Technical Change, Barriers to Entry and Market Structure," *Economica*, 45:347–61.

Loury, G. C., "Market Structure and Innovation," *Quarterly Journal of Economics*, 18(3):395–410.

Mansfield, E., J. Rapoport, A. Romeo, S. Wagner, and G. Beardsley, "Social and Private Rates of Return from Industrial Innovations," *Quarterly Journal of Economics*, May, 1977, 221–40.

Mansfield, E., "R & D and Innovation: Some Empirical Findings," in Griliches et al., *R & D, Patents and Productivity*, 1984.

Nelson, Richard R., "The Simple Economics of Basic Scientific Research," *Journal of Political Economy*, 67 (1959): 297–306.

Nordhaus, W., *Innovation, Growth, and Welfare: A Theoretical Treatment of Technological Change*, MIT Press, Cambridge, 1969.

Reinganum, J., "Dynamic Games with R & D Rivalry," Ph.D. Dissertataion, Northwestern University, 1979.

Ruttan, V., *Agricultural Research Policy*, University of Minnesota Press, Minneapolis, 1982.

Scherer, F. M., "Nordhaus's Theory of Optimal Patent Life: A Geometric Reinterpretation," *American Economic Review* 62(1972):422.

Schmookler, J., *Invention and Economic Growth*, Harvard University Press, Cambridge, 1966.

Schumpeter, J. A., *Capitalism, Socialism, and Democracy*, Harper and Row, N.Y., 1942.

Schumpeter, J. A., *Theory of Economic Development*, Cambridge, Harvard University Press, 1934.

Telser, Lester, "A Theory of Innovation and Its Effects," *Bell Journal of Economics*, 13(1), 1982.

Telser, Lester, "Innovation: Its Public and Private Aspects and Some of Their Empirical Implications for Mergers," forthcoming.

Tolley, G., and Wilman, "The Foreign Dependence Question," *Journal of Political Economy*, 85(2):323–47 (April, 1977).

Williamson, O. E., "The Modern Corporation: Origins, Evolution, Attributes," *Journal of Economic Literature*, 19(Dec., 1981):1537–68.

II

Problems in Providing for Public and Private R & D

2
The Resource Allocation Problem in R & D*

Brian D. Wright

Without some kind of government intervention, a competitive market does not produce sufficient inventions and innovations. The reason is that, except in some cases in which secrets can be protected without legal support, producers of new ideas and processes receive an insufficient reward for their efforts in such a market. Not only was this problem understood by policymakers long before economists were around to write about public goods, but the modern solutions had been located before the aid of the economic professionals could be invoked.

Among these solutions, the patent system has attracted the most interest on the part of economists. However, a large literature on the subject [see the survey by Machlup (1958)] has added little that is useful as a guide to policy. On the one hand, the essentially agnostic conclusions of Machlup are, by his own admission, hardly the stuff on which policy shifts are based. The detailed investigation of Nordhaus (1969), on the other, resulted in a general endorsement of the system, while contributing an additional analytical justification for the widespread standard patent life limitations of around 14 or 17 years as a minor improvement in the effectiveness of the system, relative to an infinite patent life. Also, the analysis of patents in noncompetitive environments has been predominantly descriptive rather than prescriptive, and inevitably plagued by lack of generality. [See Kamien and Schwartz (1975) for an excellent survey.]

In this chapter, a new view of the problem of resource allocation in a competitive economy will be presented, which connects the old obsession, the trade-off between the excess burden of patents and the appropriability that they confer, with other sources of market failure that have attracted increased

*I would like to thank, with the usual caveat, Cindy Arfken, Martin Bailey, Steven Englander, Robert Evenson, Richard Levin, Richard Nelson, John Quigley, George Tolley, and Marguerite Alejandro-Wright for assistance of various kinds.

attention in the last decade. The new analysis shows the resource allocation problem to be much more serious and less tractable than has been traditionally believed.

The chapter is organized as follows: After a discussion of necessary distinctions between different types of inventions and innovations, a very simple research model is presented. This is used to contrast the old economics of patents with the new view of the patent instrument. This new approach casts the ancient appreciation of the role of disclosure in a new light. Then, several alternatives to the current patent system are considered, drawing on some results derived elsewhere (Wright, 1983).

FOUR CATEGORIES OF INVENTIONS AND INNOVATIONS

Research and development (R & D) programs aim to produce new useful information. Since the same item of information can be used jointly by any number of persons without depleting its factual content, the marginal cost of using it is the cost of communication. The output of R & D can be divided into four categories related to the possibility of financing its production through, in effect, selling it at a price in excess of marginal cost:

Category I: Included in this group are patentable discoveries (such as a new assembly tool) that could be exploited in productive use without divulging their nature or else patented and sold to others.

Category II: This group includes inventions like a design modification to render a product more efficient, that is patentable but can be copied at little cost by anyone who wishes to inspect the product in which the discovery is incorporated. Appropriation of the benefits of this type of invention for private gain can be made possible by legal attribution of rights or by noncompetitive "barriers to entry."

Category III: In this group are discoveries like a new method for analyzing petroleum exploration data, which need not be divulged by attempts to exploit them, but which could not be patented. Thus, the inventor can conceivably obtain a reward for the embodied invention through the free market, but only as long as secrecy is maintained.[1]

Category IV: This group contains discoveries that cannot be exploited by embodiment in a specific process or marketable product. An example is the theory of relativity, or, on a more mundane level, many theoretical results published in scholarly journals.

[1]Hirshleifer (1971) points out that the value of inventions could in principle be appropriated using futures markets. But the additional gains from speculation are limited when the discovery is protected by a patent or secrecy. For example, under a run-of-the-mill patent of the type considered below, profit-maximizing exploitation of the discovery does not cause a change in product prices, and no opportunity for additional gain through the futures market exists.

If these four categories of invention were always produced by distinct processes, the advantages of direct government allocation of research aimed at the fourth would be rather clear, whereas the private sector would be equally clearly a feasible candidate for furnishing the first and the third. The second category could also be achieved "privately," but the necessary role of government would extend beyond the normal legal protections accorded to decentralized production.

With respect to inventions in categories I and II, the government role in private R & D most generally takes the form of public attribution of exploitation rights to private persons and the protection of these rights. Such publicly bestowed rights, in the form of patents, antedate the beginnings of modern economics. The economic analysis of optimum R & D incentives is dominated by the study of patents, which seem to hold a special fascination for members of this profession.

The second and third sections of this chapter are devoted entirely to patents, because despite the mass of economic research that has been dedicated to their study, no adequately clear and comprehensive analysis of their general economic effects is available. But this chapter considers patents as just one of several means of optimizing R & D. To accommodate treatment of this wider set of means of controlling research in the latter part of this chapter, attention has been restricted to the starkly simplistic invention model outlined next, which fortunately incorporates in stylized form characteristics that determine the relative efficiency of competitive R & D activity in different allocation systems.

A SIMPLE RESEARCH MODEL

The purposes of this study are served by a very simple model of research toward a well-defined goal. This goal is discrete, and one might think of it as knowledge of a new process that, on discovery, reduces the marginal cost of production of some nonpublic good from MC_0 to MC_1, as in Figure 2.1. An example could be a more efficient means of energy extraction or conversion, which lowers the cost of the energy produced. The demand curve for the output (energy) is AR; the marginal revenue curve is MR.

Imagine initially that the new discovery is a category II invention, as defined above. Assume that research imparts no knowledge that could be used for any other purposes, including further research. To simplify the exposition, distributional considerations will be ruled out by assuming that all consumers are identical. If the cost-reducing information is discovered and freely available, its social value is the increase in consumer surplus, approximated by the

[2]The value of the prospective invention is assumed to be small relative to total income. Hence, the problem of compensation in economic surplus calculations can be neglected. [For a rigorous justification, see Willig (1976).]

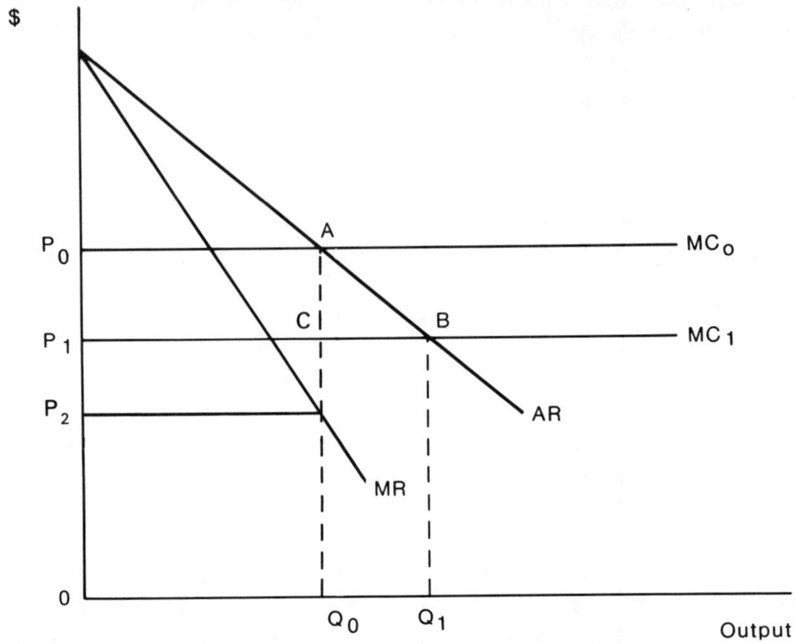

FIGURE 2.1. The Welfare Cost of a "Run-of-the-Mill" Patent Caused by Restriction of Use

area P_0ABP_1 in Figure 2.1, which is defined as equal to B dollars.[2] Though these benefits occur over time, the analysis presented below loses little importance and gains considerably in simplicity by assuming that B accrues in a single period.

The total amount of research effort is composed of m units of research activity supplied by competitive researchers who are of similar ability and, in common with society at large, assumed to be risk neutral. The aggregate cost of research $C(m)$ and the probability that at least one researcher will succeed $P(m)$ are assumed to be continuous and twice differentiable with $C'(m) > 0$, $C''(m) \geqslant 0$, $P'(m) > 0$, $P''(m) < 0$. The expected benefits of research are $R(m)$, where

$$R(m) \equiv BP(m). \quad (1)$$

The optimal allocation of resources to research in a model of this type is illustrated in Figure 2.2 as m^*, the point that maximizes the difference between expected benefits and cost, where

$$R'(m^*) = BP'(m^*) = C'(m^*) \quad (2)$$

and the expected net social benefit is equal to the distance AF.

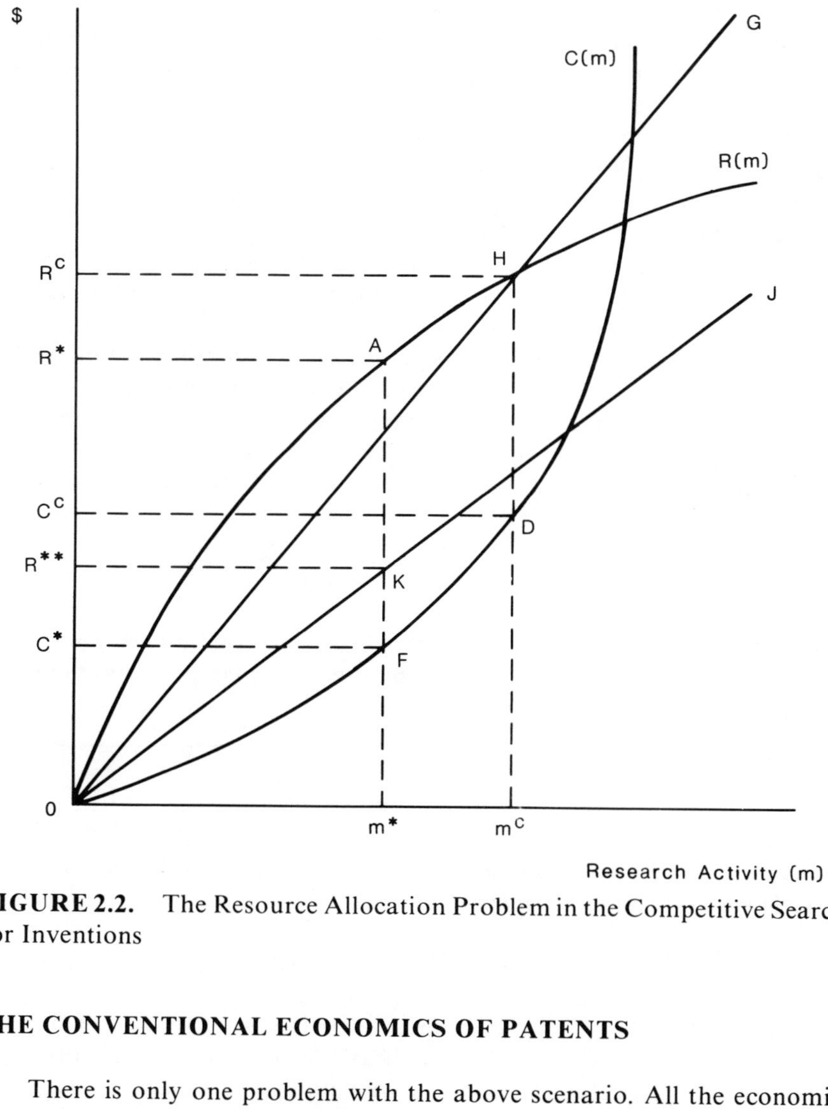

FIGURE 2.2. The Resource Allocation Problem in the Competitive Search for Inventions

THE CONVENTIONAL ECONOMICS OF PATENTS

There is only one problem with the above scenario. All the economic benefits are passed on to the users of the product (energy in the above example), and none are reaped by the producer of the invention that made the cost saving possible, except insofar as gained in the role as a user of the product. In this situation, an invention bestows its maximum economic benefit on society, but not many inventions are likely to occur without some more specific encouragement to the inventor, if the process of invention requires scarce resources as inputs.

This problem may be solved by the availability of an exclusive patent that enables the discoverer to appropriate the social benefit B. The holder of an unlimited patent maximizes profits by limiting use of the discovery to production of $0Q_0$ units of the good.[3] Profits are then represented in Figure 2.1 by area P_0ACP_1. This is the entire net social benefit of the invention under the patent system, since price remains at P_0 and consumers are no better off than if the invention had not occurred. Therefore, the invention has less social value if it is exploited by a patent holder than if it is freely available for use, the difference being represented by $L \equiv$ area P_0ABP_1 – area P_0ACP_1 = area ABC. L is called the "excess burden" or "welfare cost" of the patent.

In practice, patent lives are limited, in the United States, to 17 years. Although Posner (1977, pp. 54–55) suggests that a life limitation is essential for administrative reasons, the conventional economic rationale is quite different. The essentials of the analysis of Nordhaus (1969) are represented in Figure 2.3, using the simple model developed above. [Linearity of $C'(m)$ and $P'(m)$ is assumed to make the diagram easier to draw.] The social optimum when knowledge is freely available is m^*, as in Figure 2.2. Under an unlimited patent, the competitive equilibrium research effort, according to this analysis, is m_1, where

$$(B - L)P'(m_1) = C'(m_1). \tag{3}$$

When the patent life is limited to T years, the present value of profits and excess burden are both modified by a multiplicative factor α. Assuming the annual returns will be constant forever,

$$\alpha(T, r) = \int_0^T e^{-rt} dt, \tag{4}$$

where r is the rate of interest, assumed constant. The equilibrium under a patent of duration T^0, given $\alpha(T^0, r)$, can be represented in this atemporal model as occurring at m_2, where

$$\alpha(B - L)P'(m_2) = C'(m_2). \tag{5}$$

The marginal social value of research, given α, is $\alpha(B - L)P'(m_2)^1$. This is the equation for the straight line through M and N in Figure 2.3. The difference between the social value of the patent with a life of T^0 years and that of the infinite patent is represented in Figure 2.3 as the difference between $\alpha LP'(m_2)$, represented by the hatched area $MNDA$, and the area DEF, the social cost of the reduction in research activity from m_1 to m_2, if the patent excess burden

---

[3]Only run-of-the-mill inventions are considered here. This means that cases in which marginal cost in Figure 2.1 falls below P_2, and optimal exploitation of the patent right involves an increase in Q are excluded. Minor cost-reducing inventions will generally be of the run-of-the-mill type. [Nordhaus (1969, pp. 70–73) provides a clear discussion.] Note also that price discrimination by the monopolist is ruled out here.

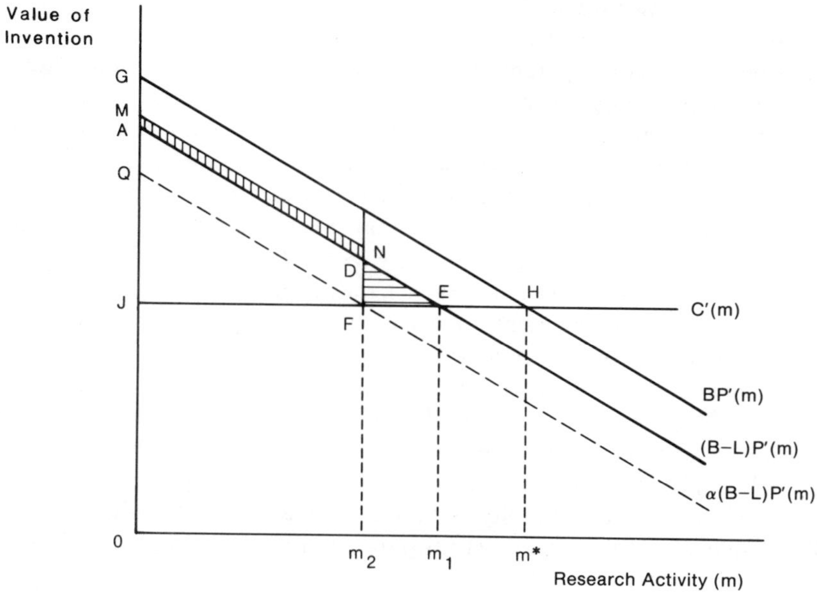

FIGURE 2.3. The Old Economics of Patents: Determination of Patent Life

remains equal to L. Assuming L is positive, as α decreases from 1 (i.e., as T decreases from infinity), this difference is initially positive, and a maximum occurs at some life T^* where the increase in the area of triangle DEF equals that of $MNDA$.

The magnitude of the potential returns from the reduction of T from infinity is limited to some fraction of $P(m_1)L$, which is itself a fraction of the gross expected benefits at m_1, $P(m_1)B$. In Figure 2.1, L/B equals the ratio of the area ABC to the area P_0ACP_1. More generally, the following approximation holds:

$$\frac{L}{B} \approx \frac{\frac{1}{2} dP \cdot dQ}{dP \cdot Q} \tag{6}$$

$$= \frac{1}{2}\, \eta^D \frac{dP}{P}.$$

Thus, the value of L/B for a category II (cost-reducing) invention depends on the elasticity of demand η^D *for the product that has its production cost lowered, as well as on the degree of cost reduction dP*. To take an example considered typical of run-of-the-mill inventions by Nordhaus (1969, p.81), if the demand elasticity is -1 and the cost reduction is five percent, $L/B = 0.025$.

More generally, the potential gain from adjusting T is typically a small percentage of the gross expected benefits of research.

The relation between patent life and the social value of the patent, under the old view of patents, is illustrated for several cases in Figure 2.4. Cases IA and IB show the relation between net expected social gain from invention and the life of the patent using an example like the one illustrated in Figure 2.3,[4] with $r = 0.15$, $B = 1$, and L/B values of 0 and 0.1, respectively, the latter being chosen as a relatively "high" value. Note that the optimal patent life T^* (the value of T at the peak of the curve) is 17 years for $L/B = 0.1$ but infinity for $L/B = 0$. [For $L/B = 0.025$ (not illustrated), the optimal life is 23 years.] Cases IIA and IIB illustrate the relation when the (constant) marginal cost of research is 50 percent higher than in the previous example, for $L = 0$ and $L = 0.1$, respectively.[5] These cases represent a line of research of lower expected productivity.[6] Optimal patent life for $L = 0.1$ is 23 years.

Although optimal patent life is sensitive to L/B in both cases shown, cases IA through IIB show that social welfare is remarkably insensitive to T over a large range. Other examples yield similar results. [See Nordhaus (1969, p. 84) for an examination of numerous parameter combinations in a similar model.]

These results imply that choosing a statutory patent life is a relatively simple problem. Because precision in the choice of T is unimportant, a standard statutory life can be chosen for all patents without significant diminution of the expected social value of each invention. The administrative economy (if not absolute necessity) of such a broad rule is obvious to anyone remotely familiar with the patenting process. Further, Figure 2.4 shows that the loss function for errors in T has a happy asymmetry—large losses can occur only if a fairly short patent life is chosen.

Thus, the prescription of this analysis is straightforward. The fixed patent lives of 17 years in the United States and from 14 to 20 years in many other countries are quite acceptable, since they come close to maximizing the social value of competitive research processes over a wide range of relevant parameters. The above analysis obviously indicates that the standardization of patent lives, which brings enormous administrative benefits, comes at negligible cost. Further, attempts to determine the optimum standardized life appear unlikely to be worth the effort involved. But we shall see below that the

---

[4]The actual functions are $C(m) = 0.005m$ and $P(m) = 0.01m - 0.0001m^2$. At equilibrium with $L = 0$, the latter curve has elasticity of two thirds with respect to m.

[5]In Figure 2.4, curves IA and IIA converge on the single dotted line to the top right of the figure.

[6]At $L = 0$ and unlimited patent life, expected benefits exceed costs by one-sixth in this case, whereas the equivalent figure for the previous case was one-half.

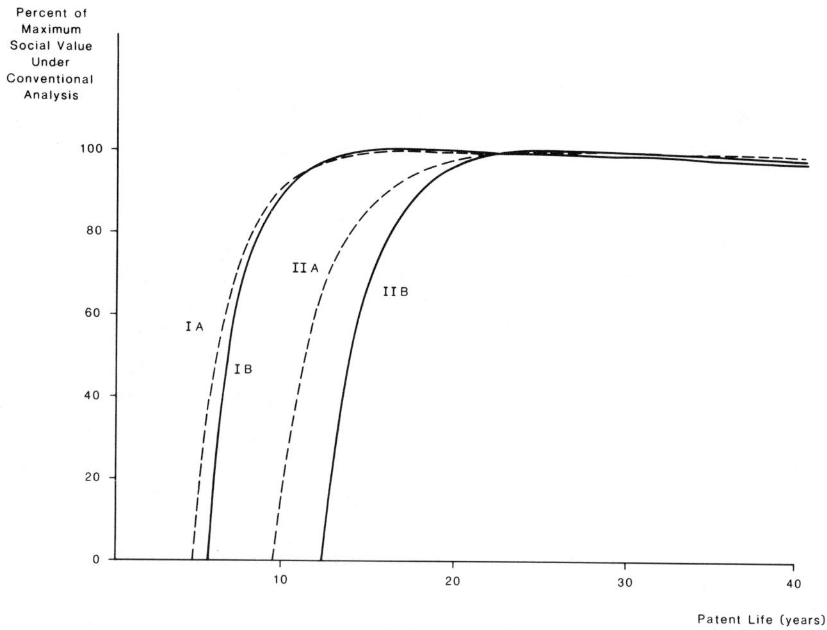

FIGURE 2.4. The Effect of Patent Life on the Social Value of Research: The Conventional Patent Economics. (Elasticity of supply of research effort is assumed to be infinite.)

above analysis and its unusually happy public policy implications are unfortunately incorrect, especially when research is highly responsive to incentives.

THE "COMMON POOL PROBLEM" AND THE NEW ECONOMICS OF PATENTS

The conventional economics of patents assumes that the production of inventions is like other productive activities that use private inputs under competitive profit maximization. But using the model developed above, it is easy to show that this is not the case. Since all of the competitive researchers are equally proficient in this model, each has an equal chance of success. Hence, each will perceive the marginal and average return for each unit of effort (each "ticket" in the "invention lottery") as $[(B - L)P(m)]/m$, the expected average return. The researchers, being rational profit maximizers, will set marginal cost equal to this expected return:

$$C'(m) = \frac{(B - L)P(m)}{m}. \tag{7}$$

If L is negligible, this equilibrium occurs at point H in Figure 2.2, where the slope of $C(m)$ equals the slope of the ray OG. Net social benefit is HD, which is by construction less than the optimal net social benefit AF. If the total cost curve $C(m)$ were linear (i.e., if research effort were supplied at constant cost), it is easy to see that research would yield no net social benefit at all under this scheme.

This misallocation, which was noted by Usher (1964), is similar to the problem of overexploitation of an unregulated fishery (Gordon, 1954). It is also akin to what is understood in the popular literature as the tragedy of the commons (Hardin, 1968), to other rent-seeking behavior (Krueger, 1974), and more generally to directly unproductive profit-seeking (DUP) behavior (Bhagwati and Srinivasan, 1984). The dissipation of the benefits of research by the competitive production of inventions before the socially optimal time (Barzel, 1968; Kitti, 1973; Loury, 1979; Dasgupta and Stiglitz, 1980; Dow, 1984) is a dynamic intertemporal version of the same type of market failure. The related problem of wasteful duplication of research effort is documented and discussed by Beck (1976, 1981).

Attention to this type of resource misallocation may have been reduced by empirical evidence showing private rates of return to R & D in the 1950s and 1960s of 30 percent or more.[7] But a recent study (Pakes and Shankerman, 1979) concludes that the private return on R & D is only between 3 and 5 percent higher than the return on other capital. They explain this differential as a modest risk premium. The contrast with earlier results arises mainly from their estimate of at least 18 percent for the depreciation rate of the private value of a discovery. Previous studies assumed that the depreciation rate was equal to the much lower rate of decay of physical productivity of other capital. Though Pakes and Shankerman attribute the low rate of return to the increasing difficulty of preventing appropriation of inventions by competitors, the model presented here shows why one might expect their result regardless of the significance of that problem, if the supply of research is reasonably elastic.

There are two ways of correcting the misallocation of research resources in the model developed above.[8] The first (and less practical) solution is to

---

[7]See, for example, Mansfield (1965) or Griliches (1980).

[8]Barzel (1968), Kitti (1973), Beck (1981), and Yu (1981) consider schemes in which a researcher bids at auction for the right to protection from wasteful competition in a specified line of research. It is by no means clear that empirical implementation would incur fewer distortions of resource allocation than the current patent system. Kitch claims that his "prospect theory" of the patent system implies that the preemption of future research under patent protection reduces competitive resource misallocation. A critique of this theory based on legal authority and empirical evidence is found in Beck (1983). Kingston (1984) proposes "Innovation Warrants" awarded prior to the achievement of the innovation, on the grounds that such protection from the threat of competition will encourage innovation. See Wright (1985) for some comments on Kingston's proposal.

change the rules so that the patent is awarded only when just one successful outcome is achieved, for only then is the successful effort marginally productive. If several researchers discover the same discrete objective considered here, the marginal social value of each of their efforts is zero. In this static context, all researchers would submit their results to the Patent Office. Competition should prevent collaboration between researchers to mask multiple successes, since verification would require communication of the result with no guarantee that the receiving party has really made the same discovery.[9]

In the real world, this system might be much more difficult to administer than, for example, the current patent system, which is itself perceived by some legal authorities as being in serious trouble owing to the cost and inefficiency of legal enforcement. In continuous time, the invention process has no determinate end period; it is cumulative and continuous. The marginal social contribution of inventors lies in advancing the introduction of their discovery. In practice, distinguishing this marginal contribution might well be an impossible counterfactual exercise. Because of these questions about its administrative feasibility, this alternative is not considered further here, although market incentives awarded under this criterion otherwise dominate conventional patents, as shown in the more technical discussion presented by Wright (1983).

The second method of correcting this problem is to reduce the award sufficiently to obtain the optimal resource allocation. Ignoring the welfare cost L for the moment, the necessary reduction factor is a fraction α_0, the elasticity of $P(m)$ with respect to m:

$$\alpha_0 = h[P(m)] \equiv \frac{mP'(m)}{P(m)}. \tag{8}$$

In Figure 2.2, the slope of OJ equals $R'(m^*)$ and $C'(m^*)$. Assuming L=0, the value of the patent should be reduced by a fraction $(R^* - R^{**})/R^*$ of the value of the discovery, so that equilibrium occurs at point K. If several researchers are successful, this reduced reward is bestowed randomly to one of them or is shared by all. In practice, this would be achieved by limitation of patent life, which is usually justified by economists (e.g., Nordhaus, 1969; Scherer, 1972) only as a means of achieving an optimal tradeoff between the excess burden of the patent restriction and the supposed advantages of awarding successful researchers the full social value of a discovery, as discussed above. This new view of the role of the patent life limitation was recognized by Kitti (1973). It builds on insights found in Usher (1964) and Barzel (1968).

---

[9]The interested reader can compare this solution with the "Clarke Tax," proposed as a mechanism for obtaining honest revelation of preferences for public goods (Clarke, 1971; Tideman and Tullock, 1976). Susan Rose-Ackerman drew my attention to an analogy between the two schemes.

The relation between patent life and the social contribution of R & D, according to this new view of the patent incentive, is illustrated in Figure 2.5, where cases IA through IIB illustrate the same cases used in Figure 2.4. Note that optimal patent life increases with L in this case, in contrast to the old patent economics analysis of Figure 2.4. Clearly, the patent welfare cost L has much less significance for the optimal patent life T^* in Figure 2.5 than in Figure 2.4. But the magnitude of L and the length of patent life are both much more crucial for patent system efficiency than suggested in the latter.

In contrast to Figure 2.4, large losses can result when too long a patent life is chosen. For cases IA and IB, a patent life of 17 years (as in the United States) wastes over 60 percent of the maximum expected net social value. (If the current practice of providing tax incentives to R & D through expensing of capital inputs were also taken into account, the discrepancy would be even greater.) For case IB, the loss incurred at optimally adjusted T, due to the welfare cost L of the patent system, which has been the focus of much of the literature, is only about one-half the loss caused by a nonoptimal 17-year patent life. (This number cannot be read from the graph, because of the proportional scaling of the vertical axis.) For case IIB, on the other hand, a

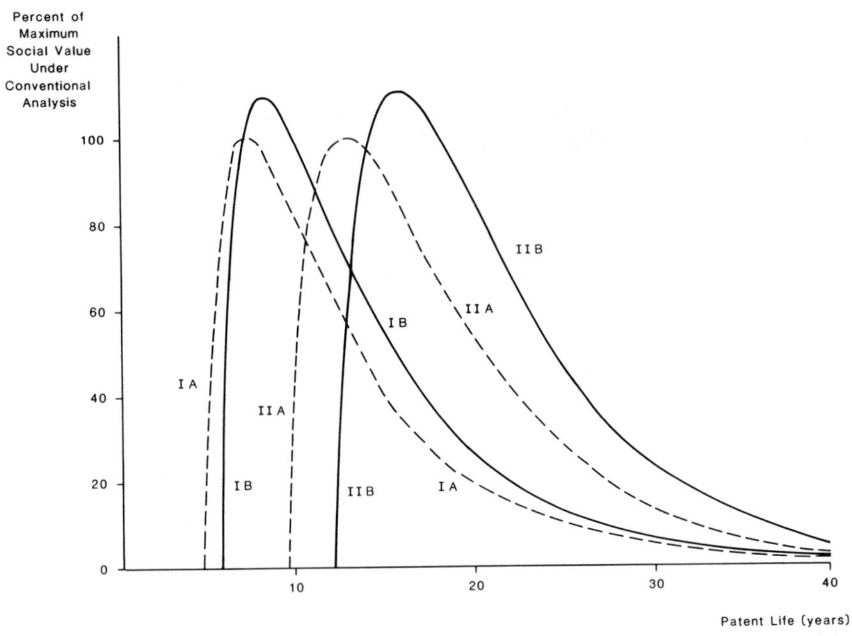

FIGURE 2.5. The Effect of Patent Life on the Social Value of Research: The New Patent Economics

17-year life limit is almost optimal. The welfare cost of $L/B = 0.1$ causes a 55 percent loss in the (lower) potential social value of research in this higher-cost case.

Although T is less sensitive to L/B than in Figure 2.4, accurate estimation of L is more important in this new analysis. In Figure 2.4, mistakenly assuming that L/B equals 0 when it really equals 0.1 means a large error in T but a trivial loss in potential social benefit of research. In Figure 2.5, the same mistake means a much smaller error in T. But an error of only a few years in either direction in choosing T can destroy a large portion of the expected net social value of the invention process. If the optimal T is chosen assuming case IIA (which assumes $L = 0$) when case IIB ($L = 0.1$) actually holds over 40 percent of the maximum social value is lost.

Most serious of all, the efficiency of a given choice of T is also very sensitive to the parameters of the invention model. If T is chosen with case II in mind, the greater part of the potential social value expected from the invention process is lost if costs have been overestimated by 50 percent, for then case I applies. If the reverse mistake is made, all of the potential contribution of the invention process is wasted, since no research takes place, in case II if T is set at the optimal level for case I.

For a given success function $P(m)$, the sensitivity of the expected social benefit to patent life is highest when the supply elasticity of research effort is infinite, as in the above examples. For example, if case I is altered so that the supply curve is unit elastic (i.e., a straight line through 0 and H in Figure 2.3), then the relation between patent life and expected social benefit is shown, for a "typical" L/B value of 0.025, in Figure 2.6. This case, denoted case III, looks much more like the relation derived for cases I and II using the conventional patent economics in Figure 2.4, and accuracy in the choice of patent life is less crucial than for case I and II.

The three cases examined are sufficient to show that if research supply is elastic, the cost of a uniform patent life is much greater than the old patent economics indicated. Even though cases I and II differ only in the level of costs, a standard patent life to cover both would waste at least 20 percent of the expected benefits of one or the other. More extreme examples would only reinforce the conclusion that the administrative advantage of a uniform-life patent system is a potentially costly convenience.

Of course, if the relevant parameters were known to the Patent Office, individual optimal patent lives would be tailor-made for each definable area of research. If the optimal lives were correctly calculated, the achievable welfare for $L > 0$ could conceivably be higher than implied in the conventional analysis outlined in the previous section, for shorter patent life reduces the present value of the patent excess burden. For example, the optimum for case IIB illustrated in Figure 2.5 shows a net expected welfare of almost 110, or nearly 10 percent higher than the maximum gain reported for case IIB in

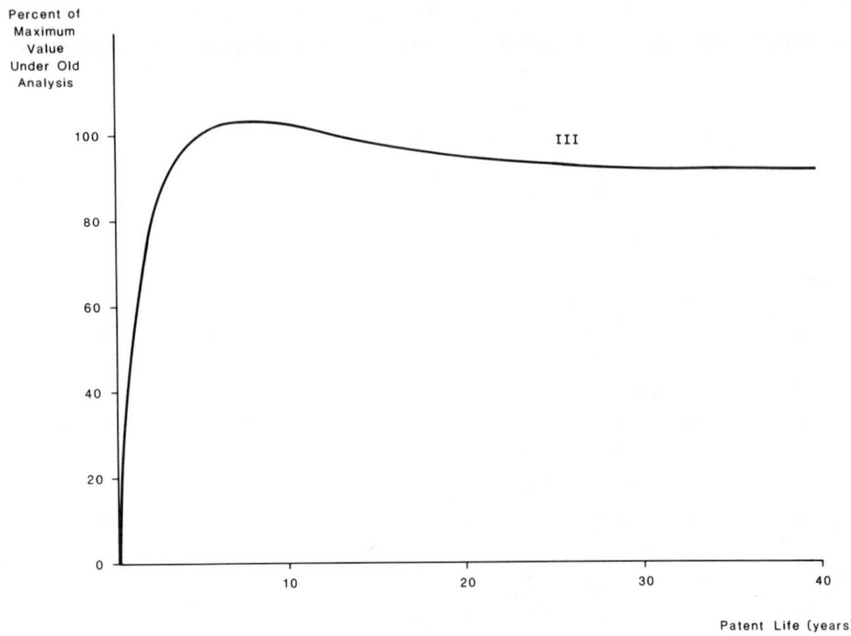

FIGURE 2.6. The Effect of Patent Life When Supply of Research Is Unit Elastic

Figure 2.4. Hence, given that patents were the chosen means of encouraging research, the common pool problem would arguably be a (small) blessing if all pertinent information were freely available and administration were costless. But would *any* kind of patent system be the best means of encouraging research under these conditions? We will return to this question below.

A REEVALUATION OF THE ROLE OF DISCLOSURE

The above analysis of the existing patent system refers exclusively to category II inventions. But the system does not appear to have been adopted with inventions of this type in mind. Rather, the classical analysis of patents implicitly assumes that most discoveries are a composite of category III with category II and/or I inventions. Discovery of a specific process or product (a category I or II invention) is often accompanied by information about the prospects for similar lines of investigation (a category III or IV discovery).

When a patent is awarded, the value of the category II or I element of the discovery is (in the run-of-the-mill case—see above) awarded to the inventor under government protection. But the unpatentable element of the discovery may be made freely available to all others by the description of the invention, filed for public inspection, from which the patent system derives its name. Traditionally, defenders of patents have stressed this role of the patent system as a means of disclosure, given that a discovery has been made.

When the common pool problem is taken into account, these two roles of the patent system can be highly complementary. Disclosure of the category III element of the discovery means that the holder of a patent does not receive all of the social benefits of his or her discovery. But to prevent overallocation of resources to research, some reductions in the realized benefits are generally desirable, as the examples given earlier showed. If, as is likely to be the case, the optimal reduction is greater than that effected by the 17-year patent life limitation, then some loss of patent value through disclosure would be socially beneficial because of its effects on the allocation of research resources.[10]

Of course, the required reduction varies with the relevant parameters of the research model. There is no reason to expect that disclosure leads to the optimal adjustment of the research benefits discussed below. However, if the supply curve of research is horizontal for all positive levels of research, disclosure can only improve the allocation of research resources relative to infinite-life patents without disclosure, since in the latter case, expected net social benefits are zero. More generally, if supply has positive elasticity, some degree of disclosure is always beneficial.

Before concluding this discussion of disclosure, it should be pointed out that though administrative constraints have been recognized by assuming that all patents have a standard length of life, the characterization of the patent system remains rather idealized. In existing patent systems, protection of category I and II inventions is incomplete, because litigation to prevent violations is costly and competitors can often "invent around" a patent, reducing its value. On the other hand, the disclosure provisions are also imperfect—in fact, some writers argue that they have little practical value (see Kitch, 1977). Though these qualifications must be recognized, no evaluation of their importance will be attempted here.

Despite the possible positive contribution of the disclosure function, a patent system with fixed patent life cannot be expected to be nearly as efficient as the old economics of patents had indicated. In the next section, the relative merits of possible alternatives to the current patent system will be considered.

[10]This benefit of disclosure is recognized by Barzel (1968).

ALTERNATIVES TO THE CURRENT PATENT SYSTEM

Choices Requiring Greater Administrative Control

It was noted earlier that if patent life could be "tailor-made" at no cost for each type of research process, and if all relevant information were freely available, then the social value of research under patents might be much higher than under the current system. But under these conditions, the patent is clearly a nonoptimal choice. For example, direct control through public research agencies or by contracts to private individuals could ensure the performance of research tasks identical to those that would have taken place under patents, but financed from tax revenues, presumably at a lower welfare cost than that (L) of the patent restriction.[11]

To justify choice of patents over all other measures, it is necessary to change one of the assumptions of the model. Consider the case in which administration is costless but the public authority in control of research does not have all the information available to (all) researchers about the parameters of the research process. Direct acquisition of the researchers' information by the public authority may well encounter moral hazard problems. Here it is ruled out as too costly, or just downright infeasible. An informational imbalance between researchers and the government authority is incorporated in the equations for the cost of research and the benefits of inventions as follows:

$$\hat{C}(m) = (1 + \theta)C(m) \tag{9}$$

and

$$\hat{B} = B(1 + \zeta) \tag{10}$$

where θ and ζ are random shifters and

$$E(\tilde{\theta}) = E(\tilde{\zeta}) = 0,\ E(\tilde{\theta}^2) = \sigma_\theta^2,\ E(\tilde{\zeta}^2) = \sigma_\zeta^2,\ E(\tilde{\theta}\tilde{\zeta}) = 0. \tag{11}$$

For now, the welfare cost L of the patent restriction and that of financing contracts are assumed away.

This is a two-period model. In period 1, the government authority must choose the means it will use to encourage research, knowing σ_θ^2 and σ_ζ^2 but not θ and ζ, and researchers make their production commitments, given their knowledge of the relevant values of θ and ζ. The simple rational expectations assumption is made that all parties know the equations of the model (Muth, 1961), and all are assumed risk neutral.

[11] It is, of course, possible that a sufficiently irrational tax scheme would incur a higher welfare cost than L, but one needs only minimal confidence in the fiscal structure to rule out this possibility.

The rest of this discussion is a brief summary of results derived by Wright (1983). Consider the simple case where $\theta = 0$ and $\zeta = \pm\zeta^0$, with probabilities $P(\zeta^0) = P(-\zeta^0) = 0.5$. Then the expected value of the patent instrument, relative to a direct central allocation of research, is illustrated in Figure 2.7. Since the government authority does not know ζ, the best it can do is to set m equal to m_0 by, for example, contracting for m_0 units of research. If there were no common pool problem, then where $\zeta = +\zeta^0$, the new equilibrium value of m under (infinite-life) patents would be at m_1. In this case, the value of the added flexibility afforded by the patent system is the increased economic surplus represented by area *GHE*, relative to the contractual allocation of m_0. Similarly, when $\zeta = -\zeta^0$, the equilibrium level of research is m_2, and the differential value of the patent system is represented by the area *EFB*. Since both areas represent gains, if there were no common pool problem and if *L* were zero, patents

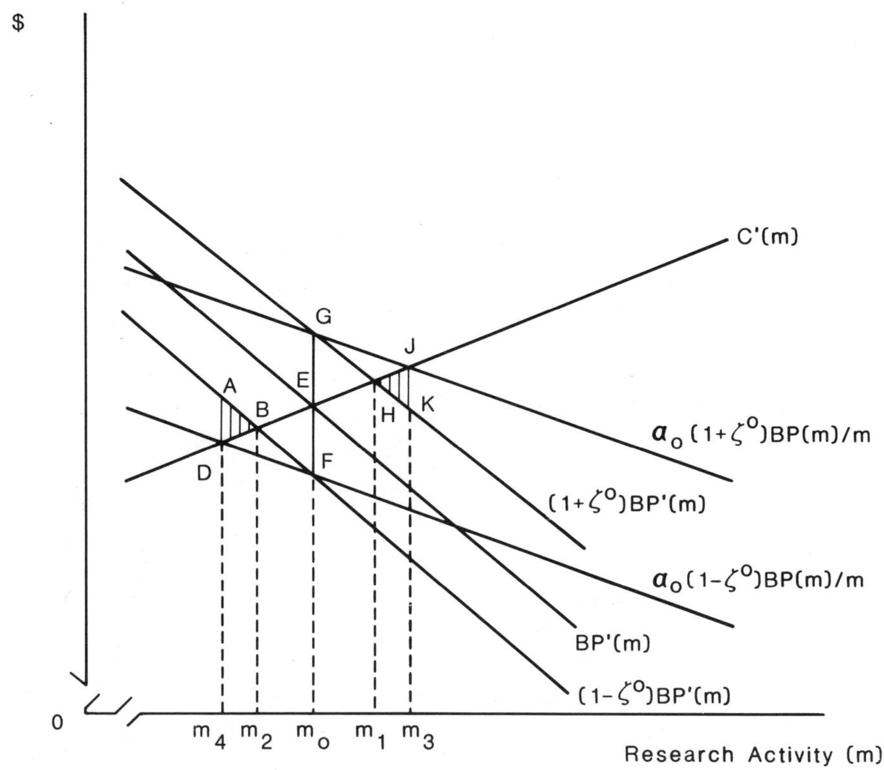

FIGURE 2.7. The Social Value of Research Under Patents Relative to Prizes or Contracts When Researchers Have Exclusive Information About Discovery Value

would always dominate contracts for category I and category II inventions because of their informational advantages.[12]

Variable-Life Patents

In a competitive model, the common pool problem does exist. If the correction factor

$$\alpha_0 \equiv h(P) \equiv \frac{mP'(m_0)}{P(m_0)}$$

is applied to the perceived incentive $(1 + \zeta)BP(m)/m$ (through "tailor-made" patent life limitation in a multi-period model), then equilibrium occurs at either m_3 or m_4 in Figure 2.7. At $\zeta = +\zeta^0$, the reduction in social benefit from the patent is represented by area *HJK*, the increase in costs net of the increase in expected benefits. Similarly if $\zeta = -\zeta^0$, the reduction in expected net social benefit of the patent is shown in area *ABD*. Depending on the relative slopes of $C'(m_0)$ and $BP'(m_0)$, the loss in areas *HJK* and *ABD* might exceed the gain in areas *GHE* and *BEF*. If that happens, then contracts are the superior instrument for getting the research done.

The case in which $\zeta = 0$ and $\theta = \pm^{20}$, with $P(\theta^0) = P(-\theta^0) = 0.5$, is illustrated in Figure 2.8. The expected net gain from the patent system relative to the contract alternative is represented by one-half the sum of areas *FHG* and *EFB* minus one-half the sum of areas *HJK* and *ABD*.

More generally, assume $\tilde{\zeta}$ and $\tilde{\theta}$ are independent and have compact distributions and small variances θ_ζ^2 and θ_θ^2. If contracts can be financed with negligible excess burden, the expected net difference between the social value of using patents and the social value of contracts is approximately (see Appendix)

$$E(D_1) = m_0C'(m_0)\left\{\frac{(\sigma_\zeta^2 + \sigma_\theta^2)}{2[(1/\eta) - h(AP)]}\left[1 + \frac{h(MP) - h(AP)}{1/\eta - h(AP)}\right] - \frac{L}{B}\right\}, \quad (12)$$

where η is the elasticity of supply of research inputs and $h(MP)$ and $h(AP)$ are, respectively, the elasticities of marginal and average probabilities of success with respect to m. This expression is, in the absence of further restrictions, of ambiguous sign, even if $L = 0$. Thus, more sophisticated variable-life patents are not necessarily better than contracts, in this model, even if their lives are optimally tailored to the parameters of the problem.

---

[12]The method of analysis used here is an extension of the approach of Weitzman (1974). The material in this section follows the more detailed and comprehensive treatment found in Wright (1983), to which those readers with a special interest in this analytical approach may wish to refer.

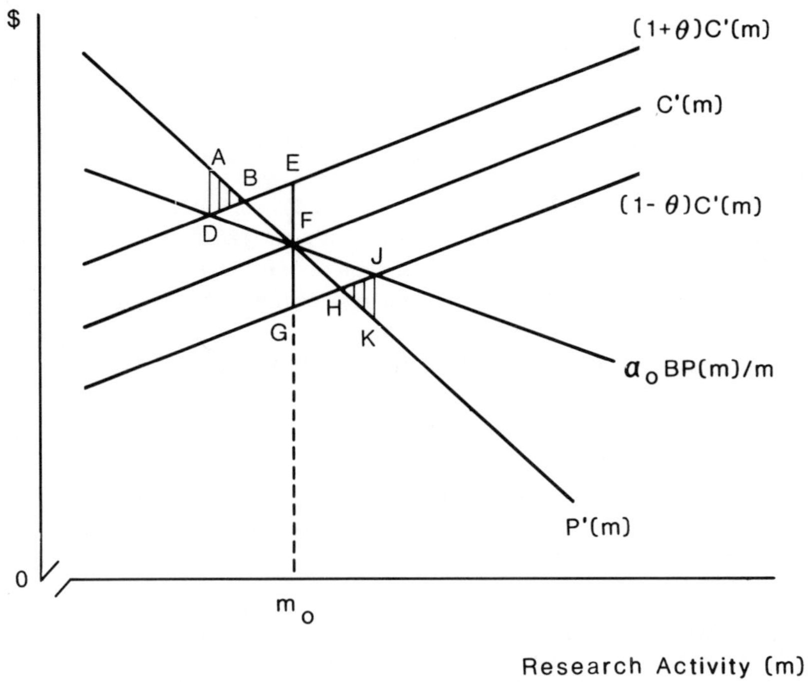

FIGURE 2.8. The Social Value of Patents or Prizes Relative to Contracts When Researchers Have Exclusive Cost Information

Prizes

By assumption, the entire welfare cost L can be avoided if the government authority offers prizes instead of patents—but the cost is that information on ζ is lost, since the reward for success is set by the central authority. The equation for the expected net difference in social welfare from using prizes rather than contracts is

$$E(D_2) = m_0C'(m_0)\left\{\frac{\sigma_\theta^2}{2[1/\eta - h(AP)]}\left[1 + \frac{h(MP) - h(AP)}{1/\eta - h(AP)}\right]\right\}. \qquad (13)$$

The sign of this expression is also in general ambiguous. Thus, if administration is costless, it is necessary to know $h(MP)$, $h(AP)$, η, L/B, σ_θ^2 and σ_ζ^2 to optimally choose between patents, prizes, and contracts. Since none of these parameters is very easy to observe, the choice of the best means of controlling research is no simple task in this context. Actually, the superiority of direct control (i.e., contracts) over the other options can be determined from just the three elasticities $h(MP)$, $h(AP)$, and η.[13] But estimation of these elasticities appears to be a real challenge, given the present state of data on R & D. Perhaps close cooperation between economists and those directly involved in R & D could help generate the data needed to inform our intuition about these parameters, at least for some of the better-understood types of research processes.

In the absence of such information, we must resort to a rather arbitrarily specified functional form for $P(m)$ to provide an example of the optimal choice between the three instruments. If each of m units of research effort can be expended on a subset of $n > m$ possible research possibilities, each with the same probability of success π, and if each researcher knows which of these are being pursued by others, so that he can avoid duplication, then

$$P(m) = 1 - (1 - \pi)^m. \tag{14}$$

In this case, the optimal choice between patents, prizes (both limited in value to eliminate the fishing problem), and contracts can be determined from Figure 2.9. Along each of the four contours, patents and prizes are equally

[13]A sufficient condition, assuming linearity, for the inferiority of contracts relative to prizes depends on just η and $h(MP)$. Contracts are inferior if the expected marginal cost curve $C'(m)$ is steeper than the expected marginal return curve $BP'(m)$, i.e., if $\eta h(MP) < -1$. This condition can be verified by constructing alternative cases similar to that illustrated in Figure 2.8. It is analogous to the condition derived by Weitzman (1974) in evaluating the simpler choice between price and quantity controls in his model.

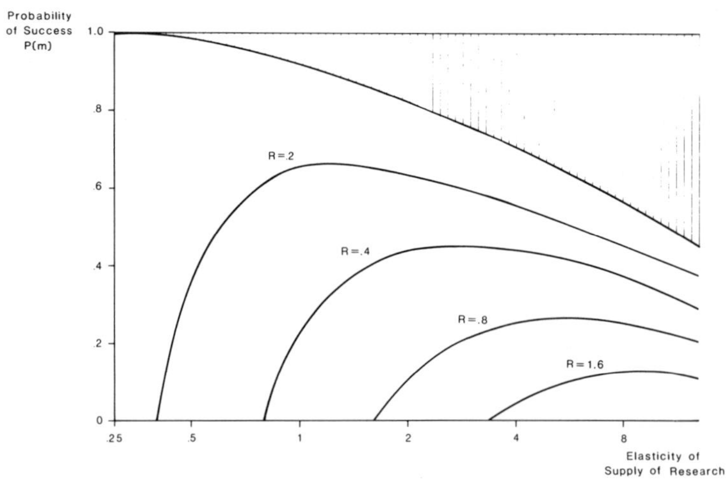

FIGURE 2.9. The Choice Between Patents, Prizes, and Research Contracts

$[R \equiv (L/B)/\sigma_\zeta^2,\ P(m) = 1 - (1 - \pi)^m$, with $\pi = 0.01]$

efficient, given the indicated value of $\rho \equiv (L/B)/\sigma_\zeta^2$. Above (below) the contour, prizes (patents) are more efficient. In the hatched region, contracts dominate both patents and prizes. As Figure 2.9 shows, prizes are most attractive when the elasticity of supply of research η and the probability of success $P(m_0)$ are both low. Contracts are best when the elasticity of supply is very high, and a high probability of success also favors contracts. The dominance of contracts is independent of the value of ρ.

Other forms of the function $P(m)$ may give somewhat different results. Most of the reasonable alternative specifications that come easily to mind would probably imply a smaller range of dominance for patents. For example, if the number of promising research alternatives is rather small, and duplication of research is more likely, the divergence between marginal and average rewards that lies at the heart of the common pool problem might be much greater than in the above example, in which case the relative attractiveness of contracts of other means of direct central control would be greater.

Choices Requiring Less Administrative Attention

Secrecy

The set of feasible alternatives for controlling research activity depends on the administrative capacity of the system and on the nature of the anticipated discoveries. If any system requiring a greater degree of public involvement (legal and bureaucratic) than the current system of awarding patents is ruled out as administratively infeasible (or unacceptably costly, which amounts to the same thing), then the only real alternative is maintenance of secrecy.

Secrecy has been discussed frequently in the literature, but has attracted little analytical attention. Though this author shall not attempt a full economic analysis of the secrecy alternative here,[14] important aspects of this alternative can be understood within the analytical approach developed above.

Obviously secrecy cannot usefully protect category II or IV inventions, which cannot be exploited without revealing the discovery to others. For other inventions, secrecy implies a welfare cost incurred owing to the profit-maximizing restriction of the use of the knowledge generated, like the patent welfare cost illustrated in Figure 2.1. The size of this cost depends on the duration of the successful defense of the secret, which depends on the extent of public protection of secrecy, on the private resources devoted to attacking and defending secrecy, and on the effectiveness of offensive and defensive measures.

---

[14]Secrecy is discussed in somewhat greater detail by Wright (1981); see also Cheung (1982).

In the two-period stochastic model used above, the efficiency of secrecy probably is bounded by the following alternative cases. If two or more independent discoverers can keep (and exploit) a secret as easily as one, then the common pool problem will tend to dissipate the social value of the research just as it does in the case of a patent with unlimited life. If two or more cannot keep a secret at all, but a single discoverer can protect his or her find, then the secrecy alternative is approximately as socially valuable as the alternative patent system mentioned above, which would award a patent only when just one researcher makes a discovery. (This patent system has been ruled out as infeasible in this chapter.) The expected advantage of this type of award over contracts is derived by Wright (1983) as

$$E(D_3) = m_0 C'(m_0) \left\{ \frac{\sigma_\zeta^2 + \sigma_\theta^2}{2[1/\eta - h(MP)]} - \frac{L}{B} \right\}. \tag{15}$$

Since a comparison with (12) above shows that $E(D_3) \geqslant E(D_1)$, secrecy can be socially attractive if two cannot keep a secret but one can, especially when the administrative economics are taken into account. Unfortunately, the data necessary to form a judgment on the extent of joint exploitation of research secrets independently discovered by different researchers are not available. Since evidence of such activity might imply criminal collusion in the United States, it would be surprising if it were easy to come by.

Unfortunately, secrecy may exacerbate another source of waste of resources, namely, duplication of research that has already been performed by others (see Beck, 1976; Kitch, 1977, p. 276). Under a patent system, the publicity of the patent award helps reduce this type of waste, by informing potential researchers that certain lines of investigation have already been covered.

Throughout this discussion, we have assumed that the potential for exploiting category I or III discoveries under secrecy is not hampered by the need for the discoverer to provide the other complementary inputs (or to find a partner or backer who will keep the secret). In practice, this may be unrealistic, especially for small, competitive research firms. To the extent that this is true, the advantages of secrecy considered in this section have been overstated.

For category I and III inventions, secrecy is always available as an alternative to the patent system. Reduction of patent lives for the allocation reasons indicated earlier will encourage abandonment of the patent system in favor of this alternative. Whether this is a socially desirable outcome depends on the net effect of the advantages and disadvantages of secrecy outlined above. It may be that no general answer is possible. If secrecy is viewed as socially undesirable, despite its administrative advantages, a natural conclusion might be that governments should not protect corporate secrets. But this apparently obvious conclusion is not generally correct. If government protection is withdrawn, it is reasonable to expect that more inventions will be patented, which is the desired result. But it is equally reasonable to expect that private resources will be devoted to attacking and defending the category I secrets that remain and the category III discoveries that by definition have no alternative protection besides secrecy. The desirability of government protection depends on the net result of these two effects. The resources expended on attacking and defending secrecy represent additional costs of secrecy, which should be taken into account in a more detailed analysis.

CONCLUSION

The benefits that society reaps from R & D may well fall far below the theoretical optimum that could be attained with perfect public knowledge of the costs and expected benefits of different research activities. Economists and policymakers have not fully appreciated the magnitude of this gap between potential and performance. R & D activity is subject to several types of market failure. Though plausible solutions can be found for each, their interaction presents problems that are much more difficult to handle and that justify a full reappraisal of the current set of public policy instruments for controlling R & D in a competitive economy.

Currently, patents, where feasible, are the favored means of encouraging research because of the administrative economies and informational efficiency associated with their relative decentralization. Their most widely recognized drawback, the welfare cost associated with the restriction of use of the patented invention, is generally considered to be of minor significance, though it has helped to justify the limitation of patent life to 17 years or thereabout. Since the social benefits in the conventional patent economics are remarkably insensitive to patent life for lives above one dozen years or so, the uniformity of the life limitation, which is such a great administrative economy, appears to come at a trivial welfare cost.

But according to the arguments presented here, supported by current empirical results, such patents should encourage competitive overallocation of resources for patentable research, unless the unpatentable "spillover" associated with discoveries is sufficiently large. Indeed, if the supply of research is elastic, this spillover, which is commonly viewed as a source of resource misallocation, may constitute the major net economic benefit of the research, a large part of the remainder of the social benefit being dissipated through wasteful duplication of results and/or research tasks. The subsidy implicit in the tax treatment of R & D may well exacerbate this problem.

It is possible to improve the allocation of research resources by adjusting patent life. In this new analysis, the social benefit of research can be highly sensitive to the accuracy of this adjustment; a mistake of a few years in either direction can lead to a heavy loss of new research benefits. In addition, optimal patent life is a function of several parameters that are difficult to observe and of the welfare cost of the patent restriction. (In contrast to the old patent economics, optimal patent life is a positive function of the latter.) Unfortunately, much of the gap between current and optimal patent performance must remain, unless different patent lives are offered for different areas of research.

Given sufficient information about the relevant parameters, each area of research could have a different patent life. But by extending the analysis to recognize very plausible informational asymmetrics, it has been shown that if some information about the costs or rewards of research remains hidden from the public authority controlling research, direct government contractual control might be superior to patents. This is more likely when the supply of research effort is elastic. Paradoxically, high economic responsiveness can penalize the more decentralized alternative. In this situation, the administrative advantages of the current uniform-life patents would be largely lost. Further, even if this adjustable-life patent system were administratively feasible, prizes, which are now offered mainly for nonpatentable discoveries, might be the best type of incentive, especially if the supply of research effort is inelastic.

Of course, the administrative economy of a fixed-life patent system may well outweigh any theoretical advantages of the above alternatives, for most types of applied research. If that is the case, further work to determine the best patent life and the optimal tax treatment of R & D certainly appears to be justified. The above analysis has suggested that the alternative of protecting discoveries through secrecy, where practicable, might in fact be the socially desirable alternative in certain situations.

This appraisal of resource allocation in R & D should be understood as tentative and even speculative. Important facts of life, like risk aversion and monopoly, as well as dynamic considerations, have been assumed away. The main point is that getting the greatest net return from this sector is much trickier than we have hitherto believed. In fact, it may be one of the most difficult allocation problems of modern society. The problem is clearly important enough to justify further investigation by economists and others concerned with public policy—encouraged, presumably, by explicit or implicit prizes and/or research contracts.

APPENDIX

The Social Value of a Variable-Life Patent

The variable-life patent is awarded to a successful inventor, or shared by all successful inventors, in period 2. The common pool problem is avoided by reducing the value of the patent by the factor α (the atemporal version of the "patent life limitation") announced in period 1. The analysis that follows is presented in more detail by Wright (1983), to which article the interested reader is referred. The cost of research is

$$C(m) = (1 + \theta)[\bar{C} + a(m - m_0)] + \tfrac{1}{2}b(m - m_0)^2, \tag{A.1}$$

where $\bar{C}$ is the cost of research when $\theta = 0$ and $m = m_0$ —the optimal allocation if ζ and θ are fixed at zero. The social value of an invention $\hat{B}$ is

$$\hat{B} = B(1 + \zeta), \tag{A.2}$$

where B is assumed to be independent of m. The probability that at least one research effort will succeed is

$$P(m) = \bar{P} + e(m - m_0) + \tfrac{1}{2}f(m - m_0)^2, \tag{A.3}$$

where $\bar{P}$ is the probability of success at m_0.

Assume that there are no administrative costs and that revenue can be raised with no excess burden. Then, in the nonstochastic case, the equilibrium allocation m_0 can be achieved by direct government purchases at the price

$$R'(m_0) = \alpha_0 \frac{B\bar{P}}{m_0}, \tag{A.4}$$

where

$$\alpha_0 = h(P) \equiv \frac{em_0}{\bar{P}}. \tag{A.5}$$

If the patent instrument is adopted in the stochastic model, the first-order difference in the incentive from Eq. A.4, evaluated at $\alpha = \alpha_0$, $m = m_0$, $\zeta = \theta = L = 0$, is

$$E_c\left[\alpha_0 \frac{R(m)}{m} - R'(m_0)\right] = \tag{A.6}$$

$$E_c\left\{\alpha_0 \frac{B}{m_0} P'(m_0)(m - m_0) + \frac{B\bar{P}}{m_0}\left[\alpha_0\left(\zeta - \frac{L}{B}\right) + (\alpha - \alpha_0)\right]\right\}$$

where E_c denotes the expectation of competitive researchers as of period 1. Inventors determine m in period 1 based on their knowledge of the stochastic terms and the announced value of α:

$$m = t(\zeta, \theta, \alpha). \tag{A.7}$$

A first-order approximation to the equilibrium change in marginal cost, evaluated at $m = m_0$ and $\theta = 0$, is

$$E_c[C'(m) - C'(m_0)] = \theta a + b(m - m_0). \tag{A.8}$$

Equating Eqs. A.6 and A.8, discarding higher-order terms, and using Eq. A.7,

$$t(\zeta, \theta, \alpha) - m_0 = \frac{a\theta - 1/m_0[\alpha_0(B\bar{P}\zeta + \bar{P}L) - B\bar{P}(\alpha - \alpha_0)]}{\alpha_0/m_0(Be - B\bar{P}/m_0) - b}\,. \tag{A.9}$$

The patent administration chooses α in period 1 to maximize expected net social benefits, given that it knows the parameters of the model and σ_ζ^2 and σ_θ^2, but not ζ and θ. Assuming an interior maximum and that the second-order conditions are satisfied, expected consumer and producer surplus is maximized at

$$\begin{aligned} &E_G\left[(1 + \tilde{\zeta})(1 - L/B)B\left\{e + f[t(\zeta, \theta, \alpha) - m_0]\right\}\right] \\ &\quad = E_G\left\{(1 + \tilde{\theta})a + b[t(\zeta, \theta, \alpha) - m_0]\right\}, \end{aligned} \tag{A.10}$$

where E_G denotes the expectation of the patent administration as of period 1. Since, in the nonstochastic case, equilibrium by definition occurs at m_0,

$$Be = a. \tag{A.11}$$

Substituting Eq. A.9 in Eq. A.10, using Eq. A.11, and eliminating higher-order terms,

$$\begin{aligned} &B\bar{P}\,(\alpha - \alpha_0) = \\ &\frac{aL/B[\alpha_0(a - B\bar{P}/m_0) - bm_0] - \sigma_\zeta^2\alpha_0\bar{P}B^2f - ab\sigma_\theta^2 m_0}{(B - L)f - b} + \alpha_0\bar{P}L. \end{aligned} \tag{A.12}$$

Substituting Eq. A.12 in Eq. A.9 and using Eqs. A.11 and A.5,

$$\begin{aligned} t(\zeta, \theta, \alpha) - m_0 &= \left[\zeta - \theta + \frac{\sigma_\zeta^2 Bf + \sigma_\theta^2 b}{(B - L)f - b}\right] \\ &\times \frac{a}{\alpha_0(a/m_0 - B\bar{P}/m_0^2) - b} + \frac{aL/B}{(B - L)f - b}\Bigg]. \end{aligned} \tag{A.13}$$

The expected cost of the patent distortion is reduced by the same fraction α as the expected value of the patent. So the expected social gain from using the patent incentive rather than a direct allocation of m_0 units to research is, using Eq. A.7,

$$E(D_1) = E_G\{R(t) - R(m_0) - [C(t) - C(m_0)]\} - \frac{\alpha P(m)L}{B}. \quad \text{(A.14)}$$

Substituting Eq. A.13 in Eq. A.14, using Eq. A.5, and eliminating terms of higher order than σ_ζ^2 and σ_θ^2,

$$E(D_1) = m_0 C'(m_0)\left(\frac{\sigma_\zeta^2 + \sigma_\theta^2}{1/\eta - h(AP)}\left\{1 - \frac{1/\eta - h(MP)}{2[1/\eta - h(AP)]}\right\} - \frac{L}{B}\right) \quad \text{(A.15)}$$

where $C'(m_0) = a$ from Eq. A.1 and η is defined as the elasticity of the supply of inventive effort at m_0:

$$\eta = \frac{a}{bm_0}, \quad \text{(A.16)}$$

h(MP) is defined as the elasticity of the marginal probability of success:

$$h(MP) = \frac{fm_0}{e}, \quad \text{(A.17)}$$

and *h(AP)* is the elasticity of the average probability of success:

$$h(AP) = \frac{em_0}{\bar{P}} - 1. \quad \text{(A.18)}$$

Rearranged, Eq. A.15 becomes Eq. 12 in the text.

REFERENCES

Barzel, Yoram, "Optimal Timing of Innovations," *Review of Economics and Statistics* (August 1968): 348–55.

Beck, Roger L., "Patents, Property Rights, and Social Welfare: Search for a Restricted Optimum," *Southern Economic Journal* 43, no. 2 (October 1976).

Beck, Roger L., "Competition for Patent Monopolies," *Research in Law and Economics* 3 (1981): 91–110.

Beck, Roger L., "The Prospect Theory of the Patent System and Unproductive Competition," *Research in Law and Economics* 5 (1983).

Bhagwati, Jagdish N., Richard A. Brecher and T.N. Srinivasan, "DUP Activities and Economic Theory," Chapter 1 in David C. Colander, Ed., *Neoclassical Political Economy*, Cambridge, Mass: Ballinger, 1984.

Cheung, Steven N.S., "Property Rights in Trade Secrets," *Economic Inquiry* 20 (1982): 40–52.

Clarke, E.H., "Multipart Pricing of Public Goods," *Public Choice*, 11 (Fall 1971): 17–33.

Dasgupta, P., and J. Stiglitz, "Uncertainty, Industrial Structure and the Speed of R & D," *The Bell Journal of Economics* 11, no. 1 (Spring 1980): 1–28.

Dow, Gregory K., "Pools and Streams," *Journal of Economic Dynamics and Control* 8 (1984): 117–133.

Gordon, H. Scott, "The Economic Theory of A Common-Property Resource: The Fishery," *Journal of Political Economy* 62 (April 1954): 124–42.

Griliches, Zvi, "Returns to Research and Development in the Private Sector," in J.W. Kendrick and B. Vaccara, eds., *New Developments in Productivity Measurement and Analysis* (Chicago: University of Chicago Press, 1980).

Hardin, Garrett, "The Tragedy of the Commons," *Science* 13 (December 1968): 1243–48.

Hirschleifer, J., "The Private and Social Value of Information and the Reward to Inventive Activity." *American Economic Review* 61 (1971): 561–74.

Kamien, Morton I., and Nancy L. Schwartz, "Market Structure and Innovation: A Survey," *Journal of Economic Literature* 13, no. 1 (March 1975): 1–37.

Kitch, Edmund W., "The Nature and Function of the Patent System," *Journal of Law and Economics* 20, no. 2 (October 1977): 265–90.

Kingston, W., "Innovation Warrants: A Lifeline to Industry?" *Creativity and Innovation Network* January–March 1984.

Kingston, W., *Direct Protection of Innovation*, Report to the European Economic Community D–G XIII, forthcoming.

Kitti, Carole, "Patent Policy and the Optimal Timing of Innovations," Ph.D. Dissertation, University of Chicago, 1973.

Krueger, A.O., "The Political Economy of the Rent-Seeking Society," *American Economic Review* (June 1974).

Loury, Gleen C., "Market Structure and Innovation," *Quarterly Journal of Economics* 93, no. 3 (August 1979): 395–410.

Machlup, Fritz, *An Economic Review of the Patent System*, Study No. 15 of the Subcommittee on Patents, Trademarks, and Copyrights of the Committee on the Judiciary, U.S. Senate, 85th Congress, 2nd Session (Washington, D.C., 1958).

Mansfield, Edwin, "Rates of Return from Industrial Research and Development," *American Economic Review Papers and Proceedings* 55 (May 1965): 310–22.

Muth, John F., "Rational Expectations and the Theory of Price Movements." *Econometrica* 29, no. 3 (July 1961): 315–35.

Nordhaus, William D., *Invention, Growth and Welfare* (Cambridge: MIT Press, 1969).

Pakes, Ariel, and Mark Schankerman, "The Rate of Obsolescence of Knowledge, Research Gestation Lags, and the Private Rate of Return to Research Resources," National Bureau of Economic Research Working Paper No. 346 (1979).

Plant, Arnold, "The Economic Theory Concerning Patents and Inventions," *Economica* 1 (1934): 30–51.

Posner, R.A., *Economic Analysis of Law*, 2nd ed. (Boston: Little, Brown and Co., 1977).

Scherer, F.M., "Nordhaus' Theory of Optimal Patent Life: A Geometric Reinterpretation," *American Economic Review* (June 1972): 422–27.

Scherer, F.M., *The Economic Effects of Compulsory Patent Licensing,* New York University Graduate School of Business Administration, Center for the Study of Financial Institutions, Monograph 1977-2 (New York: New York University, 1977).

Tideman, T. Nicolaus, and Gordon Tullock, "A New and Superior Process for Making Social Choices," *Journal of Political Economy*, 84, no. 6 (December 1976): 1145–59.

Usher, Dan., "The Welfare Economics of Invention," *Economica* 31 (1964): 279–87.

Weitzman, Martin L., "Prices vs. Quantities," *Review of Economic Studies* 41, no. 4 (1974).

Willig, Robert D., "Consumer's Surplus Without Apology," *American Economic Review* 66, no. 4 (September 1976): 589–97.

Wright, Brian D., "Is Protection of the Secrecy of Research Socially Desirable?" Paper presented at the annual meeting of the Eastern Economics Association, Philadelphia, PA, April 10, 1981.

Wright, Brian D., "The Economics of Invention Incentives: Patents, Prizes, and Research Contracts," *American Economic Review* 73, no. 4 (1983): 691–707.

Wright, Brian D., "On the Design of a System to Improve the Production of Innovations," in William Kingston, ed., *Direct Protection of Innovation*, forthcoming report to the European Economic Community, D–G XIII.

Yu, Ben T., "Potential Competition and Contracting in Innovation," *Journal of Law and Economics* 24 (October 1981): 215–38.

3

Patent Life and the Optimal Timing of Innovations*

Carole Kitti

The patent system provides a legal/institutional framework for encouraging the production and financing of a public good—the knowledge embodied in innovations—by the private sector.[1] This type of incentive system allows the private sector to make such decisions as the level of innovation, the time of introduction of new innovations, and the length of the research and development (R & D) period. These private decisions are constrained by the length of the legal patent life and by competition in the form of free entry into the prepatent stages of R & D activity. This chapter examines the extent to which the patent system can encourage, through adjustments in the length of the patent life, private R & D decisions to be in the public interest.

Theoretical economic models developed by Barzel (1968), Kamien and Schwartz (1972, 1974), Nordhaus (1969, 1972), and Scherer (1967, 1972) have looked at interactions among the level of innovative activity, the time of introduction of innovations, the length of the development period, the length of patent life, and competition in R & D activity, but each model has

*I am indebted to Larry A. Sjaastad of the University of Chicago for his helpful comments and for encouraging my interest in science and technology policy.

[1]In terms of the usual distinction between invention (discovery of a new product or process) and innovation (commercial use of an invention), the incentive effect of the patent system lies in allowing inventors to capture financial returns on their invention when it is used. The patent system does not provide a financial reward to a discovery itself, but rather it permits inventors to receive rewards on discoveries that are put into commercial use.

emphasized different features. For purposes of this chapter, the key assumption of the Kamien and Schwartz, Nordhaus, and Scherer models is that an innovation is profitably introduced immediately (at least for the social costs and benefits). Barzel, however, considers the set of innovations that are not profitable now but will be in the future because benefits are increasing, say, owing to increasing population or incomes. The assumption of an increasing benefit stream means that the appropriate time of introduction is an economic problem.

In Barzel's model, freedom of entry into the prepatent stages of R & D provides an incentive for a firm to introduce an innovation when that innovation is just profitable (zero net present value) rather than at the optimal time (at which net present value is maximized). This premature introduction is induced by competition for a patent that then grants exclusive rights to control an invention. Firms are willing to accept less than the competitive return on their capital costs in the early years after introduction because the later benefits will provide more than the competitive return.

This chapter extends Barzel's model of innovation by taking into account the effects of competition on the length of the R & D period and on the scale of innovative activity (measured as the size of cost reduction provided by the invention selected for commercial introduction). In addition, it explores the use of legal patent life as a policy tool, deriving the length of patent life that will yield the most socially desirable time of introduction of an innovation. The model developed here allows for the possibility of a growing benefit stream, providing a general case; the other models of innovation under a patent system can be treated as special cases with zero growth in benefits. The optimal length of patent life is shown to be independent of the innovation's costs and benefits, depending only on the rate of growth of benefits, the discount rate, and the ratio of private to social benefits received during the life of the patent. An increase in the length of patent life tends to give earlier introduction of an innovation but leaves the most profitable scale of innovation unaffected.

The commonly recognized defect of a patent system—the loss to society arising from the temporary monopoly of the patent holder—is treated implicitly rather than explicitly. Nordhaus (1969) has already derived an optimal length of patent life based on the trade-off between the social loss from the temporary monopoly and the social benefits from obtaining an innovation that allows a lower real resource cost of production. This chapter adds another dimension to society's trade-off by considering the time of introduction of the innovation.

The chapter is divided into three major sections. In the first section, the socially optimal and the privately competitively determined introduction times and durations of an R & D project are derived for a single cost-reducing innovation. The concept of the socially optimal length of patent life is introduced, and the optimal patent life is derived. The second section looks at the social and private choices of scale of innovation, explicitly considering the effect of patent life on private decisions about the size of cost reduction to market. In the final section, the social welfare effects of a patent system that has the optimal length of patent life as developed here are compared with the welfare effects of an auction system for allocating rights to do research.

The results of the model suggest that a patent system cannot eliminate all sources of welfare loss even if the optimal length of patent life is chosen. The competitively induced compression of the R & D process (which shortens the duration of the R & D project) cannot be stopped, but given these research costs, the introduction time that maximizes the social net present value of the innovation can be obtained by choosing the appropriate length of patent life. The scale of innovation that maximizes the private net present value is unaffected by the length of patent life, so the socially and privately optimal scales are the same. However, if firms inefficiently produce innovations by reducing the duration of their R & D projects to increase their chances of obtaining a patent, then the same incentives can operate so that a nonsocially optimal scale of innovation may result.

OPTIMAL INTRODUCTION TIME FOR A SINGLE INNOVATION

Let there be a given cost-reducing innovation that if now in existence would generate benefits of B in the current time period. These initial social benefits depend on the size of the cost reduction and on the number of units of the product sold. The demand for the product is assumed to be increasing over time, say, owing to increasing population or increasing incomes, so that the benefits increase monotonically with calendar time (i.e., independent of the innovation's age) at an exponential growth rate of p. Instantaneous adoption of the innovation is also assumed, so that the full benefits accrue immediately upon adoption. The model developed here deals only with a single innovation with no substitutes.[2] The relevant discount rate, or social opportunity cost of capital, for both private and social decisions is assumed to be r where $r > p$ (otherwise net present value would increase without reaching a maximum at a finite introduction time). The discounted value of the benefits evaluated as of the present for an innovation to be introduced t years from now equals

$$\int_t^\infty Be^{-(r-p)y}\,dy.$$

[2]See Kitti (1973) for an extension of the model developed here. It considers the possibility that after a patent is granted and an invention is put into commercial use, a superior substitute innovation will be introduced and will end the economic life of the first.

The cost side is less straightforward. Let the production function for this innovation be given implicitly as $f(D, I) = 0$, where D is the duration or length of time over which research is conducted and I is the research intensity or amount of resources used at each point in time. Whereas realistically intensity would vary over the different years of the duration, the simpler assumption of constant intensity is enough to show the nature and direction of the biases. The production function for innovation is such that

$$f_I > 0, f_D > 0, \text{ and } f_{D,I}\Big|_{\substack{\text{output}\\\text{constant}}} < 0,$$

so that if the innovations are measured as cost reductions, the size of the cost reduction increases as more resources or time is used, but to produce a given cost reduction, there is a trade-off between duration of the project and the physical resources used. More specifically, the intensity, or the research inputs required to obtain the innovation, is a function of the amounts spent per period on R & D by individual firms in the industry. The total expenditure or cost per period by all firms in the industry, denoted C, may involve some duplicate research, so the intensity obtained is less than the total expenditure. Therefore, let $I = I(C)$ and $0 \leqslant V_{I,C} \leqslant 1$, where $V_{I,C}$ is the elasticity of the function.

Although in later discussions a single relationship is assumed, there is in effect a family of functions for intensity and expenditures depending on institutional arrangements. The highest curve can be associated with all of the firms acting as one or with no secrecy about the results of research efforts. As there is more duplication of research efforts with excess resource costs imposed on society, the intensity or net research obtained from a given expenditure is reduced. Institutional factors like the patent system, trade secret protection, and the degree of enforcement of antitrust laws will affect the intensity-expenditure relationship and so are assumed constant. Because this model is concerned with the introduction of an innovation under a patent system where there is free entry into research, the social costs are not those of only a single firm but are the costs of all firms that have decided to conduct research. The minimum social costs are thus defined as all firms using the lowest cost combination of intensity and duration of research. This interpretation of minimum social costs comes up later in the comparison of the patent and auction systems.

Socially Optimal Solutions

Before continuing the mathematics of the model, Figure 3.1 shows diagrammatically the determination of the socially optimal introduction time

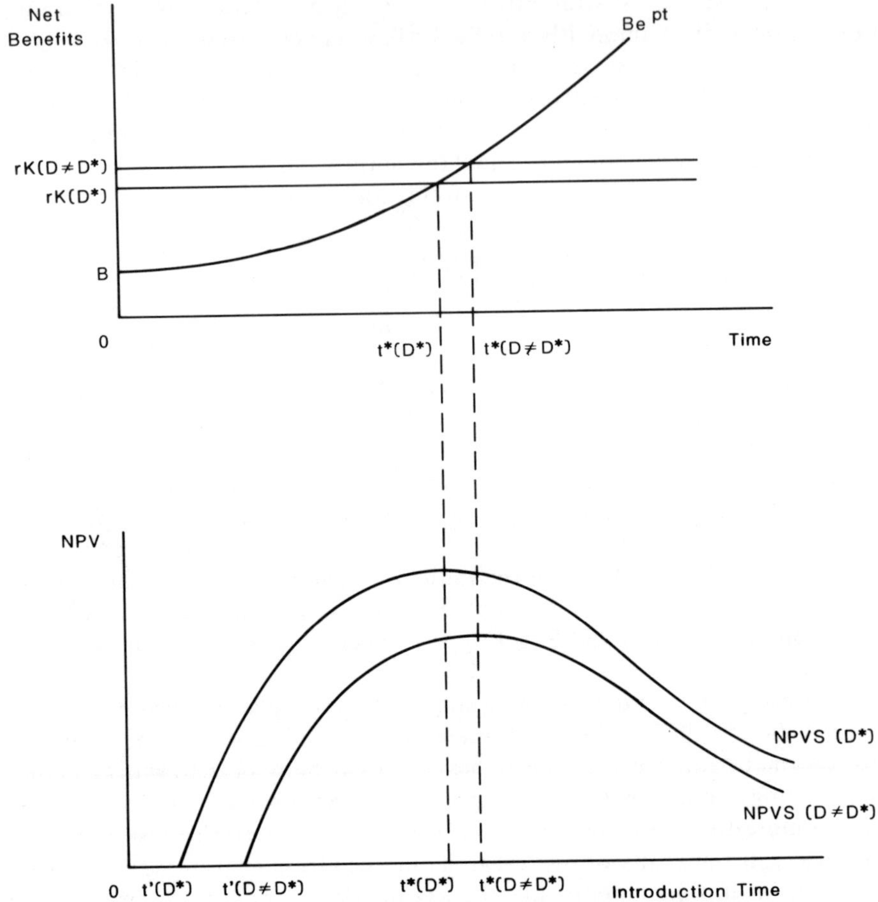

FIGURE 3.1

and the change in this time as research costs increase. The upper part shows the undiscounted potential benefit stream, which is received only on the introduction of the innovation. The capital costs K accumulate over the length of the research project and so are a function of the duration of the project, and duration D^* has been found to give the lowest research costs. These accumulated capital costs, like the benefit stream, are not discounted back to the present, but are converted into a perpetuity, with the interest on the capital cost providing a continuing cost. The optimal time of introduction t^* is where the first year's benefits of the project just equal the interest on the capital costs—the earlier benefits provide less than the market rate of return, whereas the benefits after t^* provide a greater rate of return and should not be foregone. If capital costs increase, here because an inefficient project duration is used, the interest due on these accumulated capital costs also increases and delays the most profitable introduction date.

The lower diagram in Figure 3.1 has the innovation's costs and benefits discounted to the present and expressed as net present values for introduction at different times. For a fixed benefit stream, increasing the accumulated capital costs lowers the net present value curve and shifts it to the right. The net present value curve illustrates the difference between the profit-maximizing introduction time t^* and the introduction time t' that just gives the competitive rate of return.

To determine mathematically the socially optimal values of timing, intensity, and duration for a given cost-reducing innovation, the social net present value ($NPVS$) is maximized:

$$NPVS = \int_t^\infty Be^{-(r-p)y}\,dy - \int_{t-D}^{t} Ce^{-ry}dy \qquad (1)$$

$$f(D, I) = 0 \qquad (2)$$

$$I = I(C). \qquad (3)$$

Taking $\partial NPVS/\partial t = 0$, to find the introduction time that maximizes net present value,

$$t^* = \frac{\ln C(e^{rD} - 1) - \ln B}{p}. \qquad (4)$$

Taking $\partial NPVS/\partial C = 0$,

$$\frac{1 - e^{rD}}{rD} = -V_{D,I}V_{I,C}, \qquad (5)$$

where $V_{D,I}$ is the elasticity of $f(D,I) = 0$ and is less than zero and $V_{I,C}$ is the elasticity of $I = I(C)$ and is greater than zero. Taking the derivative of $NPVS$ with respect to D necessarily gives us the same implicit function for D, the solution of which will be called D^*.

To see that the duration D^* gives the lowest development costs, the cost function can be examined as duration changes. But instead of looking at costs evaluated as of the present (shown in Eq. 1 as $\int_{t-D}^{t} Ce^{-ry}dy$), the accumulated capital costs evaluated as of the time of introduction t can be written as

$$K(t) = \frac{C(e^{rD} - 1)}{r}. \qquad (6)$$

To see how the trade-off between duration and intensity affects the accumulated capital (the compounding effect versus the total outlay effect), take

$$\frac{\partial K(t)}{\partial D} = \frac{C}{e^{rD}} \times \frac{1 + rD\, V_{D,I} V_{I,C} - e^{-rD}}{rD\, V_{D,I}\, V_{I,C}}.$$

At D^*, $\partial K(t)/\partial D = 0$. As D increases beyond D^*, $\partial K(T)/\partial D > 0$, and when $D < D^*$, $\partial K(t)/\partial D < 0$. Thus, D^* minimizes the capital at charge function. The time t^* that maximizes social net present value was earlier determined to equal $[\ln C(e^{rD} - 1) - \ln B]/p$. Since $C(e^{rD} - 1) = rK(t)$ and going from the optimal D^* increases $K(t)$, the use of a nonoptimal duration and intensity will mean that the time at which net present value is maximized is put further into the future (see Figure 3.1, bottom). In Figure 3.1, introduction time t^* is the time at which benefits Be^{pt} first equal the interest on the accumulated capital costs rK. This may be seen by simply rewriting Eq. 4 so that $Be^{pt*} = C(e^{rD} - 1) = rK(t^*)$. (This is shown in Figure 3.1, top.)

Market-Determined Solutions

In a system with patent protection of innovations, the private benefits of an innovation are unlikely to equal the social benefits. The length of the private benefit stream is assumed to be effectively restricted to a patent life of L years. The private benefits in each period can be expressed as some proportion m of the social benefits. This fraction m will depend in large part on the pricing policy used in charging for the use of a patented technique. If the user price for technology is less than the cost reduction, the private benefits will be less than the benefits to society, which include the gain to consumers from the price reduction. Unless the grant of a patent facilitates collusion in production and monopoly pricing, a price larger than the reduction in resource cost cannot be charged for the use of an innovation because there is the alternative of producing by the old method. The proportion m may also be a government policy variable to the extent that subsidies or taxes change m from its market-determined value. For simplicity, m is assumed constant over the life of the patent.

The cost side of the model is as described before, with private and social costs the same. The private firms each face the same research production function required for the social net present value, $f(D, I) = 0$ (Eq. 2), and the aggregate of the private costs is $I = I(C)$ (Eq. 3). Thus, the equation for the private net present value ($NPVP$) aggregated for all firms is

$$NPVP = \int_t^{t+L} mBe^{-(r-p)y}dy - \int_{t-D}^{t} Ce^{-ry}dy.^{3} \qquad (7)$$

[3] If there are n identical firms in the industry, then each firm's expected benefits are $1/n\int_t^{t+L} mBe^{-(r-p)y}dy$. If the firms also have the same costs, then each firm's costs are $1/n\int_{t-D}^{t} Ce^{-ry}dy$. Equation 7 gives the aggregate result.

There is assumed to be free entry into the prepatent stages of R & D so that competition will induce entry into the production of potential innovations until the expected net present value is zero. (The one firm that is granted the patent will get the full private benefits each year of the patent's life, not the smaller expected value, and will have incurred only its own costs. But the total costs of all firms will offset the total private benefits, so that the aggregate private net present value is zero.) However, a positive net present value can be eroded by introducing a technique too soon (moving along a net present value curve with duration and accumulated capital costs held constant) or by using nonoptimal durations and intensities (shifting to lower net present value curves).

An introduction time t_1 can be derived such that $NPVP = 0$, or

$$t_1 = \frac{\ln C(e^{rD} - 1) - \ln B - \ln m + \ln (r - p)/r - \ln [1 - e^{-(r-p)L}]}{p}. \tag{8}$$

Rewriting Eq. 8 and discounting back to the present gives

$$\frac{mBe^{-(r-p)t_1}(1 - e^{-(r-p)L})}{r - p} = \frac{e^{-rt_1}C(e^{rD} - 1)}{r}. \tag{9}$$

where the left side is clearly the present value of the private benefit stream that begins at a value of mB, grows at a rate p, and stops after L years. Thus, for introduction at time t_1, the present discounted value of the benefits equals the present value of the costs.

Taking the derivatives of Eqs. 4 and 8 with respect to D and C to see how t^* and t_1 change as the duration of or expenditures on the research project change gives

$$\frac{\partial t^*}{\partial D} = \frac{\partial t_1}{\partial D} \text{ and } \frac{\partial t^*}{\partial C} = \frac{\partial t_1}{\partial C}.$$

This means that as the costs incurred by private firms and borne by society change, the social and private net present value curves will both shift by the same amounts, keeping the same relative positions.

Assuming that firms somehow cooperated so as to minimize collective discounted costs, the resulting duration would be the previously determined socially optimal duration D^*. However, if firms compete by trying to introduce an innovation earlier than the others in the industry, then we may want to assume, as Scherer (1967) does in his N-firm case, that "potential innovator Firm i takes into account parametrically only the product introduction date (and when all firms begin development at $t = 0$, the development time) T_j of a representative rival firm j" (p. 389). But in this model, if only the product introduction date is given, say, t_j, a firm still has control over duration and intensity subject to the constraint that $t_j - D \geqslant 0$. If others have already begun work on the project, then a maximum D is given and rivalry will require a shorter duration and earlier introduction date. But a duration shorter than the cost-minimizing D^* will mean net present value first becomes nonnegative at a later time. The use of the optimal duration will give the earliest time at which $NPVP = 0$, but if 0 $NPVP$ indicates that a firm is indifferent about undertaking a project, then the research may be delayed. This delay of the research increases its net present value upon introduction, if the lowest-cost research project duration is chosen. Nevertheless, any attempt to compress the development period will increase the research costs, tending to keep the expected private net present value at zero, which may again lead to the delay of the research project. Without some additional information or specification of the firm's behavior, the date of introduction of an innovation will depend on chance.

A plausible solution to this problem of indeterminacy of introduction date is to specify a probability distribution for dates of introduction. If a typical firm believes that actions of its competitors will drive the expected net present value of a particular research effort to zero, there is no reason to believe that the probability of that firm's initiating a research project will vary systematically with time once (the maximum obtainable) private net present value is nonzero. In other words, if a firm is indifferent about undertaking a project when the expected net present value is zero, then the initiation probability associated with indifference should be the same for all possible introduction times—even those times at which net present value would be positive if it were not for the actions of the firm's competitors. Hence, the probability would be a constant, giving the Poisson probability distribution for the probability of introduction of the innovation. The probability distribution of different time intervals until introduction, with the condition that the innovation has not already been introduced, is given by the negative exponential, which takes the form:

$$p(t) = \theta e^{-\theta(t - t')}$$

where $p(t)$ is the probability of introduction at time t, given that t' is the first point at which introduction is feasible (present value is nonnegative).

Derivation of the Optimal Patent Life

Because of the argument that private net present value will tend to zero because of premature introduction and competing attempts to shorten duration, which increase capital costs, the private net present value for the lowest capital costs at any introduction date will show the amount available to be eroded or competed away by excess resources. This will be a cost to society of a patent system with free entry into the performance of research. Given this institutional arrangement, it is in the interests of society to maximize what will not and cannot be eroded by inefficient production of innovations, that is, the part of the social benefit stream that private firms cannot capture.

Figure 3.2 shows the private and social net present value curves for a given innovation produced with the lowest research costs, denoted by the duration D^*, and for a given patent life and ratio of private to social benefits. As in Eqs. 4 and 8, introduction time t^* maximizes the social net present value, and t_1 makes the private net present value equal to zero. The vertical difference between these two curves, or the nonerodible social surplus, shows the social benefits that will not be eroded by the use of excess resources in research. If patent life is changed and shifts the private net present value curve so that t_1 and t^* are the same times, the vertical difference is maximized. Taking into account the probability that introduction will be later than t_1, a patent life can be derived such that the expected social surplus is maximized—this is the optimal patent life. Not only does the optimal patent life maximize the expected nonerodible social surplus, it also provides the socially optimal introduction time, given the actual research costs incurred. This optimal patent life is independent of the absolute size of the costs and benefits of the innovation, because only a distortion between the private and social net present value is needed. The optimal patent life will be derived mathematically below.

To maximize the vertical difference between the net present value curves in Figure 3.2, i.e., to maximize the nonerodible social surplus, Eq. 1 and 7 give

$$NPVS(D^*) - NPVP(D^*) = \frac{Be^{-(r-p)t}\{1 - m[1 - e^{-(r-p)L}]\}}{r - p} \tag{10}$$

and

$$\frac{\partial[NPVS(D^*) - NPVP(D^*)]}{\partial t} = -Be^{-(r-p)t}\{1 - m[1 - e^{-(r-p)L}]\} < 0,$$

so the difference is decreasing as t increases. Because the innovation will tend not to be introduced when $NPVP < 0$ before t_1, $NPVP$ may be arbitrarily set equal to zero before t_1, so the time that maximizes Eq. 10 is introduction time t_1. Although Eq. 10 was derived for the lowest costs, the difference does not depend on the costs, so t_1 maximizes the social surplus whatever the cost incurred.

If the $NPVP$ curve could somehow be shifted so that $t_1 = t^*$, then the nonerodible social surplus ($NPVS - NPVP$)[4] would equal the maximum

[4]To simplify notation, the term D^*, which indicates the lowest costs of innovation, will be dropped from $NPVS$ and $NPVP$.

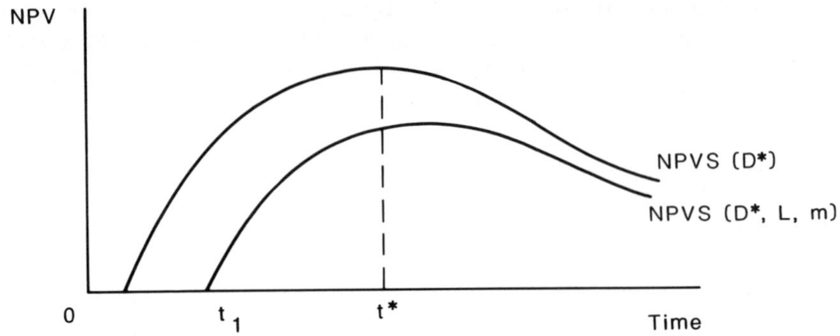

FIGURE 3.2

social net present value. Since accumulated capital costs are being held constant, the only way to shift *NPVP* is to change either patent life L or the ratio m of private to social benefits. The equation for the patent life needed to set t_1 equal to t^* (Eqs. 4 and 8) is

$$L^* = -\frac{\ln[1-(r-p)/mr]}{r-p}. \quad (11)$$

Inasmuch as there is a trade-off between m and L along a fixed *NPVP* curve, which can be seen by taking the total differential of *NPVP* for variables m and L, once the *NPVP* function has been decided on, fixing m will determine a patent life. Therefore, the m^* that equates t_1 and t^* gives the same function as L^* does.

By rewriting the patent life L^*, a convenient economic interpretation of what this patent life does to the private benefit stream is obtained. Equation 11 in exponential form, multiplied through by Be^{pt_1}, becomes

$$\frac{mBe^{pt_1}[1-e^{-(r-p)L^*}]}{r-p} = \frac{Be^{pt_1}}{r}.$$

Combining this expression with Eqs. 9 and 6 gives

$$\frac{Be^{pt_1}}{r} = K(t_1).$$

But this says that the benefits at introduction time t_1 are just equal to the interest on the accumulated capital costs, or that t_1 is now the optimal time of introduction from the social point of view.

Because t_1 is the time at which private net present value first becomes nonnegative, it is not very likely that this will be the market-determined time of introduction. As developed previously, the probability distribution of introduction times of the innovation will be characterized by the negative exponential probability function. Therefore, the L and m that maximize the expected value of the nonerodible social surplus must be found. Because the probability distribution should begin as soon as introduction is first profitable (at the earliest t_1), the lowest-cost net present value curves are needed. The equation for the expected social surplus (z) becomes

$$z = E[NPVS(D^*) - NPVP(D^*)] \tag{12}$$

$$= \frac{\int_{t_1}^{\infty} \theta e^{-\theta(y - t_1)} B e^{-(r-p)y} \{1 - m[1 - e^{-(r-p)L}]\}}{r - p}\, dy.$$

Taking $\partial z / \partial L = 0$,

$$\bar{L} = \frac{\ln[1 - (r - p)/mr]}{r - p}. \tag{13}$$

Comparison of the $\bar{L}$ that maximizes the expected social surplus with the L^* that maximizes the social surplus shows that they are the same. Although this result for $\bar{L}$ may appear suspiciously simple, as it does not seem to account for the expected time of introduction being later than t_1, nevertheless it follows from the mathematical properties of the model.[5]

A more economic reason for patent lives $\bar{L}$ and L^* being the same, and an important point in itself, is that the value of $\bar{L}$ in no way depends on D and C, the duration and costs, respectively, of the research project. As shown earlier, $\partial t^*/\partial D = \partial t_1/\partial D$ and $\partial t^*/\partial C = \partial t_1/\partial C$, so a change in either component of the capital cost will shift both the *NPVS* and *NPVP* curves by the same amount. Thus, if initially, say, for the lowest accumulated capital cost, t_1 is shifted so it equals t^*, this remains true even if costs are increased by the inefficient performance of research (by excessively shortening or lengthening the development period). When the probability distribution of various introduction times is used with a given social surplus function, the probability that this social surplus will be reduced by excess production costs is being described. Because t^* remains equal to t_1 for changes in D or C, the optimal patent life $\bar{L}$ gives the socially optimal introduction time for the costs actually incurred, not

[5]Since both the social surplus function (Eq. 10) and the probability function for introduction times are decreasing functions beginning at t_1, and the social surplus functions for different patent lives do not cross, the only way to maximize the expected value (which involves the product of these two decreasing functions, one of which is assumed fixed) is to maximize the social surplus. The points on the social surplus curves are being compared for the same intervals until introduction, not for the same introduction times.

only for the lowest costs. However, the expected value of the nonerodible social surplus does depend on the research costs, and this point comes up later in the comparison of a patent system with optimal life with an auction system.

Along a given private net present value curve, there is a trade-off between *L*, the length of patent life, and *m*, the ratio of private to social benefits obtained during the life of the patent, because both are a source of divergence between the private and social benefit streams. The diagrammatic expression of the optimal patent life shown in Figure 3.3, also reflects this trade-off. Each curve in Figure 3.3 show the combinations of *m* and *L* that maximize the expected social surplus and give the optimal time of introduction for the innovation. The position of the curve depends on the relative values of *p*, the rate of growth of benefits, and *r*, the discount rate. Holding the ratio *m* of private to social benefits constant and for a given discount rate, Figure 3.3 shows that as the benefit growth rate *p* increases, the length of the optimal patent life decreases. This can be explained by noting that $NPVP = 0$ when the present value of the benefits equals the present value of the costs and that the costs are independent of *p*. A larger growth rate of benefits means the benefits

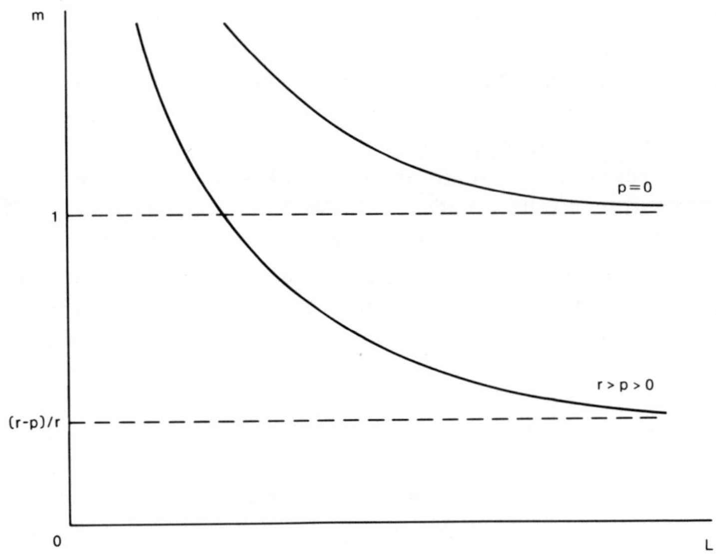

$$\bar{L} = -\frac{\ln[1 - (r - p)/mr]}{r - p}$$

for $mr > r - p$

$$\lim_{p \to 0} \bar{L} = -\frac{\ln(1 - 1/m)}{r}$$

FIGURE 3.3.

after the respective t^* values ($= t_1$ values) are larger when p is larger. Therefore, the stream of larger benefits must have a relatively shorter patent life to have the same present value as its costs.

When there is a zero growth rate of benefits, the time of introduction is not an economic problem (the project should be done right away or never), so incorrect timing is not an issue. With a finite patent life, even if $m = 1$ (so private firms get all the social benefits), a socially beneficial project may not be undertaken. This is in effect the situation considered by Nordhaus and others and explains why subsidies to research, which could raise m above 1, are often recommended.

Because the ratio m of private to social benefits accruing during the life of the patent can be changed by taxes or subsidies, Figure 3.3 also indicates the trade-offs among taxes, subsidies, and patent life that can give introduction of an innovation at the socially optimal time. For example, the grant of a subsidy requires a shorter patent life to avoid changing introduction time. This becomes an important policy alternative when the social loss from inefficient pricing for the use of the innovation is considered.

THE OPTIMAL SCALE OF COST REDUCTION

In this section, the socially optimal size of cost reduction is determined and the effect, if any, that the use of the optimal patent life has on the choice of scale is examined. A basic assumption of the following analysis is that larger amounts of (minimum) capital costs K accumulated over the research period produce larger initial benefits B, all of the benefits growing at the same rate p. It is also assumed that there is no substitution once a particular scale of innovation has been introduced, so that the length of the social benefit stream is infinite.

As an example of the costs and benefits to be considered, Figure 3.4 describes the case for two different sizes of cost reduction, the subscript 1 denoting the smaller cost reduction and the subscript 2 indicating the larger one. Times t_1^* and t_2^* are the socially optimal introduction times of innovations 1 and 2, respectively, and in this figure t_2^* is later than t_1^*, but this may not always be the case. The difference between rK_2 and rK_1 shows the yearly equivalent of the additional capital costs required by the larger innovation. Because an innovation is assumed to be introduced as soon as its research is finished, these additional capital costs, accumulated over the research period, are incurred just before introduction time t_2^* and not earlier. Another cost of the larger innovation is the difference $(B_1e^{pt} - rK_1)$ between t_1^* and t_2^*, showing the earnings above the opportunity cost of capital that would have been earned by the smaller cost reduction but that are foregone if innovation 2 is introduced instead of innovation 1 but at innovation 2's optimal time. The

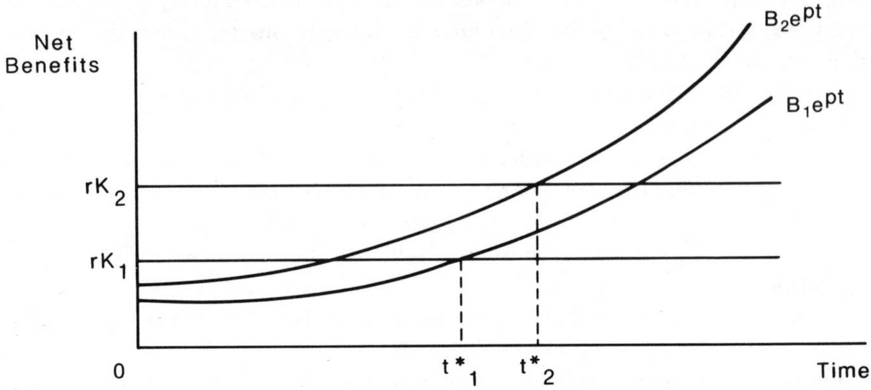

FIGURE 3.4

marginal social benefits of the larger innovation are the difference between B_2e^{pt} and B_1e^{pt} and are received after t_2^*.

The equation for the present discounted value of the marginal costs of innovation 2 is

$$PVMC = \int_{t_2^*}^{\infty} r(K_2 - K_1)\, e^{-ry}dy + \int_{t_1^*}^{t_2^*} (B_1e^{py} - rK_1)\, e^{-ry}dy,$$

and that for the present value of the marginal benefits is

$$PVMB = \int_{t_2^*}^{\infty} (B_2 - B_1)\, e^{-(r-p)y}dy.$$

Rewriting these equations,

$$PVMC = \left(K_2 - \frac{B_1e^{pt_2^*}}{r-p}\right)e^{-rt_2^*} - \left(K_1 - \frac{B_1e^{pt_1^*}}{r-p}\right)e^{-rt_1^*}$$

and

$$PVMB = (B_2 - B_1)\frac{e^{-(r-p)t_2^*}}{r-p}.$$

The scale of innovation or size of cost reduction should be expanded until marginal costs equal marginal benefits in present value terms, or until

$$K_2e^{-rt_2^*} - K_1e^{-rt_1^*} = \frac{B_2e^{-(r-p)t_2^*}}{r-p} - \frac{B_1e^{-(r-p)t_1^*}}{r-p} \tag{14}$$

This just says that the present value of the increased costs equals the present value of the increase in benefits, taking into account the possibility of different optimal dates of introduction.

As discussed earlier for Figure 3.1, at the optimal time of introduction, an innovation's undiscounted benefits at introduction just equal the interest on the accumulated capital costs, so

$$Be^{pt^*} = rK,$$

or, in present value terms,

$$Be^{-(r-p)t^*} = rKe^{-rt^*}. \tag{15}$$

Equations 14 and 15 say roughly that

$$dK = \frac{dB}{r-p}$$

and that

$$B = rK.$$

Putting these rough equivalents into elasticity form to get the elasticity of benefits with respect to capital costs for introduction at the optimal or profit-maximizing time gives

$$V_{B,K} = \frac{(r-p)K}{B} \tag{16}$$

$$= \frac{r-p}{r}.$$

Equation 16 shows the value of the benefit-cost elasticity that must hold to give the optimal size of cost reduction introduced at the optimal time. It demonstrates that there must be diminishing returns to capital in generating larger benefit streams.

Because this elasticity derivation has been done in fairly rough terms, a more rigorous mathematical approach is used below to derive the socially optimal scale of innovation. The same elasticity form is derived, but the relationship between different values of the benefit-cost elasticity and the optimal introduction time is discussed as well.

Derivation of the Socially Optimal Scale

Instead of looking explicitly at the marginal costs and benefits of changes in scale, the size of cost reduction can be varied to find the scale that maximizes social net present value at the respective maximum points. It can be shown that both the maximum social net present values and the optimal introduction times of different scales depend on the elasticity between benefits at the time of introduction and (minimum) capital costs. For some values of this elasticity, the optimal scale becomes indefinitely large. For a finite, determinate optimal scale to exist, larger scales must become profitable at later introduction times, so that the discount rate has a chance to offset the value of the increasing benefits. This implies diminishing returns to accumulated capital costs in generating undiscounted benefits.

By rewriting t^* from Eq. 4 in terms of K from Eq. 6,

$$t^* = \frac{\ln r + \ln K - \ln B}{p}. \tag{4'}$$

The evaluation of social net present value ($NPVS$) from Eq. 1 becomes

$$NPVS\,(t^*) = \frac{Ke^{-rt^*}p}{r - p}. \tag{17}$$

From Eq. 17,

$$\frac{\partial NPVS(t^*)}{\partial K} = \frac{e^{-rt^*}p[1 - (r/p) + (r/p)V_{B,K}]}{r - p} \tag{18}$$

where $V_{B,K}$ is the elasticity of the function relating undiscounted benefits at time of introduction and the required capital costs accumulated to the same introduction time. From Eq. 18, the direction of change in net present value as the scale of innovation changes depends on the elasticity of benefits with respect to capital costs.

The change in each scale's optimal introduction time can also be expressed in terms of the elasticity of benefits with respect to capital costs. From Eq. 4′,

$$pK\frac{\partial t^*}{\partial K} = 1 - V_{B,K}. \tag{19}$$

If the elasticity has a value of less than one, then the optimal introduction time becomes later as the size of cost reduction increases. If $V_{B,K}$ equals one, the optimal time is unchanged; and for $V_{B,K}$ greater than one, larger cost reductions are best introduced earlier in time.

Next, the impacts of the benefit-cost elasticity on optimal introduction time and on the direction of change in net present value as the scale of innovation changes are combined. For $V_{B,K} = 1$, the optimal time of introduction does not change (see Eq. 19), but $NPVS\,(t^*)$ continues to increase as K increases (from Eq. 18), so the optimal scale is indefinitely large. If the proportional change in benefits is greater than the proportional change in costs so $V_{B,K} > 1$, then from Eq. 19 the optimal introduction time becomes earlier for larger scales of innovation. For $V_{B,K} > 1$, Eq. 18 shows that $NPVS$ evaluated at each scale's optimal time increases as scale increases. The change in $NPVS$ evaluated at $t=0$ for those scales whose optimal times are the present ($t=0$) or earlier must now be examined, because the earliest feasible introduction time is the present, ignoring the gestation period. The derivative of Eq. 1 with respect to K evaluated at $t=0$ equals

$$\frac{\partial NPVS(t=0)}{\partial K} = \frac{V_{B,K}B}{K(r-p)} - 1.$$

At the optimal introduction time or later, $Be^{pt} \geqslant rK$; so for $t=0$ and $t^* < 0$, $B > rK$. Thus, for $V_{B,K} > 1$, it follows that $\partial NPVS\,(t=0)/\partial K > 0$. Therefore, the net present value of larger scales increases as scale increases even though some of these larger scales cannot be introduced at their optimal times (because the present is too late). Again, the optimal scale is indefinitely large.

When there are diminishing returns so $V_{B,K} < 1$, then from Eq. 19 the optimal time of introduction becomes later as the size of cost reduction becomes larger. The net present values evaluated at the respective t^* values (Eq. 17) may increase or decrease as scale increases. Taking $\partial NPVS(t^*)/\partial K=0$ to maximize the maximum social net present value with respect to scale gives

$$V_{B,K} = \frac{r-p}{r}. \tag{20}$$

Thus, the scale of innovation that maximizes the social net present value must be characterized by an elasticity between B and K of $(r-p)/r$. If the elasticity of the function relating benefits and costs happens to be constant and equal to this value, then all scales will have the same net present value, but larger scales will have later optimal introduction times.

A situation with increasing or constant returns means that not enough is being invested in R & D, but, in the real world, expanding the scale of innovation for immediate introduction is likely to lead to diminishing returns as the prices of R & D inputs are bid up and the quality of the inputs declines. Investment should be at a rate sufficient to produce diminishing returns, and the optimal rate of investment is implied by Eq. 20. With this elasticity, the marginal social cost of a larger scale equals the marginal social benefit when introduction is at the optimal time.

Derivation of the Privately Optimal Scale

In this section the incentives that exist under a patent system with free entry into the prepatent stages of R & D for private decisions to produce the socially optimal scale of innovation are examined. It can be shown that private net present value is maximized (for diminishing returns) when $V_{B,K} = (r-p)/r$, the same elasticity that maximized social net present value. Even though the private and the social benefit streams are not the same, the factors

(m and L) making them differ are independent of the actual date of introduction. Therefore, it is reasonable to have the same elasticity maximize both the social and private net present values evaluated at their respective maximums.

The equation for the private net present value ($NPVP$) for a single innovation (Eq. 7) is

$$NPVP = \int_t^{t+L} mBe^{-(r-p)y}dy - \int_{t-D}^{t} Ce^{-ry}dy.$$

Taking $\partial NPVP/\partial t = 0$ to find the introduction time t^*P that maximizes private net present value and using the accumulated capital cost expression (Eq. 6) to express the private net present value at its maximum value,

$$t^*P = \frac{\ln r + \ln K - \ln B - \ln m - \ln[1 - e^{-(r-p)L}]}{p}$$

$$NPVP(t^*P) = \frac{Ke^{-rt^*P}p}{r-p}.$$

Taking $\partial NPVP(t^*P)/\partial K = 0$ to find the scale of innovation that maximizes private net present value, the scale can again be expressed as the elasticity

$$V_{B,K} = \frac{r-p}{r}.$$

Because of the earlier argument that competition for a single patent would tend to encourage introduction when $NPVP = 0$ rather than when it is maximized, time t^*P is not likely to be the introduction time. Nontheless, the appropriate marginal conditions within the firm still involve expanding production of sizes of cost reductions until marginal costs equal marginal revenues, but this is what the elasticity $V_{B,K} = (r-p)/r$ says.[6] Therefore, there should be the tendency for a private firm to introduce the socially optimal scale of innovation.

Scale Under the Patent System

Consistency with an earlier discussion creates a problem for the last statement about the tendency to optimal scale. Previously, the argument was

[6]The elasticity in Eq. 20 was derived in terms of the social benefits, and the private marginal benefits differ from the marginal social benefits by the proportional factor m and the patent life L. But if the finite private benefit stream is converted into its equivalent perpetual stream with, say, the single proportional factor w, giving $B^P = wB^S$, then the private marginal condition is $(dwB/wB)/(r-p) = (dK/K)/r$ or $(dB/B)/(r-p) = (dK/K)/r$.

made that firms may not efficiently (satisfying the appropriate nonprobabilistic marginal conditions) produce innovations, because by reducing the duration of a research project, they increase their chances of obtaining a patent. Therefore, there may be a similar incentive for firms to introduce a scale of innovation smaller than optimal at an earlier time (assuming diminishing returns so smaller cost reductions become profitable earlier) to improve their chances of obtaining a patent. If this kind of incentive is operating, then society may not get the optimal size of cost reduction. The policy tools—patent life, taxes, and subsidies—considered in this chapter are ineffective in encouraging the optimal scale of innovation. This ineffectiveness suggests that some other method of encouraging innovation might well be considered.

WELFARE EFFECTS OF OPTIMAL PATENT SYSTEM AND AUCTION

In his discussion of premature introduction of innovations due to competition, Barzel (1968) suggests that "a conceptual way of overcoming this kind of misallocation is by granting (or by auctioning) monopoly rights on potential innovations before resources are committed to the innovating activity" (p. 352, n. 11). Since he did not elaborate on this suggestion, an idealized auction system is described here. (The system described abstracts from the real world problems such as technical and market uncertainties and the difficulty of setting bounds to an area of research before any work has been done.) The auction system is then compared to the standard patent system with the optimal length of patent life in terms of their influence on four factors affecting social welfare: the time of introduction of an innovation; the use of excessive amounts of resources to produce innovations; the pricing policy used in the sale of technology; and the scale of innovation.

The idealized auction would allow a competitive bidding process for the right to do research in a certain area, and a patent would be granted if the research proved successful. The bidding process would involve a payment, the size of which would depend on the expected costs, the expected revenue from the use of the innovation, and the time of introduction of the innovation. Although the successful bidder and innovator would have a monopoly position in the sale of the innovation, the capitalized value of the monopoly return would go to the government so that the firm earns only the competitive rate of return. In effect, the auction method is designed to provide competition for the market rather than within it.

The advantages of the auction are that it gives the socially optimal time of introduction of the innovation (because there is no competition in research to induce premature introduction), eliminates excess resource costs, and provides the optimal scale of innovation. To ensure the optimal introduction time, however, the auction method requires that the social benefit stream be completely appropriated by the innovator. But if an inefficient pricing method is used in the diffusion of the innovation and if full appropriability is obtained through an infinite patent life, then there is room for a large social welfare loss.

Introduction Time

The social and private net present value curves provide a convenient means of comparing the social welfare effects of the auction method with the effects of a patent system having free entry into research and the optimal length of patent life. The auction method would provide the efficiently produced innovation at the socially optimal time with the net benefits to society measured by $NPVS(D^*)$ evaluated at t^*. The optimal patent system provides a probability distribution of introduction times (possibly with excess costs), with the net benefits to society defined earlier in Eq. 12 as $z = E[NPVS(D^*) - NPVP(D^*, \bar{L}, \bar{m})]$. The comparison of the auction and patent net present values can be expressed in ratio form as $NPVS(t^*, D^*)/z(\bar{L})$. With the optimal patent life times t_1 and t^* the same and making the appropriate substitutions from Eqs. 1, 4, 12, and 13, the comparison becomes

$$\frac{NPVS(t^*,D^*)}{z(\bar{L})} = 1 + \frac{r-p}{\theta}. \tag{21}$$

This shows that the patent system even with the optimal length of patent life is inferior to the auction method. Introduction under the patent system with the optimal life is at the optimal time given the actual costs incurred, but θ reflects the possibility that the actual costs are excessively high.

Excess Resources

The use of excessive amounts of resources in R & D projects comes about in two ways: through the use of nonoptimal durations and resource intensities, which increases the accumulated capital cost; and through the duplication of research efforts when the programs in all firms in the industry are not coordinated. The first situation occurs under a patent system with free entry and would not occur under the auction method, because successful bidders have no incentive to reduce their profits by inefficiently compressing or extending the development period.

The second effect is incorporated into the relationship between intensity I and expenditures C in the cost function. The minimum social cost under the patent system has built into it the costs of an unspecified number of competing firms as shown by $I = I(C)$ in Eq. 3. As the amount of duplicate research falls because firms act as one or because the number of firms decreases, the expenditures associated with a given resource intensity and duration are reduced. Under the auction method, when only one firm does the research, the expenditures for a given intensity I should be less than the cost C under the patent system, giving a larger social net present value for the innovation with its optimal introduction time somewhat earlier. (The assumption of one firm's doing the research does not rule out multiple approaches to the same project; it just says that these approaches would be coordinated by a single decision maker.)

Pricing Policy

The innovations in this model are assumed to reduce the costs of production of goods or services. The prices charged for the use of these innovations can be set in various ways. One method commonly recognized in the literature as an inefficient pricing policy is to charge a price that depends on the number of units of the final product sold. This raises the price of the final product above the marginal resource cost of its other productive inputs and leads to a social welfare loss, because the knowledge behind the innovation is a public good and should not be rationed. After patent protection ends, the price of the final product falls to its resource cost, and the price for the use of the innovation falls to zero, so this welfare loss does not remain. This pricing policy does not have to be followed even when innovations are to be privately financed since a lump sum payment or a multipart pricing method could be devised. However, a price based on the number of units sold is often desired by the users of the innovation as a way of sharing the risk involved in determining its value (Behrman and Schmidt, (1959, p. 273).

If there is a social welfare loss from the pricing policy, then a shorter patent life will help reduce the loss. Optimal patent life, determined by Eq. 13 and Figure 3.3, encompasses a trade-off between m, the ratio of private to social benefits, and patent life L, with different combinations having the same impact in net present value terms. Thus, if there is a welfare loss due to an inefficient pricing policy, this can provide information for choosing among the various combinations of m and L. A subsidy along with a correspondingly shorter patent life may be preferred to a longer life with no subsidy.

When there is a welfare loss from the method of sale of technology, this loss becomes an important factor in the comparison of the patent and auction systems. The ideal auction system requires an infinite patent life to equate private and social net present values as much as possible. Also, an m value of 1 is needed so that private and social benefits are the same. A divergence between private and social net present values (such as from a price reduction to consumers) would delay introduction beyond the socially optimal time and lower the amount bid for the right to do research. So under the auction method, there exists a potential trade-off between obtaining the socially optimal time of introduction with an infinite patent life (and a possible subsidy) and reducing the social welfare loss from an inefficient pricing policy by reducing the length of patent life.

Scale of Innovation

As discussed earlier, the patent system may cause a smaller than optimal scale of innovation to be produced because production of such a scale can increase a firm's chances of getting a patent and obtaining some return on its research investment. In contrast, under an auction system, the firm proposing to introduce the optimal scale of innovation will make the highest bid, even though the actual time of introduction will be later than the times for smaller sizes. The auction system will not induce the introduction of smaller than optimal scales of innovation as long as the initial bidding process covers the whole range of potential cost reductions.

SUMMARY

When the introduction time of an innovation is an economic variable within the context of a patent system, some conventional ideas about the performance of research must be changed. It is commonly asserted that the incomplete appropriability of the social benefits of innovations leads to a misallocation of resources, in that a socially useful invention may not be introduced if the private benefits are too low relative to the costs. Although this is true in a no-growth environment, the situation changes when the benefits from innovation are growing over time. A divergence between private and social benefits from incomplete appropriability will make the privately most profitable introduction time later than the socially optimal time. The divergence will not eliminate the introduction of the innovation, but it will delay its times of profitable introduction.

Since the patent system allows free entry into the prepatent stages of R & D, Barzel (1968) has argued that this will tend to give introduction when private net present value is equal to zero (so the competitive rate of return is earned) rather than when it is maximized. The privately premature introduction of an innovation tends to offset the distortion caused by the inappropriability of the entire social benefit. By combining both of these effects, the socially optimal distortion between the social and private net present values of an innovation can be found. This distortion ensures that the privately premature introduction of an innovation will be just at the socially optimal time of introduction. The optimal divergence between the social and private benefits may be expressed in terms of the length of the legal patent life, the market-determined ratio of private to social benefits accruing during the life of the patent, and any taxes or subsidies that change this ratio. Thus, patent life, taxes, and subsidies are alternative government policy tools that can be used to encourage the socially optimal time of introduction of an innovation.

Competition among several firms to get a patent first may cause them to reduce the duration of their R & D projects at the cost of increasing the accumulated capital costs. The inefficient production of potential innovations will reduce their private as well as social discounted values. This source of inefficiency cannot be eliminated, but use of the optimal patent life will give the socially optimal time of introduction for the actual resource costs incurred, not just for the minimum production cost.

The socially optimal size of cost reduction or scale of innovation has also been derived. The optimal scale gives the largest social net present value (evaluated at the socially optimal times of introduction), and the same scale is both privately and socially most profitable. An important potential problem is the possibility that competition may encourage smaller than optimal sizes of cost reductions to be produced as a result of the firms' competitive attempts to get a patent. Unlike the problem of introduction time, the currently available policy tools of patent life, taxes, and subsidies are unable to encourage the socially optimal size of cost reduction. This may explain the often-noticed pattern of many small cost reductions as opposed to major innovations, because the small improvements may provide immediate patent protection as well as erode the profitability of the optimal size of cost reduction (by reducing its marginal cost reduction).

An idealized auction of the right to do R & D has certain advantages over the current patent system, even if the system is modified to include the socially optimal patent life. The auction can give the socially optimal introduction time, eliminate the use of excessive research inputs, and provide the optimal scale of innovation. An important disadvantage of the auction method is that a perpetual patent with its associated welfare loss is required to get the advantages just listed.

In short, neither institutional change considered in this chapter provides even a theoretically ideal way to eliminate inefficient production and marketing of innovations. But if a patent system with free entry into the prepatent stages of R & D is maintained, the use of the optimal patent life can give the socially optimal time of introduction for the resource costs actually incurred.

REFERENCES

Barzel, Yoram, "Optimal Timing of Innovations," *Review of Economics and Statistics* 50 (August 1968): 348–55.

Behrman, Jack N., and Wilson E. Schmidt, "Royalty Provisions in Foreign Licensing Contracts,' *Patent, Trademark, and Copyright Journal of Research and Education* 3, no. 3 Fall 1959: 272–302.

Kamien, Morton I, and Nancy L. Schwartz, "Timing of Innovations Under Rivalry," *Econometrica* 40 (January 1972): 43–60.

Kamien, Morton I, and Nancy L. Schwartz, "Patent Life and R & D Rivalry," *American Economic Review* 64 (March 1974): 183–87.

Kitti, Carole, "Patent Policy and the Optimal Timing of Innovations," Ph.D. Dissertation, University of Chicago, 1973.

Nordhaus, William D., *Invention, Growth, and Welfare: A Theoretical Treatment of Technological Change* (Cambridge: MIT Press, 1969).

Nordhaus, William D., "The Optimum Life of a Patent: Reply," *American Economic Review* 62 (June 1972): 428–31.

Scherer, F.M., "Research and Development Allocation Under Rivalry," *Quarterly Journal of Economics* 81 (August 1967): 359–94.

Scherer, F.M., "Nordhaus' Theory of Optimal Patent Life: A Geometric Reinterpretation," *American Economic Review* 62 (June 1972): 422–27.

4

Patent Enforcement: The Uncertainties of Patent Litigation

Ronald L. Engel

The value of a patent is obviously linked to the prospects for enforcing the patent. A number of studies have reported that a substantial percentage of adjudicated patents are held invalid. These statistics are erroneously viewed as an adverse reflection on the value of patents in general and tend to undermine confidence in the patent system. The attrition rate of adjudicated patents is a major uncertainty of patent litigation, but is not a meaningful measure of the value of most patents.

Assessment of the attrition rate requires some understanding of the nature of patent litigation, which is admittedly both costly and time consuming. Legal fees incurred in a typical patent infringement case can easily run into six figures. When the stakes are high and the parties are well financed and determined, fees of 1 million dollars or more are a distinct possibility. Substantial indirect costs are also imposed by major litigation.

In addition, patent litigation tends to be complex and therefore very time consuming. According to the Administrative Office of the United States Courts (1978), the median time interval from filing to disposition of a civil case in the U.S. district courts for cases disposed of during a 12-month period ending June 30, 1978, was 10 months, with 10 percent of the cases taking 31 months or more from filing to disposition. For patent cases, the median time to disposition was 12 months, with 10 percent of them taking 41 months or more. With respect to cases that proceeded to trial, the median time from filing to disposition for all civil cases was 19 months, with 10 percent of them taking more than 43 months. By contrast, the median time from filing to disposition for patent cases that proceeded to trial was 32 months, with 10 percent taking 66 months or more. In fact, for cases that proceeded to trial, patent cases took longer to dispose of than every other class of civil case analyzed in the 1978 *Annual Report*.

THE DATA REGARDING PATENT LITIGATION

These cost and duration burdens of patent litigation are compounded by a high attrition rate of patents subjected to litigation. Several statistical studies of the judicial invalidation of patents indicate that at least half of the adjudicated patents are invalidated. Four of these studies exemplify the issue.

One study (Banner, 1978), prepared for the U.S. Senate and reported by then-Commissioner of Patents and Trademarks Donald W. Banner, analyzed patents litigated during the period from 1968 through 1972. The study found that 2,025 patents had been litigated during the five-year period. Of 638 patents that were adjudicated to a finding of validity or invalidity, 54 percent were held invalid.

Another study, which was prepared by Koenig (1976), reported that for the period from 1953 through 1972, 53.3 percent of patents adjudicated by the U.S. district courts were held invalid. With respect to courts of appeals, the Koenig study found that 59.7 percent of the patents adjudicated during the period 1953–72 were held invalid.

The Koenig study also included an analysis of 150 patents selected at random from all patents held invalid during 1953–67. With respect to these, Koenig analyzed the reasons relied on by the courts in declaring the patents invalid. One of the most significant conclusions reached was that uncited prior art (i.e., prior art that is not considered by the U.S. Patent and Trademark Office in evaluating a patent application) plays a major role in decisions invalidating patents. Of the 150 patents studied, 46 percent were invalidated based on consideration of both cited and uncited prior art, and an additional 27 percent were invalidated based on uncited prior art alone. Thus, uncited prior art played a role in the invalidation of 73 percent of the patents considered in the study. Although the sample on which this study was based was small, Koenig concluded that uncited prior art does play an important role in patent invalidity holdings.

A third study, which was prepared by Baum (1974), covers decisions in the courts of appeals and district courts for the period from 1921 through 1973. Baum's statistics show that for this period, 55 percent of the patents adjudicated by the U.S. district courts were held invalid. For the more recent period 1961–73, Baum found that 61 percent of the patents adjudicated by district courts were held to be invalid. A breakdown of the 1961–73 data for district courts on a circuit-by-circuit basis reveals that the variation in the percentage of patents held invalid between courts in the various circuits ranged from a low of 27 percent (in courts in the tenth circuit) to a high of 82 percent (in courts in the third circuit).[1]

With respect to courts of appeals, for the period from 1921 through 1973, Baum found that 65 percent of the patents adjudicated were held invalid. The same percentage of patents (65 percent) was held invalid by courts of appeals for the 1961–73 period. A circuit-by-circuit breakdown of appellate court holdings for the 1961–73 period reveals that the percentage of patents held invalid by the courts of appeals ranged from 30 (in the tenth circuit) to 89 (in the eighth circuit) percent.

A fourth study was prepared by the Patent and Trademark Office (U.S. Patent and Trademark Office, 1979). This report shows for the interval 1973–77 a 48 percent invalidity rate in the district courts and a 69 percent invalidity rate in the courts of appeals.

Interpretations of the Litigation Data

Differences in statistical methodology and in data base selection seemingly account for the variances in invalidation rates suggested by these studies. However, a generalization that can be reached from the representative studies summarized above is that approximately 50 percent of litigated patents are judicially invalidated at the trial level (with a tendency toward an even higher attrition rate at the appellate level).

Many factors contribute to the uncertain outcome of patent litigation as reflected in these statistics. Patents that are litigated are selected by a complex process, not mere chance. Thus, litigated patents do not provide a representative sample of all issued patents. In most instances, both the patentee and the alleged infringer are represented by competent and rational counsel. As a result, patents that are either clearly valid or clearly invalid are usually not litigated.

If a patent is clearly valid, counsel for the accused infringer will advise the client to either design around the boundaries of the patent or to take a license if one is available. Given the expense of litigation, it is rare for an accused infringer to spend large sums of money fighting an uphill battle against the validity of a patent that the attorney has advised is valid. Conversely, a patentee who has been advised by counsel that the patent is invalid will generally avoid its enforcement. Moreover, economic realities will encourage the owner of a marginal patent to license the patent rather than to risk a result of invalidation in litigation.

Generally, the only patents that are litigated to final judgment are those for which a legitimate difference of opinion exists as to whether or not it will

[1]These variations are a factor in the forum shopping that is often a characteristic of patent litigation.

be upheld. Accordingly, the percentage of adjudicated patents that are held invalid should be substantial. However, this does not necessarily mean that litigated patents should be held valid precisely 50 percent of the time. For example, if an accused infringer would be forced out of business if he or she failed to establish invalidity, and if the patentee has offered a license on terms that permit the accused infringer to continue in business, presumably the accused will risk litigation only if the chances of a successful defense are rated above 50 percent. Another factor is that patents are generally obtained on an ex parte basis, whereas patents in litigation are subjected to all the assaults that an adversarial system can muster. Thus, a court often has available to it evidence of invalidity that simply is not available to the Patent and Trademark Office when it considers the merits of a patent application. Undoubtedly, other mechanisms operate to affect the expected percentage of patents held invalid. Accordingly, the true significance of statistics on the validity of adjudicated patents cannot be evaluated until the process that determines which patents are litigated to final judgment is better understood.

The significance of statistics regarding the validity of adjudicated patents is further weakened when they are considered in the context of the large number of patents in force at any given time. Chief Judge Markey of the Court of Customs and Patent Appeals attributes a great deal of the present concern about the condition of the U.S. patent system to statistics that purport to reflect the percentage of existing patents that are invalid (Markey, 1977). According to Judge Markey, the number of appellate patent decisions is simply too small to be statistically significant as a measure of overall patent validity. He argues that for the period 1968–72, the number of patents adjudicated by appellate courts represented only 11 percent of those on which suit was filed and less than 0.2 percent of the number of patents issued during that period. When account is taken of the fact that, at any given time, almost all patents issued over the preceding 17 years are subject to litigation, it is clear that the number of patents litigated represents a very small percentage of the number in force. For example, for the 12-month period ending June 30, 1978, there were 904 patent cases filed, and 145 patent, trademark, and copyright cases appealed (Administrative Offices of the U.S. Courts, 1978). During this period, there were approximately 1.2 million patents in force. Thus, Judge Markey correctly points out that the sample of adjudicated patents is not large enough to serve as a basis for a broad conclusion as to the worth of patents in general.

More importantly, Markey notes that, for reasons that he cannot explain, only 50 percent of the decisions holding a patent valid are reported, whereas 92 percent of those holding one invalid are reported. Accordingly, use of reported decisions as a basis for evaluating the value of patents (as is typically the case in these types of studies) is questionable at best. Furthermore, Markey points out that holdings of patent invalidity are appealed far more often than those of patent validity.[2] Since the courts of appeals currently reverse fewer than 20 percent of the cases they hear (Administrative Office of the U.S. Courts, 1978), appellate court statistics on the percentage of patents held invalid are not a direct reflection on the quality of issued patents.

The illogic of using statistics on adjudicated patents to make generalizations about the validity of all patents is highlighted by the variation in the validity holdings among the various circuits as revealed by Baum's study. As discussed above, the percentage of patents found invalid varies from 30 to 89 percent among the courts of appeals and from 27 to 82 percent among the district courts (by circuit). This variation is obviously not solely a result of a variation in the quality of patents considered by the courts. Rather, the phenomenon of patent validity statistics is a reflection of the operation of the judicial process on the very small number of issued patents that are considered by the courts.

Recommendations for a Better Patent System

In spite of the doubtful legitimacy of generalizing patent invalidity statistics to conclude that patent quality in general is poor, these statistics are useful when viewed in the proper perspective. In particular, the Koenig study found that uncited prior art figures in the result in approximately 73 percent of the cases in which patents are held invalid. This statistic is significant for several reasons. First, the present state of the Patent and Trademark Office's search facilities and staffing is inadequate. Thus, an accused infringer with substantial potential liability for infringement is likely to be able to conduct a far more comprehensive prior art search than an examiner in the Patent and Trademark Office. This state of affairs suggests a significant weakness in the patent system, which can and should be corrected. However, the pertinence of uncited prior art also points out that a patent applicant can take the initiative to improve the probability that the validity of the patent will be upheld. This can be done by ensuring that the prior art presented to the Patent and Trademark Office is as complete as the applicant can afford to make it. By investing in a search of the relevant art and presenting the search results to the examiner, the presumption of validity enjoyed by the patent can be significantly strengthened.

The uncertainties of patent litigation reflect in part inherent weaknesses in the patent system. Part of the problem is clearly attributable to insufficient

---

[2]This phenomenon may be explained by the substantial incentive that exists for accused infringers to accept an offer of settlement after a patent has been held valid by a district court. Thus, the parties are likely to compromise their claims rather than risk an appeal. Conversely, if a patent has been held invalid, there is relatively little incentive for an accused infringer to accept a license on any terms, given the likelihood that the court of appeals will affirm the district court.

funding received by the Patent and Trademark Office. The significance of the office's lack of funds was highlighted by former Commissioner of Patents and Trademarks Banner (1979) as contributing to its difficulties in ensuring patent quality. Because the office's funding in real dollars has been declining over the last several years, patent search files, the principal tool utilized by the examiner in determining the patentability of inventions, have been deteriorating. Prior art searches are still conducted in reliance on the contents of files that are found to be incomplete with alarming and increasing frequency. Foreign patents are available to only a limited extent, and many patents are organized in out-dated classifications that impair their accessibility to the examiners. Thus, relevant prior art is often missed by the Patent and Trademark Office, and it is usually not until an accused infringer with a substantial economic incentive conducts a more comprehensive search that invalidating or otherwise relevant prior art is located. The inadequacy of the Patent and Trademark Office's funding and facilities is further highlighted by the fact that many examiners still send out their office actions written in longhand, and the office cannot afford to maintain duplicate copies of its application files. For these and other reasons, the ability of the Patent and Trademark Office to process patent applications is declining.

For the patent system to perform its constitutionally mandated function of promoting the progress of science and the useful arts, some assurance must exist that a patent will be enforceable. At the same time, the system must be free to purge itself of invalid patents. The available statistics do not establish that most or even a substantial percentage of issued patents are invalid. Nevertheless, perceived uncertainty regarding the enforceability of patents, combined with the substantial time, expense, and risk involved in challenging a patent, threaten to distort the role of the patent system and inhibit innovation. One step toward alleviating this problem is to recognize that statistics regarding the validity of adjudicated patents do not reflect on the quality of the majority of issued patents and therefore should not discourage innovation or the patenting of inventions.

The great majority of patents, those that represent legitimate inventions, are not affected by the whims of litigation, since the threat of enforcement is effective either to deter infringement at the outset or to encourage settlement of those claims that do arise. Thus, the actual cost of enforcement when implemented is too remote to be a legitimate negative influence on innovation. In addition, the "uncertain" outcome of patent litigation is simply not a reflection on the enforceability of patents in general. Clearly, enforceable patents can and do serve their function without ever being subjected to actual enforcement. However, given the fact that one of the principal reasons courts hold patents invalid is that the Patent and Trademark Office did not consider the most relevant prior art, or was otherwise not apprised of all relevant information at the time it passed on the application, patentees have under their own control the ability to improve the reliability of their patents. If patentees take the initiative in ensuring that the record presented to the Patent and Trademark Office is as complete as possible, the enforceability of the patent that results should be substantially increased. Thus, investment in research and development, and the innovation that it generates, should not be allowed to decline in the name of uncertainties of patent litigation.

REFERENCES

Administrative Office of the United States Courts, *Report to the Director,* 1978 (annual).

Banner, D.W., "Address to the American Bar Association Patent, Trademark, and Copyright Section," *Journal of the Patent Office Society* 60(1978):477.

Baum, Lawrence, "The Federal Courts and Patent Validity: An Analysis of the Record," *Journal of the Patent Office Society* 56(1974):758.

Koenig, Gloria, *Patent Invalidity—A Statistical and Substantive Analysis,* 1976.

Markey, "The Status of the U.S. Patent System—Sans Myth, Sans Fiction," *Journal of the Patent Office Society* 59(1977):164.

Since this article was first written, jurisdiction in patent cases has changed. Today, the Court of Appeals for the Federal Circuit, which is the successor to the Court of Customs and Patent Appeals, has exclusive appellate jurisdiction in patent cases. This consolidation, which eliminated the differences in the interpretation and application of patent law that had previously existed between the circuits, might be expected to reduce some of the uncertainties of patent litigation. Unfortunately, the consolidation is too recent for any empirical research of the kind referred to by Engel to have been done. Engel's main points, however, are as valid today as when they were first written: 1) Statistics on adjudicated patents do not reflect the validity of patents in general; 2) patent litigation remains slow and expensive; 3) the Patent and Trademark Office is as poorly funded today as in the past; 4) patentees can still improve the reliability of their patents by ensuring that the record presented to the Patent and Trademark Office is as complete as possible.

5
The Role of National Laboratories in R & D*

Joseph G. Asbury

The origins of the complex of Department of Energy (DOE) multiprogram laboratories can be traced to early work on nuclear weapons development. The responsibility of the laboratories expanded during the late 1940s and the 1950s, as the Atomic Energy Commission (AEC) charged them with major roles in the development of civilian nuclear power and with national trust missions in the physical sciences and in radiobiological and nuclear medicine research. Under the Energy Research and Development Administration (ERDA) and the DOE, the missions of the laboratories were broadened further. By 1980, they were conducting research on most of the major energy technologies and collectively accounted for a significant part of the energy research and development (R & D) supported by the federal government.

As a matter of policy, each of the laboratories was established as a federally owned and funded facility to be operated and staffed by a private contractor. The private contractor arrangement has provided a degree of independence and flexibility, especially in personnel policies and practices, not available at government-operated facilities. Nevertheless, the dependence

---

*The author is solely responsible for the views and ideas presented in the chapter and for any errors of fact. None of the material contained herein should be construed as necessarily representing the position or the policies of Argonne National Laboratory or the U.S. Department of Energy. Through this chapter, the term "DOE multiprogram laboratory" will be applied to the nine laboratories so designated by the Energy Research Advisory Board. These are Ames Laboratory, Argonne National Laboratory, Brookhaven National Laboratory, Los Alamos National Laboratory, Lawrence Berkely National Laboratory, Lawrence Livermore National Laboratory, Oak Ridge National Laboratory, Pacific Northwest Laboratory, and Sandia Laboratories.

of the laboratories on the parent agency for most of their funding support and for approval of major research initiatives has meant that they have generally behaved, and have been treated, as agents of the parent organization. Thus, there has been a close historical relationship between the role and missions of the laboratories and those of the parent agency.

The reformulation of federal R & D policy under the Reagan administration brought an abrupt change in the R & D mission of the DOE. Previous policy had included a strong commitment to the development and commercialization of near-term technology. Under the new policy guidelines, federally supported work on civilian technology would be concentrated on the upstream end of the R & D cycle, that is, on longer-term, higher-risk research activities. Federal support would extend into downstream development work only through the proof-of-concept stage. Nearer-term technical support would be limited to cases in which the government had a unique resource or capability. The private sector would generally be responsible for demonstration plants and for commercializing new technologies as they became economical.[1]

Like their parent agency, the multiprogram laboratories, which had mobilized to support the priorities and objectives of previous administrations, came under intensive review.

Two reviews of the multiprogram laboratories have recently been completed. The review by the Energy Research Advisory Board (ERAB) of the DOE examined the capabilities of the DOE's multiprogram laboratories and made recommendations about the appropriate roles of the laboratories and the department's policies and procedures regarding the use of the laboratories.[2] Another review, conducted by the Office of Science and Technology Policy (OSTP), was charged with examining the missions and effectiveness of all the national laboratories, including, but not limited to, those supported by the DOE.[3] Although the scopes of the two reviews were different, their findings and recommendations with regard to national laboratories generally (OSTP) and to the DOE multiprogram laboratories specifically (ERAB) were similar in several essential respects.

Both reviews concluded that there was a need for clearer statements and assignments of missions for the individual laboratories and for a clearer

---

[1]These general principles, which were to guide federal R & D policy, were apparently first issued in a budget document by the Office of Management and Budget. See *Energy Daily*, February 6, 1981. The guidelines are more fully elaborated in "Annual Science and Technology Report to the Congress: 1981," Office of Science and Technology Policy in cooperation with the National Science Foundation (April 1982).

[2]U.S. Department of Energy, "The Department of Energy Multiprogram Laboratories: A Report of the Energy Research Advisory Board to the Department of Energy" (September 1982).

[3]Office of Science and Technology Policy, Executive Office of the President, "Report of the White House Science Council" (May 1983).

delineation of the laboratories' roles vis-à-vis those of the university and industrial research communities. At the same time, the reviews recommended greater information and personnel exchange with these communities to facilitate manpower training and technology transfer. Both faulted federal parent agencies for micromanagement of laboratory programs and unnecessary administrative burdens and called for the conferring of greater programmatic responsibility and discretion on the laboratories' managements.

The recommendations for improving the usefulness of the laboratories to the private sector deserve special mention because of their implications for the future role of the laboratories. To improve the accessibility of laboratory facilities and to promote technology transfer, the ERAB recommended several specific actions, including the establishment of user groups for all major programs, vigorous implementation of the recently liberalized patent policy governing federally sponsored research, more joint ventures with industry, and the opening up of the laboratories for more reimbursable work for other sponsoring agencies. These recommendations present an opportunity and pose a challenge to the DOE and the laboratories' managements. They offer a path, especially in the applied and base technology research areas, to the development of important new research initiatives. On the other hand, the initiatives will be politically feasible, and the resulting programs sustainable, only to the extent that they can be made responsive to the private sector's needs.

It is worth noting that the general principles advanced by the Reagan administration to guide federal R & D policy with regard to civilian technology were adopted either explicitly or implicitly by the review panels. These principles, in fact, appear to have taken hold throughout the federal R & D establishment.

The reformulation of federal R & D priorities has taken place against a backdrop of growing concern about the nation's technological competitiveness in the international marketplace. The importance of this issue to the future roles of the multiprogram laboratories probably cannot be overstated. The many recent R & D policy and funding initiatives by governments throughout the industrialized world stem from a widening consensus that a nation's economic, military, and political standing is determined largely by the comparative quality of its scientific and technological accomplishment.

In the long run, U.S. success in the technological competition is likely to depend on many factors, including the nation's success in improving the quality of technical education in its primary and secondary schools and its ability to maintain a decentralized and efficient industrial economy. In the intermediate run, there are likely to be increasing pressures to improve the productivity of available R & D resources, including the multiprogram laboratories.

In this chapter, we try to delineate, more sharply than heretofore, appropriate roles for the DOE multiprogram laboratories. The discussion begins with a description of the laboratories, including a brief review of their history and the scope of their energy R & D programs. Then, recent changes in federal R & D policy are described, causes of the changes examined, and the evolution of the laboratories in the policy context traced. The role of the multiprogram laboratories is subsequently divided into four generic types of activities. The kinds of federally supported research that are likely to be performed more efficiently by the laboratories than by universities or industry are delineated. Several issues important to the future effectiveness of the laboratories in meeting industry's R & D needs are then identified and discussed.

The chapter is concerned mainly with the roles of the laboratories in general science and energy-related R & D areas. Defense-related work, which constitutes over one-half the budgets of three of the nine multiprogram laboratories, is not discussed.

THE MULTIPROGRAM LABORATORIES

Each of the multiprogram laboratories, or its predecessor institution, played an important role in nuclear weapons development. The laboratories evolved into multidisciplinary institutions because of the technical requirements of nuclear weapons development and related health and environmental research. The multidisciplinary character of the laboratories was further broadened during the 1950s when they were assigned major missions in civilian nuclear power development. The laboratories also assumed national trust missions in the physical sciences (high-energy and nuclear physics) and in the radiobiological sciences and nuclear medicine research. Especially in the physical sciences, they have served as homes for large research facilities, including a number of the nation's largest particle accelerators. Traditionally, these and numerous smaller facilities have been made available for use by university scientists and, to a lesser extent, by industry.

The activities of the laboratories expanded greatly under the ERDA and later the DOE. Whereas before, applied energy research had focused mainly on nuclear power development, it subsequently encompassed most of the important energy technologies, including fusion energy, coal conversion technologies, magnetohydrodynamics, geothermal resources, solar thermal and solar electric energy, biomass energy, and a number of end-use and conservation technologies. An indication of the breadth of the laboratories' energy R & D programs is provided by Table 5.1, which lists funding levels in fiscal year 1981 by technology and science area.

TABLE 5.1. Department of Energy Allocations to Eight Multiprogram Laboratories, by Technology and General Research Area (obligations, fiscal year 1981)

	ANL	*BNL*	*LBL*	*LLL*	*LANL*	*ORNL*	*PNL*	*SNL*
Fossil Energy	17.5	2.6	3.5	7.9	6.4	13.0	3.3	24.7
Conservation	19.5	3.0	6.9	0.7	1.8	16.0	9.1	1.2
Nuclear Energy	88.2	0.6	1.0	0.6	14.1	55.9	16.6	21.2
Electric Systems and Energy Storage	9.4	7.3	3.9	5.3	2.1	13.0	10.2	1.6
Solar Energy	8.2	2.8	5.7	1.0	2.6	7.3	13.9	64.4
Geothermal	—	1.6	4.8	1.0	15.5	1.1	1.4	9.8
Magnetic Fusion	4.7	1.3	8.3	70.2	20.0	73.7	—	2.5
Environmental	18.3	10.1	9.1	14.6	12.0	27.1	18.9	1.0
Energy-Supporting Research	34.3	30.0	20.1	4.7	8.6	40.6	5.0	10.6
General Science	14.7	106.5	46.3	1.9	36.4	16.0	0.3	—
Defense	5.1	2.4	2.1	343.3	255.3	21.2	13.9	412.9

Ames Laboratory, whose total budget of $14 million is comparatively small and for which a detailed breakdown was not readily available, was omitted from the table.

ANL, Argonne National Laboratory; BNL, Brookhaven National Laboratory; LBL, Lawrence Berkely National Laboratory; LLL, Lawrence Livermore National Laboratory; LANL, Los Alamos National Laboratory; ORNL, Oak Ridge National Laboratory; PNL, Pacific Northwest Laboratory; SNL, Sandia National Laboratories.

Source: Argonne National Laboratory, Argonne, Illinois.

Argonne National Laboratory

Although the circumstances affecting the original and subsequent development of each of the multiprogram laboratories differ significantly, some insight into their evolution can be gained by reviewing the history of one of them. The following sketches the history of Argonne National Laboratory.

Argonne is the direct descendant of the Metallurgical Laboratory established at the University of Chicago to examine the feasibility of self-sustaining nuclear reactions and their application in the production of plutonium for use in atomic weapons. By early 1944, the Metallurgical Laboratory had successfully constructed and operated three experimental reactor facilities. The first facility, which demonstrated the first self-sustaining chain reaction, was located at the University of Chicago; the second and third reactors were located near the present Argonne site southwest of Chicago.

Following the successful transfer of reactor design principles and features to the production plant in Hanford, Washington, the Metallurgical Laboratory was left without a clearly defined mission. To prevent the disintegration of an outstandingly successful research organization and to exploit further the evident promise of nuclear energy, the Manhattan District in the fall of 1945 decided to continue the Metallurgical Laboratory on a permanent basis. Acting on the recommendations of a committee of leading midwestern scientists, the government established Argonne National Laboratory on July 1, 1946.

The new laboratory was conceived "as a research organization with its program centered in the field of phenomena important to atomic energy developments."[4] This included basic work in nuclear, chemical, and materials sciences as well as in the biological and health effects of radiation. In 1948, the newly formed AEC asked it to assume major responsibilities in the nation's nuclear reactor development program.

By any measure, Argonne's contributions to reactor development have been significant. The laboratory either originated or made important contributions to all of the nuclear power systems now in worldwide use, including the pressurized light water reactor, the boiling water reactor, and the liquid metal fast breeder reactor (LMFBR). The laboratory constructed and operated the first experimental breeder reactor, EBR-I, and its successor, EBR-II, the latter serving as the nation's principal fuel test facility for breeder reactors since its completion in 1965. Currently, Argonne is the nation's leading center for LMFBR research in the physics and safety areas.

A major change in Argonne's character, from mainly an in-house AEC resource to also a user-oriented laboratory, occurred in 1957 with federal authorization for the construction of the zero gradient synchrotron (ZGS). The ZGS, which was the first major accelerator in the Midwest, contributed to the building of strong physics groups in midwestern universities and led to the development at Argonne of frontier expertise in cryogenics, magnets, high power radio frequency systems, and applied superconductivity. Although the ZGS, the laboratory's largest user facility, was retired in 1981, Argonne recently completed construction of the intense pulsed neutron source, a world-class spallation source of neutrons for condensed matter and irradiation studies, and the high-voltage electron microscope for real-time studies of structural changes in matter. The laboratory currently is constructing the Argonne tandem-linear accelerator system, a national facility for heavy ion research, and is preparing a design proposal for a synchrotron light source.

While nuclear-related R & D and facilities-based research remained the twin pillars of laboratory effort, the spectrum of its applied programs expanded during the 1970s. This stemmed partly from the broadened missions of the ERDA and then the DOE and partly from the willingness and ability of the

---

[4]For an early history of Argonne National Laboratory, see Norman Hilberry, "Elements of Basic Management Philosophy at Argonne National Laboratory with Applications to Personnel Management and Salary Administration," Argonne, Ill. (September 2, 1952).

laboratory to apply skills and experience developed in other areas to new energy-related problems. Over the last decade, the laboratory has assumed major programmatic responsibilities and made major technical contributions in such areas as advanced electric batteries, fuel cells, solar collector design, magnetohydrodynamics, Tokomak fusion reactor design, coal chemistry, and the environmental and health consequences of nonfission energy sources.[5] Although federal funding of near-term energy technology has contracted, Argonne plans to maintain its scientific and base technology programs in support of a number of energy technologies.

No one laboratory can be regarded as representative of all the multiprogram laboratories. The individual laboratories exhibit important differences with regard to historical mission, size, engineering versus scientific emphasis, geographical location, organizational structure, and management style. Nevertheless, the history of Argonne illustrates a number of characteristics common to most of the laboratories. These include early participation by the laboratory itself or by its predecessor institution in nuclear weapons development; work on civilian nuclear power development and/or in the sciences and base technology that have supported such development; an emphasis in the basic sciences on facilities, often user facilities, requiring substantial technical support and management oversight; and, in energy technology, an emphasis on large R & D programs, typically involving multidisciplinary research groups and requiring research planning and coordination.

FEDERAL ENERGY R & D POLICY

Under the traditional model of the laboratories, their mission has been basic and applied research in support of the national mission of the parent agency. Any prescriptive discussion of the role and mission of the multiprogram laboratories must therefore begin with an examination of federal R & D policy.

Role of Federal R & D

The classical arguments for public support of R & D follow from the general conclusion that private firms systematically underinvest in R & D. The principal reasons for underinvestment are limited appropriability of

---

[5]Argonne's programs and technical accomplishments are summarized in "Argonne National Laboratory: A Resource for the Nation," Argonne National Laboratory (February 22, 1982).

benefits, uncertainty of returns, and scale efficiencies that prevent individual firms from undertaking large R & D projects.[6]

There are other distortions from the ideal allocation. Several work in the direction of overinvestment rather than underinvestment. Thus, the patent and copyright systems, instituted to overcome the appropriability problem, can lead to monopoly rents and to an underutilization of the technology. Industrial secrecy, the only method of protecting the private value of an R & D investment prior to an application for a patent, unavoidably leads to the duplication of R & D effort. The problem of duplication may become especially pronounced in an international context where a number of nations are competing to develop new technological opportunities in the same field.

Whatever the arguments favoring public support of R & D, Nelson and Langlois have shown that there are great variations in the historical efficacy of public support.[7] In a case studies analysis, they found that the effectiveness of government support differs from industry to industry. However, under the appropriate institutional setting, three approaches were found to work in the past: (1) support associated with direct government procurement or with some other well-defined public sector objective; (2) support of defined nonproprietary research, with the allocation of R & D funds guided by the appropriate scientific community; and (3) support of applied R & D, coupled with the provision of an institutional structure that allows potential users to guide the allocation of funds. A fourth approach, under which government itself selects projects designed to produce winners in the commercial marketplace, was found to be ineffective.

The Historical Role

It is illuminating to apply the model of publicly supported R & D devised by Nelson and Langlois as a means of interpreting and evaluating the historical missions of the multiprogram laboratories and their parent agencies. It should be noted at the outset that none of the seven detailed case studies conducted by Nelson and Langlois, and on which they based their findings, involved R & D programs supported by the DOE or its predecessor agencies.

The early work by the multiprogram laboratories, or their predecessor organizations, on weapons and weapons-related research clearly corresponds to the Nelson-Langlois first category of publicly supported R & D. Government

[6]K.J. Arrow, "Economic Welfare and the Allocation of Resources for Invention." In *The Rate and Direction of Inventive Activity: Economic and Social Factors* (Princeton: Princeton University Press, 1962).

[7]R.R. Nelson and R.N. Langlois, "Industrial Innovation Policy: Lessons from American History," *Science* 219 (February 18, 1983): 814–18.

was the direct procurer of the devices and the information developed under these programs.

By all accounts, this work, especially the very early effort during the World War II emergency, was an outstanding technical success. Over a period of three years, three fundamentally new and different processes for producing weapons-grade fissile material were developed, tested, and constructed.[8] The gaseous diffusion and plutonium breeding processes, which were operational before the end of the war, remained the only viable sources of enriched fissile material until the recent development of centrifuge separation.

Federal support of nuclear weapons development produced a classic example of a spillover technology, namely, nuclear reactor technology for electric power generation. Although the laboratory complex was the repository of most of the early expertise in this technology, leadership for commercial applications soon passed to the utilities and their equipment suppliers. By the time light water reactors reached commercial application, several of the laboratories had already undertaken major programs in support of the fast breeder reactor.

Laboratory work in support of civilian reactor development appears to have fallen into the second and third categories identified by Nelson and Langlois. Part of the work was essentially nonproprietary, directed toward understanding such basic and generic technology phenomena as radiation effects, heat exchange properties, isotope properties, and nuclear-related health and environmental effects. Other work, which was of a more applied nature, included the design and evaluation of alternative reactor concepts, the development of advanced components and instrumentation, and the construction and operation of prototype reactors.

Although government exercised direct control over the allocation process during the 1950s and 1960s, in contradiction to the dictum of Nelson and Langlois that the scientific community and industry be granted substantial control, the contradiction is actually more apparent than real, and is tempered by the circumstances under which the nuclear industry developed. It must be remembered that nuclear technology and, in an important sense, the nuclear industry itself originated within the laboratory complex. Most of the early research initiatives were developed by the laboratories, and much of the nation's scientific and engineering leadership resided within the laboratory complex. While the AEC exercised formal control over the allocation process, it was often in the position of responding to and monitoring an allocation determined by the field. The private sector, which at first was simply the beneficiary of an enormous transfer of technology, gradually began to exercise more influence. Although never formally incorporated into an allocation

[8]Nuel Pharr Davis, *Lawrence and Oppenheimer* (New York: Simon & Schuster, 1968).

structure, its views and recommendations were sought and incorporated into the process. Technology transfer and the allocation process were facilitated by heavy personnel exchanges between industry and the laboratories. Throughout this period of civilian reactor development, it was apparent to all that the laboratories were working on the next generation of technical problems and that they were engaged in research that was broadly supportive of the nuclear industry's commercial aims.

Following the oil embargo of 1973 and the dramatic increases in energy prices, the energy R & D mission of the federal government expanded considerably. The newly formed ERDA undertook a development program that encompassed essentially all the advanced energy technologies: coal liquefaction and conversion, shale oil, enhanced oil recovery, electric batteries, fuel cells, solar thermal energy, photovoltaics, ocean thermal energy conversion, and others. The first R & D plans developed by the ERDA emphasized supply technologies.[9] However, conservation and end-use technologies were to receive considerably higher priority under the Ford and Carter administrations.[10,11]

The overriding energy policy objective during this period was to reduce the level of oil import dependence. Accordingly, R & D policy tended to emphasize those technologies that could be moved rapidly into the marketplace. Indeed, a favorite project selection criterion was oil-savings potential by the year 1985. The policy intent was most directedly expressed in legislative mandates to demonstrate the technical and economic feasibility of a host of new energy technologies, ranging from electric vehicles to solar central receivers to community energy systems. The multiprogram laboratories, representing the most convenient administrative agents available to the ERDA and DOE, assumed major programmatic responsibilities for developing the new technologies.

The emphasis on picking market winners probably peaked during the 1977–79 period. The rise in oil imports during the 1975–77 economic expansion—imports had risen to 8 million barrels per day in 1977 from about 5 million in 1973—coupled with the price shocks following the overthrow of the Shah of Iran added to the urgency of the commercialization efforts within the DOE. The objectives of the Market-Oriented Program Planning Study, conducted by the ERDA in 1977, were to "decide which technologies best suit

---

[9]Energy Research and Development Administration, "Creating Energy Choices for the Future: A National Plan for Energy Research, Development, and Demonstration," ERDA-48 (1974).

[10]Energy Research and Development Administration, "Creating Energy Choices for the Future: A National Plan for Energy Research, Development, and Demonstration," ERDA-76 (1976).

[11]Executive Office of the President, Energy Policy and Planning, *The National Energy Plan* (Washington, D.C.: U.S. Government Printing Office, 1977).

the various end-use energy needs" and then to determine which "can serve the user's needs most economically."[12] This was followed in 1979 with the establishment of a high-level commercialization group within the DOE to (1) review the portfolio of technologies then under development, (2) identify barriers to commercialization, and (3) establish milestones and timetables to commercialize the most promising technologies.[13] So far as can be determined, these efforts produced only minor changes in R & D program direction and few commercial winners.

To be sure, the federal program has achieved notable advances in such areas as magnetic confinement fusion, photovoltaic cells, and advanced electric batteries. Where the prospects for ultimate commercial success have been advanced, however, it has generally been the result of fundamentally new design concepts or new experimental findings rather than the perfection and demonstration of existing technical approaches.

Thus, the extraordinary efforts of government, acting through the ERDA and DOE, to develop and commercialize specific energy technologies appear to have borne little fruit. The experience is consistent—it is certainly not inconsistent—with the conclusions of Nelson and Langlois and others that government is ill equipped to perform this function.

The Shift Away from Near-Term Technology

When translated into R & D policy, the less-interventionist political philosophy of the Reagan administration called for a sharp reduction in government support of near-term civilian technology. The implementation of this policy in the energy area was facilitated by the federal R & D experience of the previous eight years, which provided little justification for the continuation of previous policies. Moreover, industrial support for the previous administrations' near-term programs, except for certain demonstration projects for which substantial private participation had already been arranged, was generally weak.

Adoption of the new guidelines was helped by two other developments. By 1981, forecasts of future U.S. energy requirements had been reduced considerably and oil imports had started to decline (see Figure 5.1). Although long-run prospects for domestic oil supplies had not improved, the picture for natural gas, which had been in short supply during the 1970s, had improved considerably under partial deregulation. As a result, the development and commercialization of new energy technologies had become considerably less urgent.

---

[12] "ERDA's 'MOPPS' Study Is Severely Criticized," *Energy Daily*, May 5, 1977.

[13] "Commercialization: DOE Takes the First Step," *Energy Daily*, June 19, 1978.

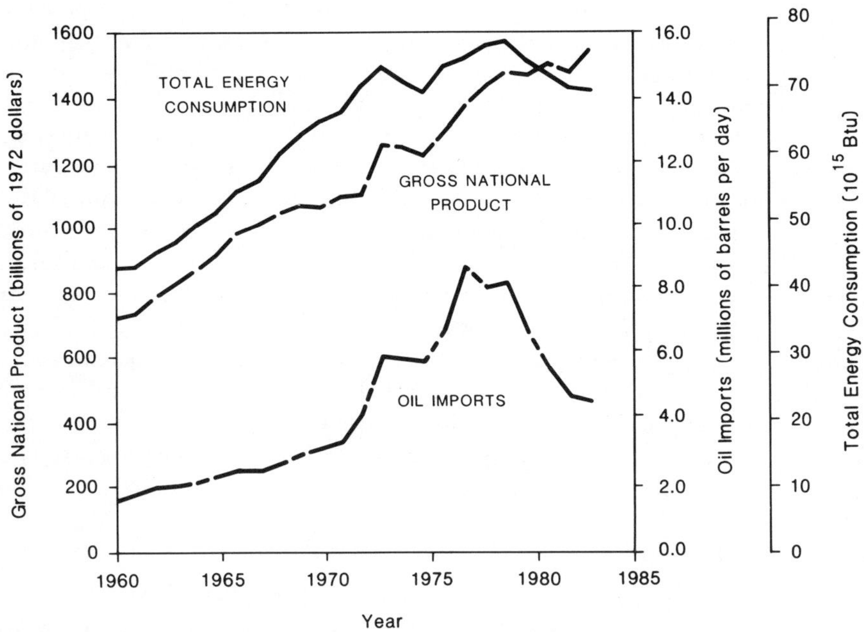

FIGURE 5.1. U.S. Energy Comsumption, Oil Imports, and Gross National Product, 1960–1983.

The second consideration that favored a backing away from near-term technology was basically a technical issue, one that could be fully appreciated only in hindsight. The problem of developing cost-competitive versions of the near-term technologies proved to be considerably more difficult than previously supposed. Despite nearly a decade of publicly and privately supported R & D and the substantial rises in costs of conventional energy supplies, in 1981 the costs of the next generation of supply technologies were still typically a factor of two higher than the costs of the conventional technologies.

The Great Plains Coal Gasification Project is a case in point. Coal gasification represents an important backstop technology for the gas industry in the United States. The Great Plains Project, finally organized during the 1979–80 period and the recipient of a \$2.0 billion loan from the Federal Financing Bank, is now nearing completion, on schedule and within the projected budget. However, the break-even price of the product gas is approximately \$8.00 per million British thermal units, roughly twice the market out wellhead prices currently mentioned by gas pipeline companies. Similarly, the SASOL coal-liquefaction plant in South Africa, while technically successful, is reportedly producing product at over \$60 per barrel, substantially more than the cost of petroleum-derived liquids.

The development of new supply and end-use technologies capable of holding energy costs anywhere near their present levels will probably require new engineering approaches based on new scientific understandings. Thus, on purely technical grounds, it could be argued that the grace period provided by the recent hiatus in energy demand growth would be more profitably spent working on fundamental improvements in the advanced technologies rather than trying to accelerate the commercialization of near-term technologies.

The magnitude of the energy problem appears to call for a reallocation of R & D resources rather than a reduction in the national effort. An indication of the cost to the economy of failing to improve the advanced technologies can be seen from Figure 5.2, which shows the trends in expenditures for electricity, natural gas, and petroleum products since 1960. Measured as a percentage of GNP, the total expenditures have more than doubled. The total in 1983 amounted to approximately $380 billion, a figure that understates the actual costs of the conventional supply technologies because of the average cost pricing of electricity and the rolling-in of old contract natural gas.

Changes in Federal Patent Policy

Another important recent development in federal R & D policy is the change in federal patent policy. The change is motivated mainly by the desire

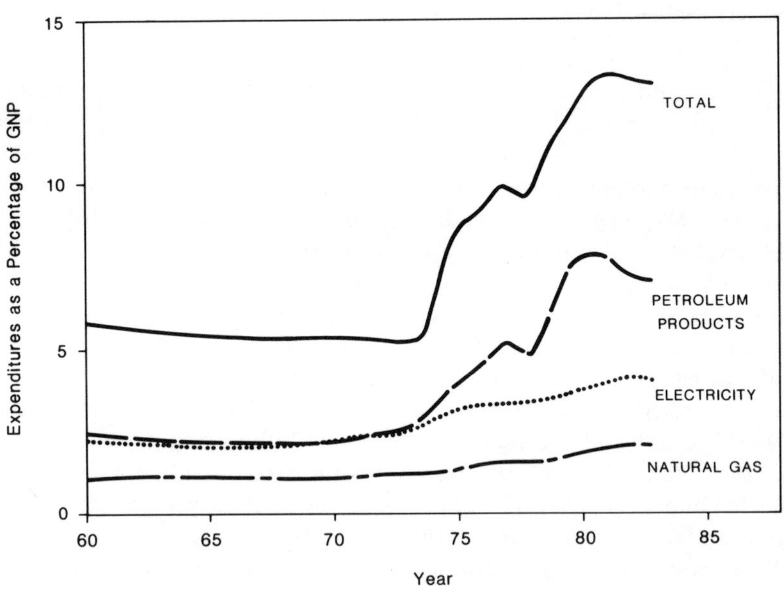

FIGURE 5.2. U.S. Expenditures on Petroleum Products, Electricity, and Natural Gas as a Percentage of Gross National Product (Expenditures on petroleum and natural gas do not include purchases by electric utilities).

to improve technology transfer from federally supported programs to the private sector.

Historically, the government funding agencies have had first claim on inventions developed under government sponsorship. As a result, neither federal laboratories nor contractors/operators have had adequate incentive to develop and exploit the commercial potential of new technologies.

The historical system has worked against both major functions of the patent system: the reward function and the prospect function. By failing to provide a reward for the discovery of technological opportunities having commercial potential, the system has not encouraged the adoption of measures that would reward such activities by the laboratories' staffs. Although private firms can obtain nonexclusive licenses comparatively easily, acquiring an exclusive license is usually a protracted, arduous process that in the end binds the licensee to a specified development and marketing program. The obstacles to obtaining an exclusive license undermine the prospect function of the patent system, which, as conceived and elaborated by Kitch,[14] bears a close analogy to the mineral claims system. Not the least of the benefits of exclusive ownership is that it provides an incentive to the owner to make investments in developing and marketing an innovation "without fear that the fruits of the investment will produce unpatentable information appropriable by competitors."[14]

The recently enacted Bayh-Dole bill now enables universities and small firms to obtain titles to patents developed under research contracts with the federal government. The bill also enables the DOE, at its own discretion, to grant patent rights to the contractors/operators of the national laboratories. Several recent bills that have been proposed, but not enacted by Congress, would extend the rights given to small firms to large firms.

Clearly, an improved method of granting exclusive rights to innovations developed at the laboratories is needed. Assigning these rights to the operators of the laboratories is probably the simplest of the alternatives. Although issues of equity are obviously a consideration, these might be ameliorated by requiring the operator to assume the cost of all patent applications, thereby also improving the efficiency of the application process.

ROLE OF THE MULTIPROGRAM LABORATORIES

The previous section sketched the evolution of the DOE multiprogram laboratories and examined the changes in federal R & D policy over the last decade. Here we outline, in fairly generic terms, appropriate roles for the multiprogram laboratories. Several of the roles represent simple extrapolations

[14]Edmund W. Kitch, "The Nature and Function of the Patent System," *The Journal of Law and Economics* 22, no. 2 (October 1977).

of past experience; others, particularly those in support of the industrial R & D needs, imply departures from previous policies and operating practices and raise a number of unresolved economic and legal issues. Several of these issues are identified and briefly discussed.

Because the laboratories represent but one of the types of candidate organizations for performing research, their roles must be defined in context with the capabilities and roles of other organizations, in particular, with those of industry, universities, and university-based research centers.

Broadly conceived, the role of the national laboratories can be divided into four categories, as following:

To Conduct Technology-Directed R & D and Basic Research That Supports the Missions of the Parent Agency

Technology-directed R & D encompasses activities ranging from research into basic phenomena underlying new technology to construction and operation of prototype facilities. Under the present R & D guidelines, it would not include demonstration projects or responsibility for commercialization efforts. The traditional criteria favoring the selection of a national laboratory, as opposed to a university or private firm, are that the nature of the work be such that (1) it is in the national interest that the disposition of the product of the work be the responsibility of the public at large, precluding performance of the work by a private organization where the conference of special benefits, the loss of general access, or the loss of public control over the product of the research would not be in the national interest, and (2) the performance of the work require a degree of technical concentration, including technical support facilities and services, not obtainable as efficiently at other institutions, for example, at universities.

Clearly, considerations incorporated under the first criterion were operative at the time of the decision to concentrate initial research to support fission reactor development at the national laboratories. Today, similar considerations would appear to favor locating generic technology work in support of fusion energy at the laboratories. Although large industrial organizations might assemble the resources to perform the work, the conferring of such privileged positions on one or only a few private organizations raises serious issues of equity, especially when the research may identify a technical approach that may eventually find massive commercial application. In the long run, economic efficiency would also appear to be better served when many firms have access to research and base technology information and when they compete on a relatively equal footing to develop technology for the ultimate market.

It should be noted that the first criterion does not preclude the performance of classified research at national laboratories. The results of such work, although not publicly disseminated, nevertheless are controlled by the public at large through its agent, the federal government. The greater assurance of institutional continuity during times of economic and political change is another consideration that is sometimes cited as favoring the location of nuclear weapons development at the national laboratories.

The arguments favoring free and open access to laboratory research findings are obviously in conflict with the attachment of private rights to technical innovations. This is less a problem in the more basic areas where the major research findings usually cannot be protected by patent. Although basic work can be a rich source of spinoff inventions, the granting of exclusive title to these technological opportunities should not present serious problems. However, in the major technology-directed areas (breeder reactor, fusion, etc.), the government may decide to retain title to prevent the accumulation of potentially massive commercial advantage and to protect the country's technological position in these areas. Clearly, the legal and economic issues raised by changing patent policy are important and complex and bear directly on the future role of the national laboratories.

The laboratories' success in developing and sustaining effective technology-directed programs is critically dependent on securing industry's participation and political support. Probably the only practical way of engaging industry participation in the R & D allocation process and thereby providing a sense of ownership is through the establishment of an advisory committee structure. Unfortunately, present federal policy, apparently motivated by concerns about the development of conflict-of-interest situations, the encouragement of lobbying efforts, and related problems, discourages the establishment of advisory committees by the federal parent agencies.[15] The DOE has only 12 standing advisory committees, hardly sufficient in the face of the broad and diverse nature of its scientific and industrial constituencies.

A central question is whether the problems commonly associated with advisory committees can be avoided. The High Energy Physics Advisory Panel, one of the 12 DOE committees, is generally regarded as having been very successful, suggesting that a sufficiently prestigious and open committee can overcome conflict-of-interest problems. Although the laboratories are not encumbered by the regulations that constrain the DOE, there is a clear need for greater industrial participation in major allocation decisions at the parent agency level.

The criteria for selecting a national laboratory for an R & D program must also take into account university capabilities. The second criterion

[15]Among the statutes and orders that guide Department of Energy policies and procedures with regard to advisory committees are the Federal Advisory Committee Act, P.L. 92-463 (1972); Section 5(c), P.L. 94-409 (1977); Section 2, P.L. 96-523 (1981); Executive Order 12024 (1977); Department of Energy Order 1130.6, "Advisory Committee Management" (1982).

advanced above could in principle be satisfied by establishing a federally supported research center on a university campus. This, of course, would amount to duplicating the capabilities that would otherwise reside at a national laboratory.

The advantages of a university-based institution would appear to include access to first-rate faculty research talent and the national benefits of improved training opportunities for university students. In practice, however, these benefits are difficult to achieve in large technology-directed programs where much of the work is facilities based and team centered. The demands of such work often are not easily met by faculty who have university responsibilities and whose academic performance is measured against criteria different from those typically employed by program managers.

The importance of the public benefits of student training is not easily dismissed, however. In situations in which the laboratories do not have a clear managerial and technical advantage, preference should be given to the universities. The laboratories should also be encouraged to expand their own student-training programs.

To Build and Operate National Research Facilities That, Because of Their Scale or Complexity, Are Beyond the Requirements or Means of Other Individual Institutions or Firms

Traditionally, new national laboratories have been established, or existing ones have been selected, as the locations for major research facilities. In keeping with their national purpose, these facilities have been made available to qualified users from industry and academic institutions.

Over the years, scientists and engineers of the multiprogram laboratories, often in collaboration with university scientists, have conceived, designed, and constructed many of the nation's major facilities for physical research. The record of accomplishment, measured in terms of innovation, cost of the machines, and productivity of the research and when compared against the international competition, has been outstanding.

Although university use of laboratory-sited research facilities has been very successful, industry participation has been minimal. In general, industry has not participated in the selection and design of facilities, and historically firms have not been able to secure proprietary rights to research they might finance and conduct at laboratory facilities.

The recent success of the Brookhaven national synchrotron light source in attracting participating research teams composed of industrial and other user groups may have established an important precedent in breaking down the barriers to greater industry use of laboratory-based facilities. Under the Brookhaven model, a participating research team finances and builds an experimental station in return for unrestricted use of the station for a prescribed fraction of the running time.

On a less structured basis, industrial organizations have gained access to research facilities at other national laboratories. For example, at Argonne, a number of companies have conducted catalysis research at the laboratory's intense pulsed neutron source, and several major oil companies have participated in materials experiments at the laboratory's corrosion/erosion test facilities.

The very fact of industrial use of laboratory facilities under present conditions establishes the existence of an economic demand for access to the facilities. Because this demand exists despite the base technology nature of the industrial research—the benefits are not fully capturable—there is clear justification for some level of federal support.

It is sometimes argued that the absence of joint industry action to sponsor facilities at institutions other than national laboratories is evidence of the lack of industry interest in such facilities. This argument is without force, because it fails to predict how industry would behave in a situation in which government support were available and industry were invited to participate. It is entirely plausible, for example, that steel-making firms desire, and collectively would benefit greatly from, a shared experimental program centered on a large device for electromagnetic casting.

Until steps are taken to engage industry participation in research at publicly supported facilities, there is no way to gauge the extent of private sector interest and to estimate the potential benefits. Once the ground is broken, it is likely that private interest will extend to upstream activities including the conception and design of the research facilities themselves.

To Make Resources Available on a Reimburseable Basis When It Would Not Be in the Public Interest to Duplicate These Resources Elsewhere

Technology-directed and facilities-based research will often lead to the development of unique research capabilities, which can be made available to other sponsors. Unlike research conducted by outside users of laboratory user facilities, work for others is typically performed on a fee-for-service, or contract research, basis. It may or may not involve a large facility.

Traditionally such work has been controlled to prevent the dilution of laboratory resources and to prevent their diversion from the mission of the parent agency. Actually, the work often strengthens the capabilities of the laboratories in meeting their commitments to the parent agency. For example, research supported at the multiprogram laboratories by the National Institute of Health and by the Environmental Protection Agency on the environmental and health effects of energy technologies has contributed to the laboratories' capabilities in areas important to the parent agency.

Whether the present relationship with DOE is maintained, or, given the desire to expand access to national research facilities, that the laboratories are opened up to work for other sponsors is a policy issue of considerable importance. Obviously, a significant policy change in this area would have major impact on the nature of laboratory work.

To Assist the Parent Agency in Its Mission by Conducting Technology Evaluations, Policy Analyses, and Other Studies and by Providing Technical Assistance When Called on to Do So

Because of their expertise and comparative independence from commercial interest in new technology, the laboratories are often uniquely qualified to assist the parent agency in assembling and integrating technical information necessary for efficient management and decision making. The future effectiveness of the laboratories in this role, however, will be compromised to the extent that they or their operators/contractors are permitted, under changes in patent policy, to capture the commercial benefits of new technologies.

SUMMARY

In its report on the multiprogram laboratories, the ERAB review panel concluded that the "laboratory complex constitutes an impressive national research and development asset."[1] Simply stated, therefore, the purpose of the panels recommendations is to improve the nation's return on this asset. The assumption underlying much of the discussion presented in this chapter is that increasingly this return will be evaluated in terms of contributions to the productivity and competitiveness of the nation's economy. The challenge before the DOE and the laboratories is to continue a tradition of excellence in the basic sciences and in a number of technology-directed fields, while simultaneously improving, in number and quality, the technological opportunities discovered and successfully transferred to the private sector.

There will be a continuing role for national laboratories in a number of publicly funded research areas. The most obvious role is to provide homes for national research facilities. The siting of a large facility amounts to the establishment of a laboratory. The clustering of such facilities to take advantage of scale economies in a host of support operations, including facilities building itself, amounts to the establishment of a multipurpose laboratory.

Although university use of laboratory research facilities has been very successful, industry participation has been minimal. Recent evidence suggests that if public funds were made available for the construction of industrial research facilities, industry would avail itself of R & D opportunities that are presently foreclosed. The research findings from facilities designed for large-scale, whole-system investigations could be shared by all participating firms. For facilities capable of simultaneously supporting a number of experimental stations, arrangements can be devised that allow individual firms to conduct proprietary research. There are few precedents in the United States for industrial participation in the development and use of large publicly financed research facilities. Until steps are taken to engage such participation, it is impossible to estimate the level of interest and the potential economic benefits.

Beyond facilities-centered research, there will be a role for national laboratories in technology-directed programs, where the required concentration of technical and management resources exceeds that obtainable at other institutions and where the government wishes to maintain certain controls over the disposition of the R & D product. Thus, major federal programs in fusion energy, breeder reactor technology, and the base technology underpinning the development in such areas as fuel cells, electric batteries, and coal conversion processes are appropriately conducted at the multiprogram laboratories.

Several policy issues identified in this chapter are likely to be critically important to the future roles of the multiprogram laboratories. These include the disposition of rights to innovations developed under federally funded programs and the design of efficient and equitable mechanisms for industrial participation in the R & D allocation process. Because of their importance not only to the role of laboratories but to the effectiveness of the nation's entire R & D effort, these issues appear to merit more attention by the social science community than they have so far received.

III

R & D Project Evaluation

6
Project Evaluation Approach to R & D

George S. Tolley and Stuart B. Townsend

Research has provided us with many new processes and ideas that can be utilized in new technologies for the production and conservation of energy. Many of these potential technologies are not profitable at present. However, rising fuel prices, improved efficiencies, and reduced production costs will increase profitability until many of the more exotic technologies become, at some time, economically feasible. Research and development (R & D) projects can accelerate this process. R & D projects can be analyzed as investment activities where the return to the R & D is an earlier stream of benefits from a new technology.

Serious assessment of the potential of any given specific innovative activity is possible, but too seldom attempted. The effects of a potential innovation on quality of life, the reductions brought about in costs of producing goods and services, the extent of the markets, the rapidity of adoption, as well as the cost of the R & D activity can all be estimated, at least to an order of magnitude. This type of assessment can be used as a basis for encouraging or discouraging particular types of activity. This chapter develops a methodology for determining which of the many R & D opportunities available offer the greatest potential returns to society.

In this chapter, the four stages of the proposed methodology will first be introduced and elaborated. Then, interdependencies among projects relevant to the selection of portfolios of projects will be discussed and methods of selecting portfolios illustrated. Finally, the mathematical basis for computerizing the methodology is developed and applied to the case of solar heat for residences.

DESCRIPTION OF THE PROPOSED EVALUATION METHOD

The purpose of the remainder of this chapter is to develop a method for the systematic comparison of energy storage R & D projects that are competing for federal funding. The objective of the government in deciding which R & D projects to fund should be to obtain the most return from public investment in energy-conserving technologies.

The complete R & D project evaluation and selection procedure should deal with:

1. The likelihood of commercial success, taking into account:
   a. The potential application of the product
   b. the size of the potential markets for the product
   c. the existence of competing products and elasticities of substitution between products
   d. the cost of manufacturing and marketing the product
   e. the return on the manufacturer's investment and to consumers
   f. the timing of the manufacturer's introduction, rates of penetration, and market saturation of the product
2. An analysis of the technical soundness of the project, including:
   a. the probability of technical success
   b. the probability of achieving product unit-cost/performance objectives
   c. project development costs and schedules
3. The need for and effects of the federal R & D support, considering:
   a. the existence of similar R & D projects in the private sector
   b. the reasons for the lack of sufficient private sector R & D
   c. the acceleration of commercial deployment due to federal expenditures
4. The potential energy resource savings to the nation, including:
   a. fuel oil and natural gas savings
   b. other resource (capital, labor, and material) savings

The methodology developed to integrate the consideration of these issues into a consistent measure of project worth is a nested cost-benefit analysis. Figure 6.1 illustrates the four stages of the methodology.

The first stage of the analysis determines the private cost savings produced by a single unit of the new innovation installed in a particular time period and location. The private cost savings are measured by the difference between the present values of the total cost of the old and new technologies. The second stage of the methodology uses the projected private cost savings per unit to estimate the rate and ultimate extent of market penetration as a function of the present value of the savings and other market factors. If it were possible to define homogeneous markets and to calculate the private cost savings for each, then market penetration would be a dichotomous decision. If the innovation would result in lower costs, it would be installed; if higher costs

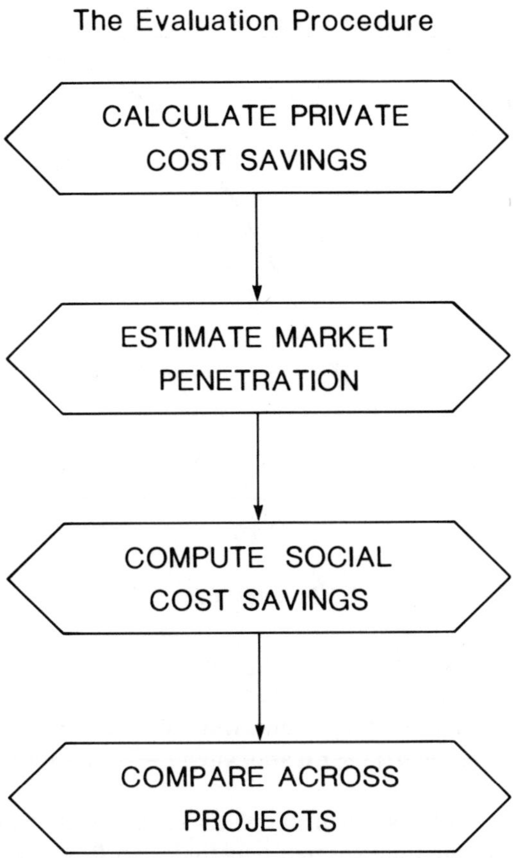

FIGURE 6.1. The Evaluation Procedure

would result, it would not be installed. Since all firms, or households, in the homogeneous market would be alike, either all or none would adopt. In practice, it is not possible to define completely homogeneous markets, and it is necessary to estimate the rate and ultimate extent of market penetration. Factors, in addition to average cost savings, which affect market penetration for the typical firm include the scale of the firm relative to the innovation, the vintage of the firm's capital equipment, the age and education of its management, and the expected growth of the industry.

Figure 6.2 illustrates one functional form used to estimate the rate and ultimate extent of market penetration, the logistic. The logistic may be expressed as

$$Y_t = \frac{a}{1+be^{-rt}}$$

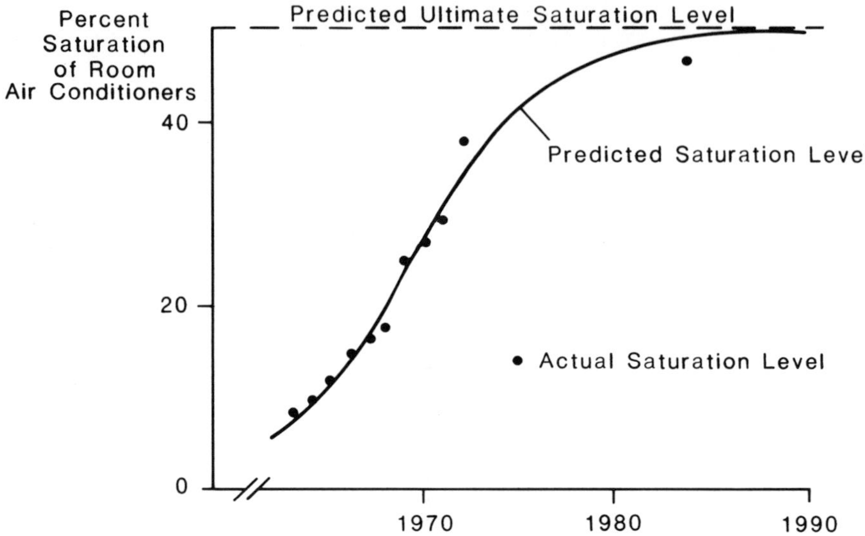

FIGURE 6.2

where a is the ceiling level as a percentage of the total, b is a constant related to the initial level, r is the rate of adoption, Y_t is the percentage of the total who have adopted by year t, and t represents time. When $t=0$, the percentage who have adopted is equal to $a/(1 \div b)$, and when $t=\infty$, the percentage who have adopted is equal to a.

The projection of market penetration is the most tenuous link in the process of determining the expected benefits of an R & D project, but some estimate must be made. The private sector makes these kinds of projections every day and must live with the outcomes. If the government is to carry out an effective R & D program directed toward the ultimate commercialization of innovations, it must also develop the capability of making reasonable projections of future markets.

The third stage of the methodology computes the present value of the social cost savings per unit by replacing the private prices, used in stage 1, with prices that have been adjusted to account for market failure and externalities. The expected present value of the social cost savings per unit for each time period is multiplied by the projected number of adopters in that period. This series is then discounted and summed to yield the total expected present value of the social cost savings generated by the new innovation.

This stage of the methodology is very important because, for a variety of reasons, the prices charged to individual consumers often do not reflect the true cost to society of various inputs. This may be due to regulatory distortions in the market or to the presence of externalities, i.e., costs that are not taken into account by consumers because they are not reflected in the price they must pay. Most often, these externalities are such things as pollution, which imposes costs on the people who are exposed to it even though they may not be receiving the benefit of the product associated with the pollution.

In the market for energy, the main causes of divergence between private and social prices are the regulation of natural gas prices, the existence of a social cost associated with U.S. dependence on imports of foreign oil that is not reflected in private prices, and the existence of environmental externalities such as pollution and risk of a major accident such as nuclear leakage.

The capital market in the United States is distorted by the corporate income tax, which increases the before-tax return to corporate capital and reduces it to capital in the remainder of the economy from the level that would prevail in the absence of the tax. Whereas the private rates of return on capital are used to estimate the expected present value of private cost savings, the social opportunity cost of capital is used to evaluate the expected present value of the social cost savings.

The fourth stage of the methodology compares the expected present value of the total social cost savings with the present value of the R & D expenditures required to realize the innovation. Ratios, such as that of the net benefit to the government R & D cost, can be used to compare the worth of various alternative projects.

This procedure, however, is correct only when there are no interactions among projects. Later in this chapter, selection procedures that should be used when there are interdependencies among projects will be discussed.

PORTFOLIO ANALYSIS

The evaluation process previously described treats a single R & D project and a single existing alternative. In reality, there are many R & D projects, each competing for several end uses. The correct unit of analysis is not the individual project, but rather the portfolio of projects controlled by the program manager. The interactions among projects during the R & D process and in the marketplace must be taken into account. A very simple example will illustrate the principles involved.

Suppose that two competing technologies exist. Should both be funded? Assume that (1) the two projects considered separately have benefits greater than costs, and (2) if one is successful, the other will have no benefits. For instance, the two projects could be alternative life support systems for space travelers or competing energy storage devices for use in 1990. The question is whether one project, or the other, or both should be funded.

Let the expected benefits from supporting each technology separately be given by

$$E_1 = VP_1 - C_1$$

$$E_2 = VP_2 - C_2$$

where V is the energy cost savings (same for both technologies), P is the likelihood of the technology coming on line in the target year, and C is the cost of developing the technology.

The expected benefits if both technologies are supported is given by

$$\begin{aligned} E_3 &= E_1 + E_2 \\ &= V(P_1 + P_2 - P_1P_2) - C_1 - C_2. \end{aligned}$$

(The term $P_1 + P_2 - P_1P_2$ results from the rule for summing two probabilities, which states that the probability of a sum is the sum of the probabilities minus the covariance.) E_3 is greater than E_1 if

$$V(P_1 + P_2 - P_1P_2) - C_1 - C_2 > VP_1 - C_1$$

$$VP_2 - VP_1P_2 - C_2 > 0$$

$$VP_2 - C_2 > VP_1P_2$$

$$\frac{E_2}{V} > P_1P_2. \qquad (1)$$

Similarly, E_3 is greater than E_2 if

$$V(P_1 + P_2) - C_1 - C_2 > VP_2 - C_2$$

or

$$\frac{E_1}{V} > P_1P_2. \qquad (2)$$

Thus, if E_1/V and E_2/V are greater than P_1P_2, the net benefits for proceeding concurrently exceed the benefits from proceeding on either project individually. A brief numerical example will illustrate the principle. Let $V =$ \$100 million, $C_1 =$ \$1 million, and $C_2 =$ \$5 million. Suppose the risk of not meeting the target year is the same for both technologies and is equal to 0.2. Then $P_1 = P_2 = 0.8$. For the first condition (Eq. 1), we have

$$\frac{E_2}{V} > P_1 P_2$$

$$\frac{100 \cdot 0.8 - 5}{100} > 0.8 \cdot 0.8$$

$$0.75 > 0.64.$$

For the second condition (Eq. 2), we obtain

$$\frac{E_1}{V} > P_1 P_2$$

$$0.79 > 0.64.$$

Thus, both conditions are fulfilled, and both technologies should be supported.

A detailed budget of the R & D project is required to facilitate the evaluation of separable components of the proposal. This will allow partial funding of projects where either budget constraints or overlapping projects indicate that full funding is not possible. The general rule for analyzing separable components of a project is that each component should be funded if, when evaluated at the appropriate discount rate, it generates positive expected net present values. Where differential funding levels of a component are possible, the incremental return from the last increase in funding should just equal the opportunity cost of those funds. Following these rules will maximize the net present value of the project.

The principles illustrated by this example may be generalized for more complex situations.

APPLICATION

In this section, the algebraic model of the methodology introduced earlier will be developed, a computer program that performs the evaluations will be described, and the results of a sample evaluation of solar heating for single-family residences will be presented.

The algebraic expressions for the private cost of the new and old technologies are shown in Figure 6.3. The term $B(t - t_1 + 1)$ is the discount factor, based on the private opportunity cost of capital. The term $\bar{p}$ is a collection of vectors, one for each time period and location couple (i, t), which contains the prices, for the specific time and location, of all inputs (capital, fuel, and labor). The $\bar{q}$s are collections of vectors that contain the input requirements for the old and new technologies, respectively. The $\bar{q}$ vectors are ordered to correspond to the $\bar{p}$ vector. $V_0(i, t_1)$ is the present value of the

PRIVATE COST WITH OLD TECHNOLOGY

$$V_0(i,t) = \sum_{t=t_1}^{t_1+T} B(t - t_1 + 1)\ \bar{p}(i,t)\ \bar{q}_0(i,t)$$

PRIVATE COST WITH NEW TECHNOLOGY

$$V_N(i,t) = \sum_{t-t_1}^{t_1+T} B(t - t_1 + 1)\ \bar{p}(i,t)\ \bar{q}_N(i,t)$$

NUMBER OF UNITS OF THE NEW TECHNOLOGY

$$M(i,t_1) = F[V_0(i,t_1) - V_N(i,t_1),\ \bar{R}(i,t_1)]$$

See text for meaning of symbols.

FIGURE 6.3

private costs associated with one unit of the old technology installed in location *i* and time period t_1. $V_N(i, t)$ is the present value of the private costs associated with one unit of the new technology installed in location *i* and time period t_1.

Market penetration $M(i, t_1)$ is a function of the present value of the private cost savings and other factors. The example described below uses a logistic function for *F*, and the other factor considered is the projected number of new housing starts in each location and time period.

Figure 6.4 presents the social costs of each technology and the formula for discounting and summing the social cost savings. The asterisk indicates that the prices and the discount factor reflect the social value of inputs and the social opportunity cost of capital. The total social benefits are obtained for 65 locations and for all years in the 40-year planning period. The 65 locations are the 65 largest standard metropolitan statistical areas (SMSAs). A computer program has been developed to perform these calculations for several types of technologies. The primary computer language used was PL/1 with provisions for using FORTRAN in some of the cost calculations if desired.

Figure 6.5 shows the elements of the system. The system resides on an IBM 370/168 in a Time Sharing Operations (TSO) environment. Control lists (CLISTS) are provided for the editor and the evaluator. A single data base contains all the price, market, and climate data for the SMSAs. A data base

SOCIAL COST WITH OLD TECHNOLOGY

$$V_0^*(i,t_1) = \sum_{t=t_1}^{t_1+T} B^*(t-t_1+1)\ \bar{p}^*(i,t)\ \bar{q}_0(i,t)$$

SOCIAL COST WITH NEW TECHNOLOGY

$$V_N^*(i,t_1) = \sum_{t=t_1}^{t_1+T} B^*(t-t_1+1)\ \bar{p}^*(i,t)\ \bar{q}_N(i,t)$$

SOCIAL BENEFITS OF NEW TECHNOLOGY (ONE REGION, ONE YEAR)

$$\omega(i,t_1) = M(i,t_1)\ V_0^*(i,t_1) - V_N^*(i,t_1)$$

See text for meaning of symbols.

FIGURE 6.4

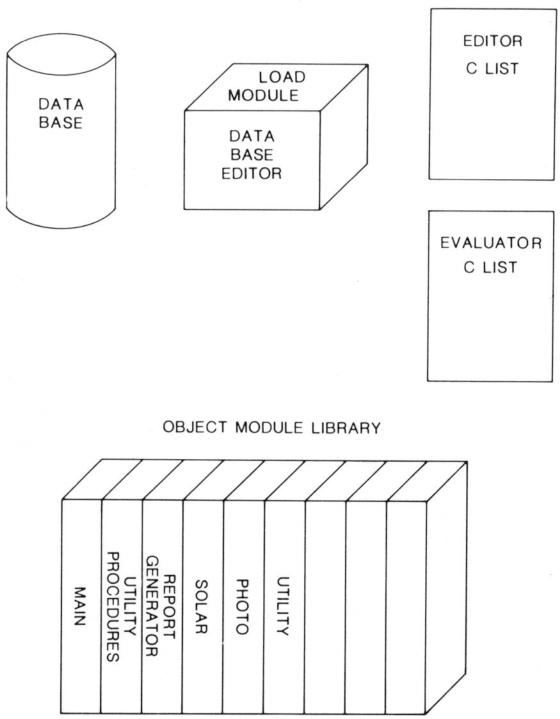

FIGURE 6.5

editor is provided for maintaining the data base and for producing reports of the information in it.

The evaluator is stored in a library of object modules. When the evaluator CLIST is executed, the user specifies which technology he or she wishes to evaluate, and TSO constructs the desired program and executes it. The program then prompts the user for a variety of information on costs. Once the calculations are completed, the user specifies the type of reports desired and the program produces them. Figures 6.6 to 6.8 outline these steps.

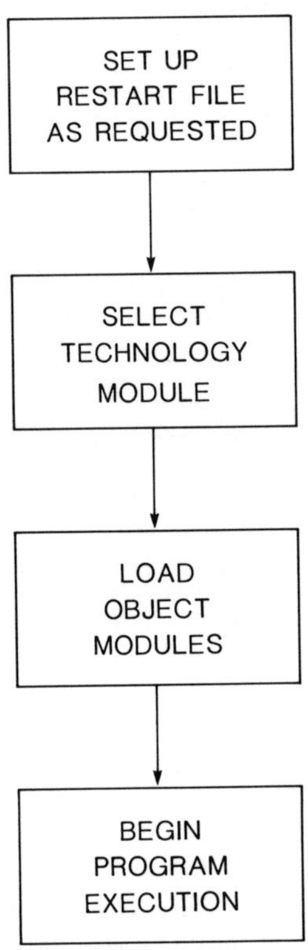

FIGURE 6.6. Preprocessor (TSO Command Language)

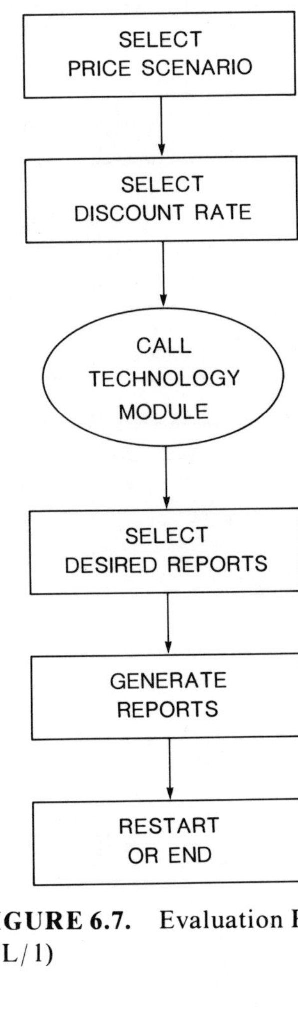

FIGURE 6.7. Evaluation Program (PL/1)

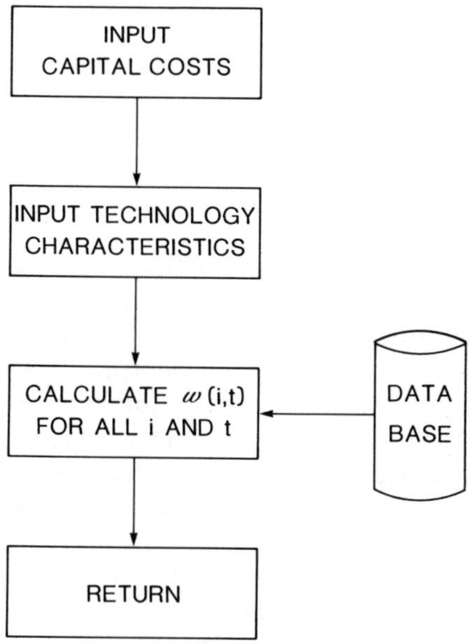

FIGURE 6.8. Technology Module (FORTRAN or PL/1)

The evaluation methodology described previously has been implemented for solar heat for single-family residences. It should be emphasized that this analysis is a prototype of a methodology for the evaluation of R & D projects and is not meant to be a thorough evaluation of the future of solar energy. The particular example chosen is the evaluation of a sample R & D program designed to reduce the energy storage costs of residential solar applications from $4 to $2 per square foot of collector between 1980 and 2000 and to $1 per square foot between 2005 and 2020 and to increase the lifetime from 10 to 20 years for all periods. The solar technology supplying energy is a water-cooled collector costing $8 per square foot between 1980 and 2000 and $4 per square foot between 2005 and 2020. The lifetime of the solar collector is 20 years. Solar energy supplies 50 percent of the heating requirements of the home and also supplies domestic hot water during the nonheating season.

The private price projections used were those implied by the National Energy Plan of 1977 as expressed in various Department of Energy reports. The social prices were derived from the private prices by correcting for taxes and subsidies and by adding pollution and foreign dependence costs where appropriate. The homeowner's real opportunity cost of capital was 1 percent, and the real social opportunity of capital was 8 percent. Table 6.1 shows the public benefits of the solar technology with and without the storage R & D activity for each time period. The present value of the total benefits of the storage R & D activity under these circumstances is $4.7 billion.

This value must be considered in the context of the uncertainty of actually achieving the postulated cost reductions and the potential erosion of the market by rival innovations.

CONCLUSION

The range surrounding these estimates must be stressed. The private and social cost savings from an improvement in technology depend on uncertain technical factors and future prices. These estimates are used to predict market penetration, which, again, has a random element. Social and private prices will tend to be correlated. Market penetration is largely a function of the private cost savings brought about by the improved technology. Errors in the estimation of private savings will thus lead to errors in both market penetration and social savings. It is important, as part of any use of the method, that a range of values be considered and the sensitivity of the results be determined.

In summary, the evaluation of federal R & D programs for the commercialization of new technologies requires a four-step analysis. The first and second steps, cost evaluation and market analysis, mimic the analysis that a private firm would perform prior to embarking on a new venture. The third step, the calculation of social cost savings, is unique to the government's point of view. Large firms such as conglomerates and the government must also consider the fourth step, portfolio analysis, in making programmatic decisions. The procedure proposed is no more accurate than the data available, but does

TABLE 6.1. Social Benefits to Residential Solar Applications With and Without An R & D Program in Energy Storage

Year	*Benefits with Storage R & D*	*Benefits without Storage R & D*	*Benefits to Storage R & D*
1980	1.2	0.2	1.0
1985	1.4	0.2	1.2
1990	0.8	0.1	0.7
1995	0.4	0.1	0.3
2000	0.8	0.2	0.6
2005	0.6	0.2	0.4
2010	0.4	0.1	0.3
2015	0.3	0.1	0.2
Total	5.9	1.2	4.7

Source: Tolley and Townsend (1979).

provide a logical method for incorporating diverse information into a consistent decision-making process.

REFERENCE

Tolley, George S. and Stuart B. Townsend, "Commercialization and the Assessment of Federal R & D," in *Federal R & D and Scientific Innovation*, American Chemical Society Symposium Series No. 105, May 1979, pp. 113–127.

7

Economic Analysis of a Technology at the Early Stages of Its Development*

Ronald G. Cummings and William Schulze

An interesting set of policy issues relevant for research and development (R & D) may be viewed as involving allocation decisions at two distinct (but interrelated) levels. At one level the concern is with the allocation of limited R & D funds between research programs for alternative technologies. For example, funds must be allocated between research programs for technology development for the fast breeder reactor, solar and geothermal energy technologies. At a second level, given an allocation to, for example, a solar program, resource allocations must be made between the specific research projects that constitute the technology development program. At issue here is that many projects may exist, each of which is focused on aspects of the technology about which more "should" be known. Allocations within the technology program presuppose some sense of priorities as to the more "relevant" lines of R & D research.

Lying at the heart of these allocation decisions between technologies and within a technology is the need of some measure for the expected success of

*The research into the economics of both hot dry geothermal and passive solar energy reported here has been supported principally by the Los Alamos Scientific Laboratory. The preparation of this chapter was supported by a grant from the Department of Energy (Contract No. DE-A504-79ET27017). The authors are indebted to a number of colleagues including Glen Morris, Jefferson Testor, Scott Noll, and Fred Roach, all of Los Alamos, Shaul Ben-David of the University of New Mexico, and James MacFarland of the University of Houston. Of course, all opinions and conclusions expressed herein are the sole responsibility of the authors.

the activity. The "between" decisions reflect the relative probabilities of success among alternative technologies, as well as the meaning (impact) of "success." The "within" decisions generally reflect the feeling that funded projects will result in the removal of uncertainties concerning technological questions that are in some sense relevant for the success of the technology. Particularly in the case of technology developments for energy, success as related to the between issue is taken to be the potential for the technology in question to meet the market test of economic feasibility—revenues will be at least as great as costs. Similarly, success for the within issues is many times taken to be the relevance of the technological question for the ultimate economic feasibility of the technology.

A major role for economic analyses at early stages of technology development may then be seen as that of providing estimates for the initial measure of success—economic feasibility. Such analyses take place within a fairly specific framework that relates to an "appropriate" economic and institutional context, e.g., management and operations practices, industry structure, and regulatory constructs. For obvious reasons, existing economic and institutional practices and arrangements are many times used as the context for evaluating the new technology; e.g., a hot dry rock (HDR) electric generating facility is viewed as being operated along the management rules used in coal-fired plants. As is demonstrated below, it is many times the case that the economic institutional frameworks appropriate for existing technologies are inappropriate for new technologies, and the delineation of such frameworks that are indeed appropriate for a technology at an early stage of development may have profound impacts on measures for success for both levels of policy issues described above.

To push this argument a bit further, there are (at least) five particularly critical issues relevant for an economic/institutional framework that would be common to feasibility studies for all energy technologies:

1. Engineering cost and technical parameters: the set of parameters required to provide an adequate technological setting for economic analyses;
2. System scale: size characteristics for the system being used as a basis for R & D efforts;
3. Management practices: management practices assumed for the hypothetical facility or activity under study;
4. Timing and location: assumptions regarding when the technology is to come "on line," and, when relevant, regions of the United States in which the technology may be usable;
5. Institutional considerations: sociocultural, organizational, and regulatory constraints assumed for the technology.

The purpose of this chapter, then, is to develop and exemplify the potential meaningful contributions of economic analyses at early stages of technology development within the context of these five issues. To allow sharper focus, primary attention is given to the ramifications of early economic analyses for the within decisions described above, although our discussions are related to between issues in the concluding remarks. Further, these discussions are centered on the issues as they relate to two specific technologies that are currently at a relatively early stage of technological development: HDR geothermal resources used for electricity generation and the passive use of solar energy for home heating.

To this end, a brief, heuristic description is given for the specific form of these five issues within the context of these technologies. Then, the divergence between conventional responses to these issues (based on the use of existing technologies) and results from the authors' research are highlighted, and attention is focused on the potential impacts of this research in terms of altering future research priorities of the within stripe.

TECHNICAL AND POLICY ISSUES

A brief, heuristic description of the HDR and passive solar technologies is given here to provide the reader with some feel for the technological context relevant for the discussion of policy issues that follow.

Technology and Policy Issues in Hot Dry Rock Geothermal Resources

HDR geothermal resources are synthetic systems wherein system characteristics, such as location and resource quality, are amenable to design and control (in contrast to liquid- or vapor-dominated geothermal resources). Given a geothermal temperature gradient[1] (hereafter referred to as simply "the gradient" and denoted ∇_T) for any given location, initial investments in a HDR resource are made by drilling wells vertically, usually into subterranean areas of hot, impermeable granite. If D (in kilometers) is drilling depth and T is the down-hole temperature of the hot granite (in degrees centigrade), T is determined simply by drilling depth as given by the following, where CT is the earth's crustal temperature:

$$T = CT + \nabla_T D$$

Having drilled the first well D kilometers, a fracture is created in the granite via massive hydrologic fracturing techniques. A second well is then

---

[1]The gradient is the average increase in the earth's temperature (in degrees centigrade) per kilometer of vertical depth for any selected point on the earth's surface.

drilled to intersect this fracture some distance above the bottom of the first well. This pair of wells and the fracture, referred to as the "HDR reservoir," make up a closed system through which water may be circulated at a pressure sufficiently high to prohibit vaporization. The flow of hot water may then be used either directly or via a secondary fluid for the generation of electricity.

The five technical/policy issues described above take the following form within the context of the technology for HDR-produced electricity.

(1) There has been considerable confusion as to the relative importance, in terms of research priorities, of a number of engineering cost and technological parameters. Among the more important of these are the character of drilling costs for drilling in granite at large depths, reservoir size and design well flow rates as they relate to resource exhaustion (temperature drawdown), and system lifetime.

(2) For any given installed capacity, a qualitative scale dimension of an HDR electric generating plant is its design temperature. Since plant costs decline with larger design temperatures, the "conventional wisdom" would suggest high design temperatures (250 to 300 degrees centigrade). This issue is clouded, however, by the fact that much deeper (and much more extensive) drilling is required to achieve rock temperatures at these levels.

(3) Engineering scientists assume that, as in the case of coal, gas, and nuclear plants, the system will be operated at design levels. Thus, initial drilling depths will be at levels required to satisfy plant design temperatures over the life of the plant; well flow rates will be maintained at design levels. Again, these issues are clouded by the fact that first, lower initial drilling depths (lower drilling costs) may be feasible if power output is allowed to occasionally dip below design levels and if future redrilling is allowed, and second, varying well flow rates through time can reduce rates of temperature draw down.

(4) Busbar costs for HDR-produced electricity are strongly dependent on geothermal gradients, which are region specific. Thus, speculation as to when HDR might come on line is inextricably related to the gradient characteristics of regions wherein demand prices are sufficiently high to cover costs.

(5) Ongoing analyses assume that, paralleling existing conditions, a fuel-supplying enterprise will develop HDR reservoirs and sell the steam to a separate entity—an electric power company.

Technical and Policy Issues in Passive Solar Home Heating

Passive solar home heating does not represent a new concept, as does HDR geothermal. Anazazi Indian cliff dwellings of the tenth century made good use of southern cave exposures to collect solar energy to mediate the temperature extremes of the Southwest. However, modern architecture—perhaps appropriately, given past availability of low-cost energy—has shown little concern for passive collection of available solar energy. Although a number of passive solar system designs have been developed, we will describe one of the simplest, the Trombe Wall. A Trombe wall system requires a south-facing "window" (aperture) to allow sunlight and heat to enter and a large thermal mass—a thick south-facing wall of masonry or concrete. An immediate gain in heat occurs because air is allowed to circulate between the wall and glass surfaces, bringing warm air into the room through natural convection. The large thermal mass of the wall is, however, essential in that solar energy available during the day is stored in the thermal mass and released during the evening hours when no direct gain is available from the sun itself.

Clearly, however, for the passive system to function, the air or room temperature in the home or structure must be allowed to fluctuate, for only as the temperature of the home drops below that of the thermal storage mass can energy be released in the evening hours. Thus, assuming a conventional backup heating system is used in the home, the lower the thermostat is set, the higher will be the percentage of total home heating supplied by the passive solar system. It is important to note that a qualitative difference exists between conventional home heating and passive solar heating, in that temperature fluctuations must be allowed (these can, however, be confined to the "comfortable" range). Although many detailed design features can improve performance (movable night insulation for windows, for example), the most important design variables are aperture, the area of south-facing window, thermal mass, and the availability of heat storage in the passive system.

The five technical/policy issues we address take the following form for analysis of passive solar home heating.

(1) A problem of special concern is determination of engineering costs, in that passive solar system costs are themselves part of the construction costs of a home. Whereas for active solar systems with "add-on" manufactured collectors, it is easy to calculate the cost per square foot of collector area, it has been claimed that passive system costs are "inseparable" from those of the home itself. A second necessary technical component for feasibility analysis is performance analysis. Most passive solar homes have not been designed in an engineering sense, but rather "ideas" of individual home builders have been embodied, with only a subjective evaluation of performance as opposed to measurement of, e.g., the fraction of the home-heating load provided by solar energy.

(2) Given knowledge of the performance and costs of passive solar systems as they relate to the two principal variables, aperture and thermal mass, the question of optimal scale arises; i.e., given the availability and costs of alternative sources of home heat, how much of a home's heating needs should optimally be met by passive solar energy? For economic efficiency, the discounted present value of the sum of backup system and solar system costs should be minimized over both aperture and thermal mass. Thus, in analyzing

feasibility and the quantity of energy provided by passive solar systems, the optimum system scale is a first question for economic analysis.

(3) A second interdependent question is the strategy for "managing" or operating the passive system. For example, as noted above, the effectiveness of such systems can be increased by movable night insulation, e.g., sheets of Styrofoam attached to collector windows in the evening. However, the added capital cost of provisions for automatically providing night insulation or the added inconvenience to owners of manual installation and removal may make such modifications of questionable value.

(4) The economic feasibility and scale of passive solar heating also have temporal and spatial dimensions. For example, with rising alternative energy prices, a large passive system might not be feasible now, but could become widely so in five or ten years. If so, R & D should almost certainly be stimulated now, given the long lags in diffusion of new technologies. Similarly, with rising prices, one would presume that larger systems (ones that provide a higher fraction of a home's heating requirements) would become feasible over time. Finally, because the quantity of available incoming solar energy (insolation) varies across the United States (highest in the Southwest, lowest in the Northwest) and because heating loads vary geographically as well, the pattern of regional feasibility is also important. Thus it may be the case that a particular region will show early feasibility and become a "testing ground" for passive solar technology.

(5) Two serious institutional constraints may well limit the acceptance and penetration of passive solar energy. First, at least for new construction, lending institutions may well not, at least initially, include passive solar costs in the appraised value of a new home and so may be unwilling to lend money for a passive solar heating system. This is likely, however, to be a temporary problem if passive solar systems prove to be truly desirable. The second institutional problem concerns the interaction of passive solar energy systems that use electricity as a backup system. Clearly, if cloudy weather persists over a period of several days, passive solar users may exacerbate any peak load problems an electric utility might have. If society has to provide the generating capacity to cover heating solar homes during periods of extended cloudy or cold weather, in any case, it is argued that solar energy may well not be economically justified since extra costs imposed on electric utilities to meet peak loads are ignored. Thus, some utilities have even now resisted serving solar homes.

IMPLICATIONS FOR POLICY ISSUES FROM CASE STUDIES OF EARLY ECONOMIC ANALYSES

Most R & D efforts for new energy technologies have been conducted and evaluated within a context that assumed that appropriate responses to the five policy issues of interest here would derive from appeal to ongoing practices used in the energy industry. In what follows, the implications of early economics research for these issues, as well as for the direction of future R & D research, are briefly described for HDR and passive solar energy.

Engineering Cost/Technical Parameters

In terms of HDR energy, early analyses demonstrate that economic feasibility is relatively unaffected by rather large variations in system lifetime, ceteris paribus. Changes in drilling costs are shown to result in much less than proportional changes in busbar costs. Variations in design well flow rates and, more importantly, reservoir size are dominant in terms of conditions required to generate electricity at potentially competitive busbar costs (in the 30- to 45-mills per kilowatt per hour range). In fact, feasibility of HDR-produced electricity is shown to turn on the proving of reservoir designs that result in relatively large surface areas. As such, priority for reservoir design projects is strongly indicated (in contrast to the current priority given to "resource assessment" projects).

For passive solar energy, a number of performance models have been developed. One of the models, that developed at Los Alamos Scientific Laboratory, is based on data collected by instrumenting and monitoring the actual performance of several passive solar structures at Ghost Ranch, New Mexico. This model served as the technical performance input for the economic analysis discussed herein. Perhaps more important, a study of the additional costs of including passive solar heating in a conventional home was funded by Los Alamos Scientific Laboratory, in part to allow economic analysis to go forward. A well-known team, consisting of a solar architect and a solar engineer, has demonstrated that passive solar costs are indeed separable by designing a passive and conventional home to the same specifications (1,500 square feet of living area, typical regional design) and costing out the two homes, attributing the differential cost as the cost of the passive feature. Thus, engineering costs and technical performance parameters for passive solar homes contain, at least in our opinion, little uncertainty at this point in time.

Scale Issues

In the case of HDR energy, early economic analyses demonstrate that drilling costs outweigh plant cost considerations as they relate to plant design temperatures. Rather than in the 250- to 300-degree centigrade per kilometer range, optimal design temperatures are shown to be in the 155- to 180-degree range in most reasonable gradient areas (less than 50 degrees centigrade per kilometer). More expensive power plants are optimal, given the savings in drilling costs associated with the lower temperatures (and therefore shallower drilling depths). Further research (as was planned) for experiments with deeper drilling and higher rock temperatures then become of questionable priority; of greater priority are projects concerned with plant designs using low-temperature organic fluid cycles.

Perhaps one of the most exciting results in analyzing optimal scale for passive solar applications is that in almost all cases, feasibility is obtained, at least for some applications, even at very small scales. As one looks across passive technologies to include increased south-facing and decreased north-facing areas of ordinary windows, one finds, at least for small changes, very good feasibility. Similarly, for the Trombe Wall, one does not find feasible scales above 40 to 50 percent of a home's needs met by solar energy even when the alternative (backup heat) is highly expensive (e.g., electric resistance heating). Broadly interpreted, our results imply that most new homes might well optimally contain some passive design elements because passive technologies are very feasible at small scales. Research priorities could then be aimed at stimulating the introduction of small-scale passive design elements into all homes as opposed to promoting purely passive solar homes as a technological oddity.

Management Issues

In the case of HDR energy, early economic research points to substantial savings in capital costs (more than 12 percent of system costs) that attend the adoption of variable management policies for drilling and well flow rates, i.e., allowing the system to occasionally operate at temperature and flow rates that are below design levels. Implications of these results suggest research priorities for projects concerned with redrilling techniques and reservoir adaptions to varying well flow rates.

Timing/Location Considerations

As mentioned above, geothermal temperature gradients play a major role in the determination of the timing at which HDR-produced electricity might come on line and, of course, the areas that it might serve. Results from a "reference case" analysis of the HDR resource wherein pessimistic characterizations of reservoir performance are used suggest the following busbar costs (in 1978 dollars) for HDR-produced electricity in areas with selected gradients:

Busbar Cost (mills/kwh)	*Geothermal Temperature Gradient (°C/km)*
80	20
55	30
42	40
25	50

Assuming an average price of electricity in the United States of 20 mills per kilowatt-hour in 1978, which increases at a real rate of 2 percent per year, the price of electricity would be sufficient to cover busbar costs of HDR-produced electricity for the above gradients in the following years:

Gradient Area (° C/km)	*Years (from 1978) at Which HDR-Produced Electricity Comes On Line*
20	100+ years
30	51
40	36
50	11

Thus, all else equal, HDR-produced electricity would be feasible by 1989 in areas characterized by hot spots, and by 2014–50 in much of the western one-third of the United States. Of course, if future research demonstrates that HDR reservoirs can be designed with larger surface areas (lower rates of temperature drawdown), these time horizons could shift forward markedly.

For passive solar heating, feasibility is highly dependent on the alternative fuel chosen for analysis. Passive solar heating is feasible now everywhere in the United States except Washington State because of cloudy weather and the availability of cheap hydroelectric power. Lack of heating demand and cheap natural gas prices in the South and cloudy weather in the Midwest make passive solar heating relatively undesirable—delaying feasibility indefinitely in these areas. This pattern of spatial and temporal feasibility might provide a number of insights for R & D policy. For example, areas of early potential feasibility might become testing grounds for technology development. In fact, passive solar technologies are developing rapidly in the Southwest and Far West. However, little progress has been made in developing passive solar technology to suit the Northeast where good economic potential appears to exist. Finally, in comparing passive with active solar home heating, the former appears to have, with few exceptions, the edge.

Institutional Considerations

Early research concerning HDR energy points to the interdependence between plant design for the electric power plant and system design for the HDR reservoirs. This raises questions as to the possibility that this new technology might require new institutional forms—an integrated fuel supply/power producer system may be superior to the existing separation between these two entities. Further, HDR facilities will likely be small, on the order of 50 to 250 megawatts(e), in comparison with the 1,000 to 3,000-megawatt(e) scale of coal-fired plants under consideration. HDR facilities, which can be as small as three to ten megawatts(e), do not, then, fit nicely into the conventional "grid" system within which power expansion plans are currently considered. Rather, HDR facilities might be local, municipal facilities. This possibility is particularly compelling given that HDR systems are (relatively) environmentally benign. Research priorities are then suggested that relate to the institutional ramifications of introducing a power source that alters the basic structure of electricity delivery systems from the current centralized grid structure to a decentralized local structure.

The feasibility analysis for passive solar homes presented above suggests that the southwestern United States will show early feasibility. In fact, a relatively large number of passive solar homes have been constructed in the region, and experience there to date suggests that as familiarity is gained with these homes, lending institutions rapidly become willing to extend mortgage money for passive solar construction. Indeed, the greater reliability of passive as opposed to active solar homes has led lending institutions to favor the former.

In contrast, electric utilities have shown mixed support in the region for passive solar designs. Public Service Company of New Mexico has supported solar energy R & D, with special concern for the solar/electric utility interface, including the peak load problem. One view of passive solar heating under exploration is quite optimistic—that storage in the form of thermal mass in the home can be used to offset peak loads. This could be accomplished, for example, by burying electric resistance heating elements in the thermal mass and heating the storage during off-peak hours. Thus, solar homes even during periods of extended cloudiness might draw electricity only during off-peak hours, reducing rather than exacerbating the peaking problem. In contrast, utilities in Colorado have actively discouraged hookups of solar homes, perhaps out of genuine concern, since only experimental solar homes to this date have employed off-peak electric power purchases.

A final institutional aspect of passive solar energy is the extent to which traditional architectural forms in the Southwest, especially in New Mexico, lend themselves to its adoption. The adobe style of architecture with massive walls provides natural thermal mass for passive system use and, in fact, represents one of the few architectural styles to exploit available solar energy. Perhaps this explains the relative lag in experimentation in the eastern United States.

CONCLUSIONS

Given the type of detailed economic/institutional analysis for new energy technologies we have described above, it is then, and we stress only then, appropriate to make comparisons between technologies. Thus, a valid comparison of, for example, passive solar home heating or HDR geothermal energy to fast breeder reactors based on analyses of relative economic feasibility requires specification of uncertainties in engineering costs and technical parameters, economically optimal scales of operation, management strategies, timing and location decisions, as well as institutional constraints. This information may then allow an educated guess as to which energy technology shows the greatest promise and deserves a larger slice of the energy R & D budget.

Of course, energy R & D policy involves more than direct subsidization of R & D to universities, research laboratories, and firms. An alternative to a "push" strategy of directly funding R & D, implicit to the above, is a "pull" strategy. A pull strategy involves incentives for R & D by subsidizing demand for a particular type of energy. HDR geothermal and passive solar energy provide a clear contrast in appropriate approaches for stimulating R & D. R & D in HDR geothermal energy has been exclusively supported by the federal government, based on concepts developed at Los Alamos Scientific Laboratory. In contrast, passive solar home heating has been principally developed by individual inventors and entrepreneurs, often on a trial-and-error basis. Clearly, no private firm or individual could supply the extensive resources necessary to try the HDR concept, and a policy of pushing R & D is appropriate. In contrast, we would argue that R & D in passive solar energy could best be furthered by stimulating consumer demand for passive solar homes. Ironically, in spite of strong evidence that passive solar home heating shows greater promise than active solar heating, federal solar incentives may well exclude all or at least some passive systems.

8

A Methodology to Incorporate Uncertainty into R & D Cost and Performance Data*

Stephen Barrager and Oliver Gildersleeve

This chapter discusses the use of quantitative analytical tools that integrate information from diverse sources and present it in a form useful to decision makers. A recent methodology demonstration at the Electric Power Research Institute (EPRI) combined these tools: modeling, sensitivity analysis, and subjective probability encoding. In this study, which compared the future costs of two pairs of closely competing technologies, models captured cost and performance relationships, while sensitivity analysis determined crucial uncertainties or issues. Uncertainty was included in the comparison by encoding subjective probability distributions for selected parameters. The final cost comparison was then expressed as a probability distribution on the cost difference. This chapter describes the approach and the results of two case studies and provides a critique of the methodology based on the results of both.

Decision makers, at the EPRI and elsewhere, are often faced with the difficult task of choosing among several directions for future work. For example, the high cost of supplying short-duration peak power demands may be reduced as a result of improving the reliability of combustion turbines (so fewer machines are necessary) or by developing a device to store electricity generated off peak by otherwise idle coal or nuclear capacity. Such choices

---

*The authors thank the persons who participated in this project, particularly William E. Balson of Decision Focus Inc. and Stan Vejtasa of the Electric Power Research Institute. We also thank the editor, Margaret Laliberte.

among technology paths usually are based heavily on anticipated costs, performance, and the resulting market competitiveness.

Uncertainty may be the element that most confuses R & D decisions. Regardless of the consistency and thoroughness of an analysis, the ultimate cost and performance estimates are uncertain, particularly for an as yet undeveloped new technology. Future materials and labor costs, inflation, the future regulatory environment, and such world developments as the price of oil are all uncertain, and all can impact the cost difference among technologies.

Within research organizations, a growing need also exists to document important decisions and to demonstrate clearly the influence of the factors considered in the decision. Shifts in research emphasis must be explainable, particularly where there are significant impacts inside and outside the organization. In some cases, the person most qualified to assess a technology's ultimate costs and performance may also have a vested interest in its continued funding. Potentially, this places the planner in the awkward position of either accepting at face value information provided by advocates or attempting to substitute personal judgment in areas outside personal expertise. To avoid this situation, the R & D planner needs a reproducible procedure that allows for open review of all information used in an analysis and gives experts confidence that their judgment and the judgment of others will be represented fairly. Planners also need a procedure that allows experts to state their degree of uncertainty at any point rather than to respond as though they were clairvoyant or to reserve judgment until all uncertainty is resolved. Decisions must be made in spite of the uncertainty.

Over the last decade, corporate planners have successfully applied decision analysis techniques to integrate diverse interests, maintain an emphasis on crucial issues surrounding a decision involving many people, and communicate the basis for difficult choices (Howard, 1966, 1968; North, 1968; Brown et al., 1974). Decision analysis is the result of combining the fields of systems analysis and statistical decision theory, a science concerned with logical decisions in simple uncertain situations. The merger of these concepts gives a methodology for making decisions in complex, dynamic, and uncertain situations.

The EPRI was aware of decision analysis concepts and sought to apply them in the inherently uncertain R & D environment. The project described here was a first step to introduce EPRI technical program managers to the expression of data uncertainties and to some of the other tools associated with the professional practice of decision analysis.

In this project, decision analysis tools were used to compare two pairs of technologies, selected to encompass both baseload and peaking power supplies. For baseload duty, the projected costs of a gasification-combined cycle plant were compared with those of a conventional subcritical steam plant with a limestone scrubber. For peaking duty, the alternatives compared were advanced load-leveling storage batteries and advanced-design combustion turbines fueled with oil.

This chapter describes the study's methodology and briefly discusses one case study to illustrate the practical aspects of that methodology. It concludes with a critique of the process and its future applications.

METHODOLOGY

The methodology described here proceeds in two sequential phases: a deterministic phase and a probabilistic phase. In the deterministic phase, the variables affecting the decision are defined, cost and performance relationships modeled, values assigned, and the importance of the variables measured, all without consideration of uncertainty. During this phase, questions such as, Which issue has a greater impact on the cost difference between technologies, plant life or fuel cost? are answered. The second probabilistic phase begins with the encoding of probabilities on a small number of selected variables. This encoding process is a way to quantify the uncertainty associated with each key variable. This phase answers such questions as, What is the probability that construction costs will exceed $800 per kilowatt? The final step in the probabilistic phase is to use models and probability distributions to calculate the probability distributions on total cost or savings.

The EPRI case studies followed the multistep procedure illustrated in Figure 8.1. Briefly, the steps are the following:

1. Setting ground rules and cost premises. The purpose of this step is to clarify both the scope of the analysis and the basis for comparison. This is done by specifying a hypothetical decision maker and explicitly stating all assumptions regarding environmental regulations, timing, technical performance requirements, financing, and R & D efforts.
2. Compiling variables and ranges. All the variables that might affect the comparison are listed for each alternative, and nominal, high, and low values are specified for each. The high and low values are intended to span a wide enough range that participants are 80 percent confident that the ultimate value is bracketed by them.
3. Specifying a cost model. This quantitative model expresses annual cost (dollars per kilowatt per year) as a function of all variables that are important to the comparison. In this case, the model is a straightforward algebraic equation relating annual cost to such factors as capital cost, heat rate (efficiency), interest rate, and fuel cost.
4. Analyzing sensitivities. Cost and performance parameters are varied separately over their ranges, from "low" to "high," to measure their impact on the annual

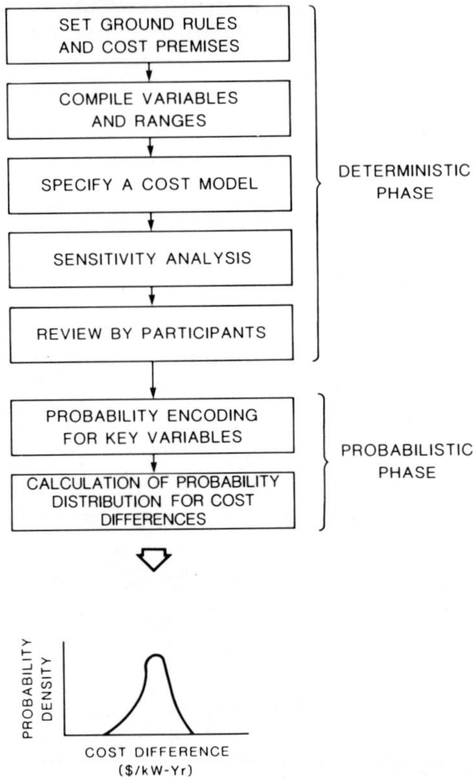

FIGURE 8.1. Outline of Procedure

cost difference between two technologies.[1] Variables are then ranked according to their impact on the cost difference.

5. Reviewing by participants. Upon completion of the sensitivity analysis, project participants review data, models, and initial results. The purpose of the review is to verify the results and select the variables to be treated probabilistically. Usually between three and six variables are selected, based on the sensitivity analysis and the degree of concern for particular issues. Variables not treated probabilistically are assigned their nominal values for the remainder of the analysis.
6. Probability encoding. Experts are selected and subjective probability distributions are encoded by a formal interview process. The techniques involved are

[1]Combinations of parameters should be varied if important probabilistic dependencies exist among them. For this study, it was assumed that important variables were independent within the ranges considered.

designed to reduce frequently occurring estimation biases (von Holstein, 1970; Hampton et al., 1973; Winkler and Murphy, 1973; Tversky and Kahneman, 1974; Spetzler and von Holstein, 1975).

7. Calculating the probability distribution for total annual cost. The encoded probability distributions on single variables are combined with the cost model to calculate a total cost distribution. This is a straightforward mathematical process, but care must be taken to account for any probabilistic dependencies that might be present. For example, capital costs and heat rates are dependent on the design of a generating plant: As heat rates go down, capital costs go up and vice versa.

The end result of this process is a probability distribution describing the uncertainty associated with the cost difference between technologies. This distribution can be displayed as a cumulative probability (Figure 8.2a) or as a probability density function (Figure 8.2b). The advantage of the cumulative distribution is that probabilities can be read directly on the vertical axis.

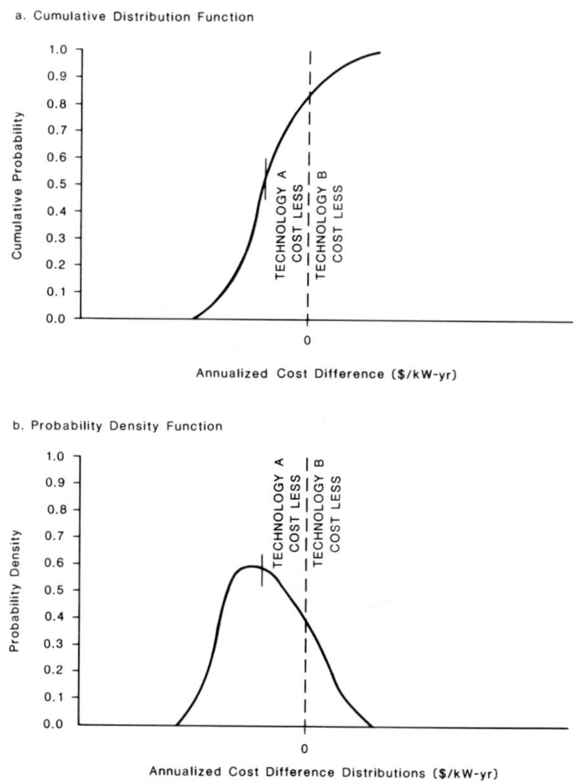

FIGURE 8.2. Probability Distribution for Cost Difference

CASE STUDY: COMPARISON OF TWO FOSSIL FUEL BASELOAD GENERATION TECHNOLOGIES[2]

Although the purpose of this project was to provide insight to R & D planners, the alternative technologies were compared from the point of view of a hypothetical utility executive faced with a new capacity expansion decision. The value of any R & D program ultimately depends on how extensively the resulting technology is implemented. In the EPRI's case, the implementation of new-generation technology depends on how decisions are made by utilities.

The study modeled the specific decision about which of the two baseload technologies should be selected for installation in 1995. An integrated gasification-combined cycle plant and a conventional coal plant with flu gas desulfurization (FGD) were compared. The assumed objective is to minimize the levelized annual cost of power from an incremental 1,000-megawatt generation station.

The results, shown in Figure 8.3, are intended to illustrate the application of the methodology and should not be interpreted as final or definitive in any way. They represent the opinions of only a small number of persons within the EPRI. Widespread acceptance of these results would require review by other experts inside and outside of the Institute. The following describe the process and intermediate steps that led to the results.

Deterministic Phase

Ground Rules

The ground rules are an explicit statement of the factors that are treated as fixed throughout the analysis. The relative cost advantage of two technologies depends on many factors, including the time when the comparison is made, R & D expenditures and results, inflation, plant size, site characteristics, fuel prices and availability, and environmental regulations. The number of factors was limited in this project because the purpose was to demonstrate a methodology rather than to perform a comprehensive market analysis. The ground rules for this case study are summarized in Table 8.1. In addition to ground rules, the design configuration of each power plant was specified before collecting cost and performance data.

Variables and Ranges

The nominal cost-performance data for each technology, along with parameter ranges, are summarized in Table 8.2. These estimates were supplied

---

[2]The material in this section was excerpted from the EPRI report, *Uncertainty Methods in Comparing Power Plants* (Balson and Barrager, 1979).

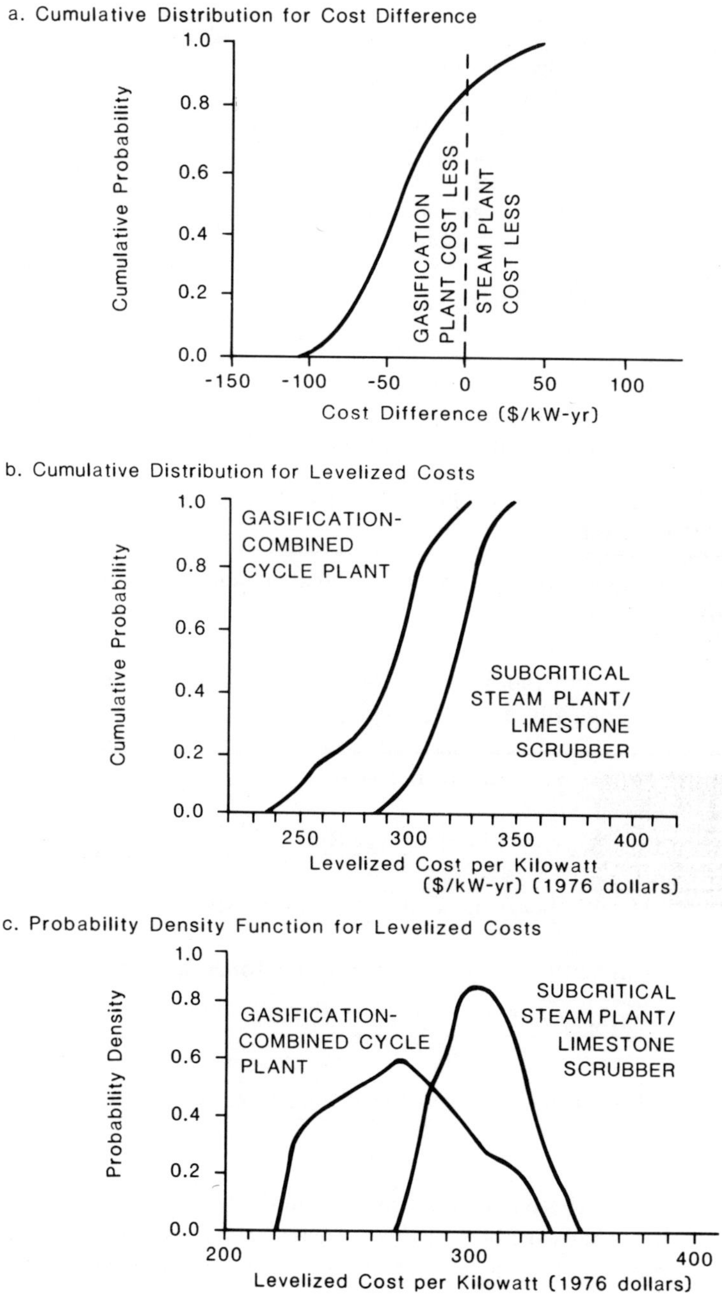

FIGURE 8.3. Case Study Number 1 Results

TABLE 8.1. Ground Rules

- Decision maker is utility executive.
- Plant construction will start in 1995.
- Orderly development and commercialization is consistent with current DOE, EPRI, and industry plans.
- 1995 costs are in 1976 dollars.
- One thousand-megawatt single-unit plants are assumed.
- Location is midwestern United States.
- Fuel is "eastern" coal.
  - 10,000 Btu/lb (2,222 Btu/kg)
  - 16% ash
  - 4% sulfur
- Capacity factor is 70%.
- Wet cooling towers are assumed.
- 1976 new source performance standards apply:
  - 1.2 lb/10^6 Btu (0.5 kg/10^6 Btu) SO_4
  - 0.1 lb/10^6 Btu (0.05 kg/10^6 Btu) particulates
  - No standard for NO_2

DOE, Department of Energy; EPRI, Electric Power Research Institute.
Source: Balson and Barrager (1979).

by program managers and reviewed for consistency by program managers as well as a technologically qualified third party.

A single equation model was used to calculate the cost of each technology, measured in dollars per kilowatt per year:

$$\text{Cost (\$/kW-yr)} = \text{Fixed Charge Rate} \times \frac{\text{Capital Costs (\$/kW)}}{\text{Capability Ratio}}$$

$$+ \text{ Fixed Operating \& Maintenance Costs}$$

$$+ \text{ Capacity Factor} \times \text{Levelizing Factor} \times 8{,}760 \text{ Hours}$$

$$\times \frac{\text{Variable O \& M Cost (mills/kWhr)}}{10^3}$$

$$+ \frac{\text{Heat Rate (Btu/kW-hr)} \times \text{Fuel Cost (\$/}10^6\text{ Btu)}}{10^6}.$$

In addition to this equation, some rudimentary calculations were used to determine that other variables, such as construction lead time, ramp rate, and water requirements, have a very small impact on the relative cost of the two technologies.

The most significant items left out of this analysis are the so-called intangible factors, such as the effects of changing environmental regulations.

TABLE 8.2. Cost and Performance Estimates and Ranges

	1976 Design Coal/Steam (Subcritical) Limestone Scrubber			Coal—Advanced Gasification-Combined Cycle		
	Low[a]	*Nominal*	*High*[b]	*Low*	*Nominal*	*High*
Capital Costs						
Process Plant Investment ($/kW)	401	424	445	439	488	610
General Facilities ($/kW)	80	85	89	42	47	58
Project Contingencies[c] ($/kW)	77	81	85	48	80	133
Process Contingency[d] ($/kW)	0	0	0	13	22	37
AFUDC ($/kW)	80	98	131	55	78	178
Total ($/kW)	638	688	750	597	715	1,016
Heat Rate (Btu/kW-hr at 100% C.F.)						
Eastern Coal	9,500	9,900	10,300	8,000	8,550	9,500
Operation						
Forced Outage Rate[e]	0.116(0.819)	0.155(0.764)	0.223(0.747)	0.087(0.859)	0.125(0.802)	0.142(0.779)
Planned Outage Rate	0.08	0.1	0.12	0.06	0.1	0.12
Minimum Load (%)	20	30	40	20	30	40
Ramp Rate (%/min.)	0.2	1	2	2	6	10
Operation and Maintenance Costs						
Fixed ($/kW-yr)	9.8	10.3	10.9	16	22.1	25
Variable (mills/kW-hr)	1.7	2.5	3.0	0.3	0.5	0.8
Planning						
Construction Period (yr)	3.5	4	5.5	2.5	3	5
Startup (yr)	0.05	0.1	0.2	0.1	0.3	0.5
Water Requirements (gal/kW-hr)	0.5	0.7	0.9	0.1	0.48	0.6

[a]"Low" is selected such that there is about a 10% chance that the actual value will be lower.

[b]"High" is selected such that there is about a 10% chance that the actual value will be lower.

[c]Usually expressed as a percentage of $^{a+b}$.

[d]Usually expressed as a percentage of ^{a}.

[e]Capability ratio in parentheses.

Source: Balson and Barrager (1979).

TABLE 8.3. Values of Variables Common to Both Technologies

	Value		
Variables	*High*	*Nominal*	*Low*
Cost of Coal ($/$10^6$ Btu)	1.10	1.00	0.90
Fuel-Levelizing Factor	2.5	1.932	1.5
Fixed Charge Rate	—	0.18	—

Source: Balson and Barrager (1979).

These aspects could not be successfully incorporated in a quantitative manner within the scope of this study.

Sensitivity Analysis

Using the cost equation, each variable was ranged from its high to its low value while each of the other variables was held at its nominal value. The values of the variables used for high, nominal, and low are given in Table 8.2. Table 8.3 gives the values of variables common to both technologies.

Table 8.4 shows the results of the sensitivity analysis. It indicates the change in cost differences between the integrated gasification-combined cycle and the conventional coal plant as each variable is moved from its high to its low value. For example, for the nominal case, the annual cost of the gasification plant was about $36 per kilowatt per year less than that of the subcritical coal plant. When the capital cost for the integrated gasification-combined cycle plant is ranged from $597 to $1,016 per kilowatt per year while keeping all other variables at their nominal values, the annual cost difference goes from $56 to –$38 per kilowatt per year, a change of $94 per kilowatt per year. The variables are ordered according to their impact on the cost difference.

The sensitivity analysis was conducted one variable at a time. This procedure is valid only if it can be assumed that all variables are independent (probabilistically). If strong dependencies exist, they can be dealt with by doing joint sensitivities; that is, variables are changed simultaneously to measure their combined effect on the cost difference.

Review Procedure

Upon completion of the sensitivity analysis, results were reviewed by all project participants. The sensitivity analysis indicates that most of the possible variations in cost difference could be explained by uncertainty in the handful of variables at the top of Table 8.4, namely, the capital costs of each technology, the forced outage rate of the conventional plant, and the heat rate of the integrated gasification-combined cycle plant. Fixed Operating & Maintenance costs and forced outage rate on the combined cycle plant are also high on the list.

TABLE 8.4. Sensitivity Analysis Results for Difference in Cost Between Case Study 1 Technologies

	Parameter Range		*Change in Cost Difference Between Technologies ($/kW-yr)*
	Low	*High*	
Capital Cost ($/kW)			
Gasification (C.C.)	597	1016	94.0
Forced Outage Rate (%)			
Pulverized Coal	11.6	22.3	31.9
Capital Cost ($/kW)			
Pulverized Coal	638	751	26.6
Heat Rate (Btu/kW-hr)			
Gasification-C.C.	8,000	9,500	17.8
Fixed O & M Cost ($/kW-yr)			
Gasification-C.C.	16	25	17.4
Forced Outage Rate (%)			
Gasification-C.C.	8.7	14.2	15.4
Variable O & M Cost (mills/kW-hr)			
Pulverized Coal	1.7	3	15.4
Planned Outage Rate (%)			
Gasification-C.C.	6	12	12.6
Pulverized Coal	8	12	12.6
Heat Rate (Btu/kW-hr)			
Pulverized Coal	9,500	10,300	9.5
Levelizing Factor	1.5	2.5	7.1
Variable O & M Cost (mills/kW-hr)			
Gasification-C.C.	0.2	0.7	5.9
Fuel Cost Eastern Coal ($/$10^6$ Btu)			
16% Ash Content	0.90	1.10	2.60
Fixed O & M Cost ($/kW-yr)			
Pulverized Coal	9.8	10.9	2.1

C.C., Combined Cycle.

Source: Balson and Barranger (1979).

Based on these results and the desire to treat both technologies at a comparable level of detail, it was initially decided that capital costs, forced outage rate, and heat rates for both technologies would be treated probabilistically. Subsequently, it was decided to ignore the heat rate uncertainty for the conventional plant because of its small impact on the overall comparison.

Probabilistic Phase

Probability Encoding for Key Variables

Experts within the EPRI were selected to provide probability assessments for each key variable. A formal interview was used to encode the probability distributions. The encoding procedure has been developed over a period of about ten years, principally by the SRI International Decision Analysis Group of California (von Holstein, 1970; Spetzler and von Holstein, 1975). The procedure involves a careful definition and structuring of the uncertain variable, followed by a series of paired comparisons used to elicit probabilities; for example, "Would you rather bet that capital costs will be above $600 per kilowatt or below that rate?" The interviewer is trained to identify and counteract modes of judgment that might bias the responses.

Often the consistent definition of terms and structuring of the variables are as important as eliciting the probability distribution itself. Terms must be clearly and unambiguously specified, and the experts should be asked to do few, if any, mental gymnastics in expressing their beliefs. The defining and structuring of capital costs, heat rate, and forced outage rates to avoid confusion and simplify judgments are described below.

Capital Cost. Although a utility must be concerned with all phases of a plant installation, a comparison for R & D evaluation is needlessly complicated by inclusion of construction factors, such as weather, management skill, intervention, escalation, labor strikes, and such site peculiarities as unexpected geological conditions. A hypothetical device, the "1995 construction bid," was invented as a means of separating the design- and development-related uncertainties from the construction-related ones. The relationship between the two and the important cost influences are diagrammed in Figure 8.4. The 1995 construction bid was defined as the bid that would be submitted to, and selected by, a utility in 1995. The bid would apply to a given set of design and performance specifications. It was conditioned on a turnkey contract that included clauses to protect the contractor from any costs incurred owing to intervention, escalation, labor strikes, or site peculiarities. These clauses have the effect of eliminating these uncertainties from the bid variable. To bound the problem further, environmental regulations and site were specified. Persons interviewed were then able to express their subjective knowledge about the

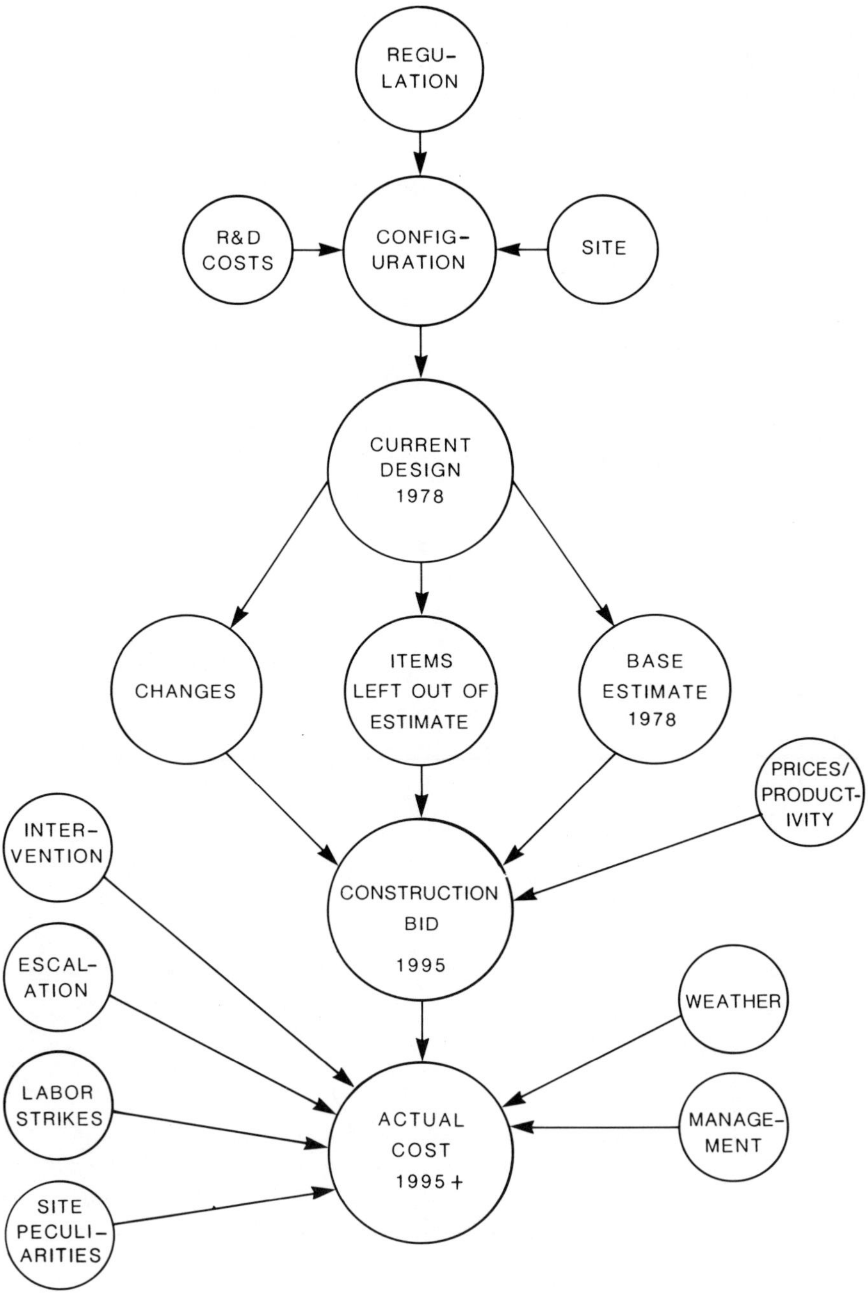

FIGURE 8.4. Influence Diagram for Capital Costs

accuracy of current cost estimates and their uncertainty about the result of future R & D efforts. (The level of R & D efforts was specified loosely in the ground rules.)

Figures 8.5 and 8.6 are the probability distributions for the capital cost of each technology encoded from the interviews with the experts. Also shown are the discrete approximations actually used in the subsequent computations.

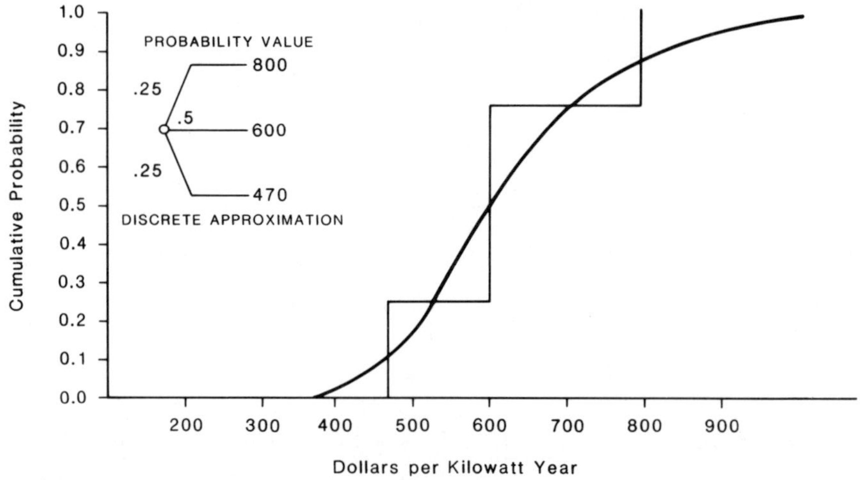

FIGURE 8.5. Cumulative Probability Distribution on the Capital Cost of a Gasification-Combined Cycle Plant

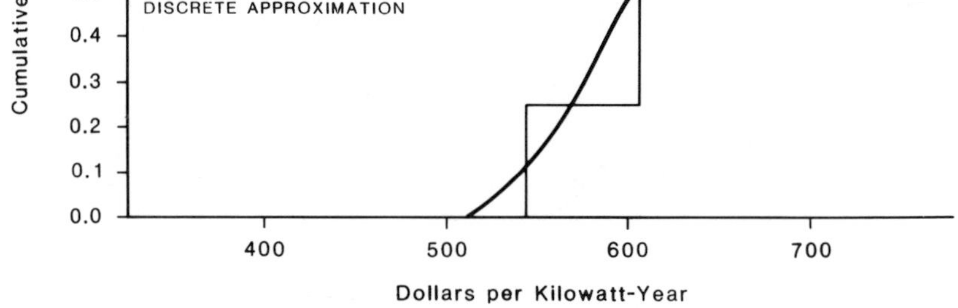

FIGURE 8.6. Cumulative Probability Distribution on the Capital Cost of a Conventional Coal Plant with Flu Gas Desulfurization

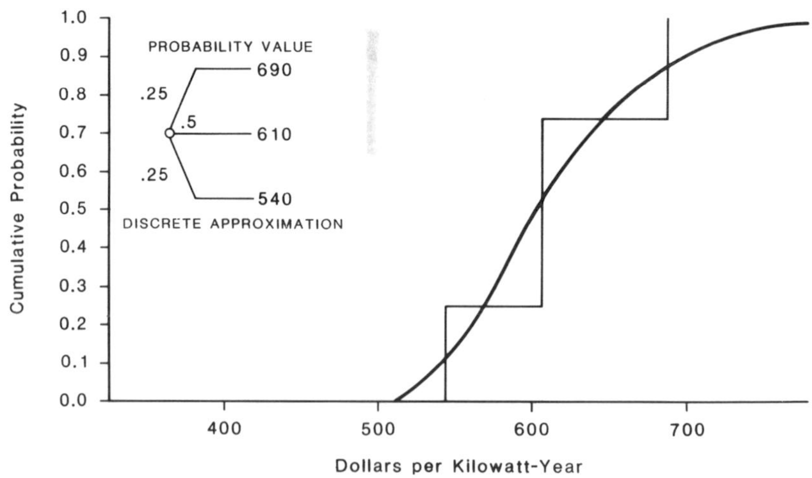

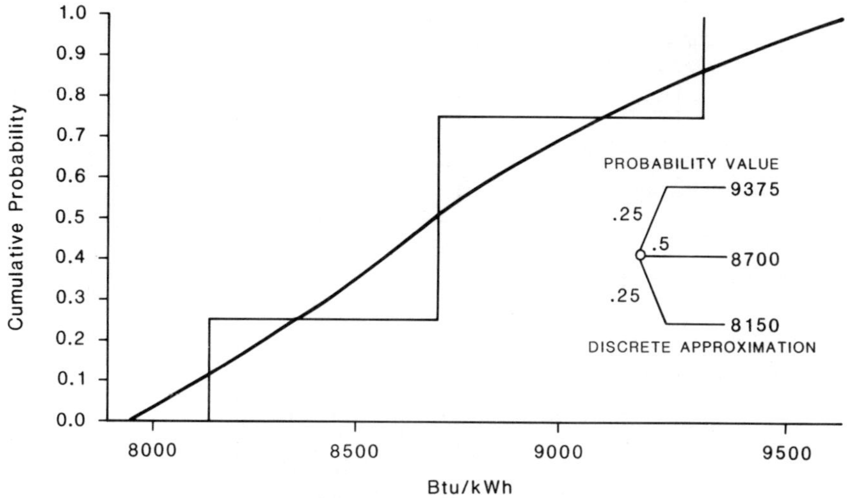

FIGURE 8.7. Cumulative Probability Distribution for the Design Heat Rate for a Gasification-Combined Cycle Plant (Nominal Design Configuration)

Heat Rate. Heat rates and capital costs are not independent. Within limits, it is usually possible to lower heat rates by spending more money on engineering and equipment. An attempt was made to decouple the costs and heat rates by fixing the design configuration (see Table 8.1) and encoding the capital costs required to meet the nominal heat rate. Likewise, when heat rates were encoded, the capital cost was fixed at its nominal value. Decision Focus Inc. of California believes this approach is valid as long as the combination of cost and heat rate is nearly optimal.

The single heat rate distribution is shown in Figure 8.7.

Forced Outage Rates. The probability distribution on forced outage rate was derived from the forced outage rates of major pieces of equipment in the plant. A sensitivity analysis was used to identify the most important equipment uncertainties, which were then encoded and combined mathematically to estimate uncertainty in the additional customer's load that each unit would meet at a fixed utility system reliability (loss of load probability). The additional customer's load divided by the unit's net capability is called the "capability ratio." It accounts for partial as well as forced outages (Garver, 1966; Gildersleeve, 1978; Poole, 1978).

In the case of the integrated gasification-combined cycle plant, the uncertainty in gasifier and combustion turbine outage rates has a greater impact on the overall capability ratio than do the heat exchangers or the steam turbine. A schematic diagram for major equipment pieces is shown in Figure 8.8a. Note that the 0.15 forced outage rate applies independently to each gasifier,

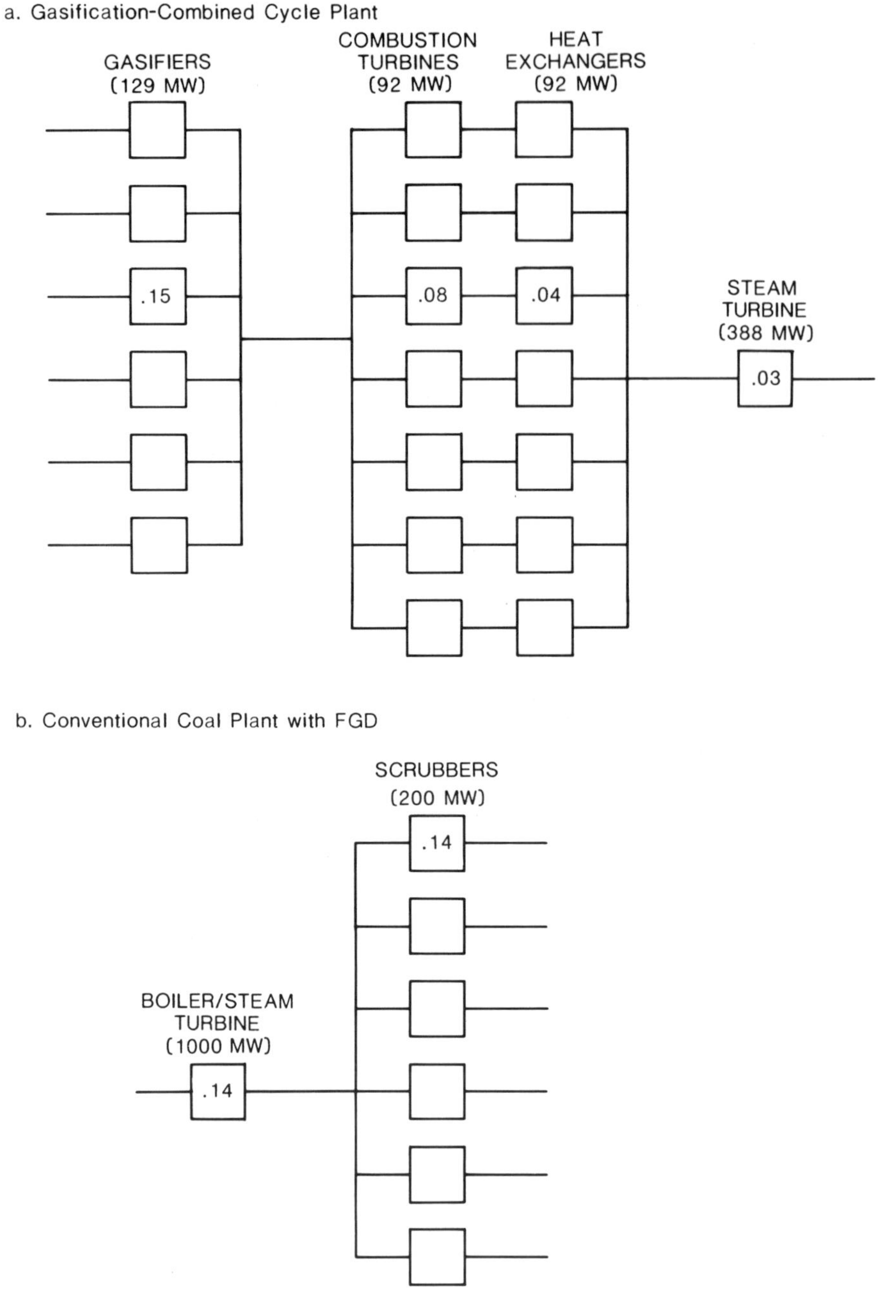

FIGURE 8.8. Schematic Diagram of Major Components of Two Case Study Technologies. (Each number in blocks indicates nominal forced outage rate of a single piece of equipment. FGD, flu gas desulfurization.)

the 0.08 rate to each combustion turbine, and so forth. As a result, gasifier and combustion turbine outage rates were treated probabilistically and encoded, whereas forced outage rates for the heat exchangers and steam turbine were set at their nominal values, 4 and 3 percent, respectively. The encoded distributions appear in Figure 8.9.

A schematic diagram for the conventional plant with FGD is shown in Figure 8.8b. Forced outage rates were treated probabilistically for both the boiler steam turbine and the scrubber. The encoded distributions are shown in Figure 8.9. The resulting probability distributions for the capability ratio of each plant are shown in Figure 8.10.

Calculation of Probability Distribution for Cost Difference

The goal of the probabilistic phase is to calculate the probability distribution for the cost difference. To this end, discrete staircase approximations are substituted for the continuous probability distributions on capital costs, heat rate, and forced outage rate. Then, a three-branch tree is constructed from the continuous distribution. The combined uncertainties are diagrammed in Figure 8.11. The five-stage probability tree in this figure is the basis for calculating the probability distributions on the difference in total annual costs. Each path through the tree represents a scenario or sequence of events. This particular tree represents 243 possible scenarios. For example, in one scenario, the gasification-combined cycle plant could have a capital cost of $800 per kilowatt,

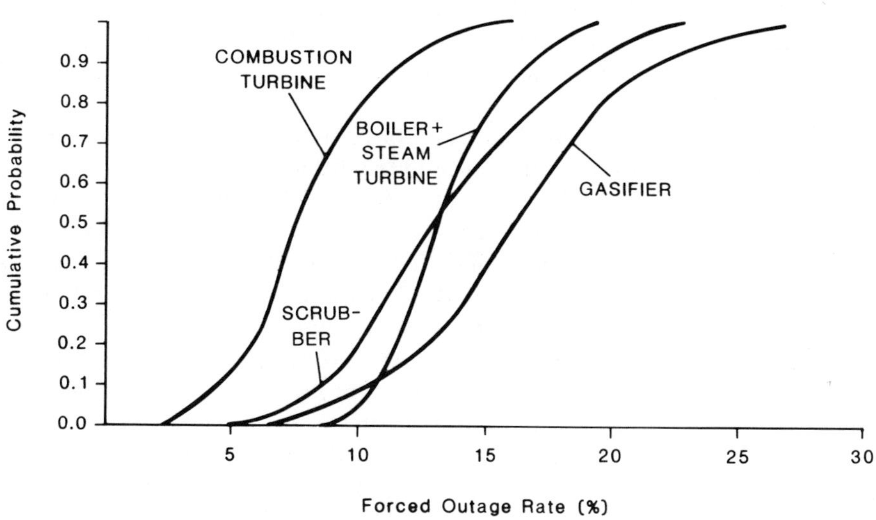

FIGURE 8.9. Cumulative Probability Distributions on Forced Outage Rates for Four Critical Items

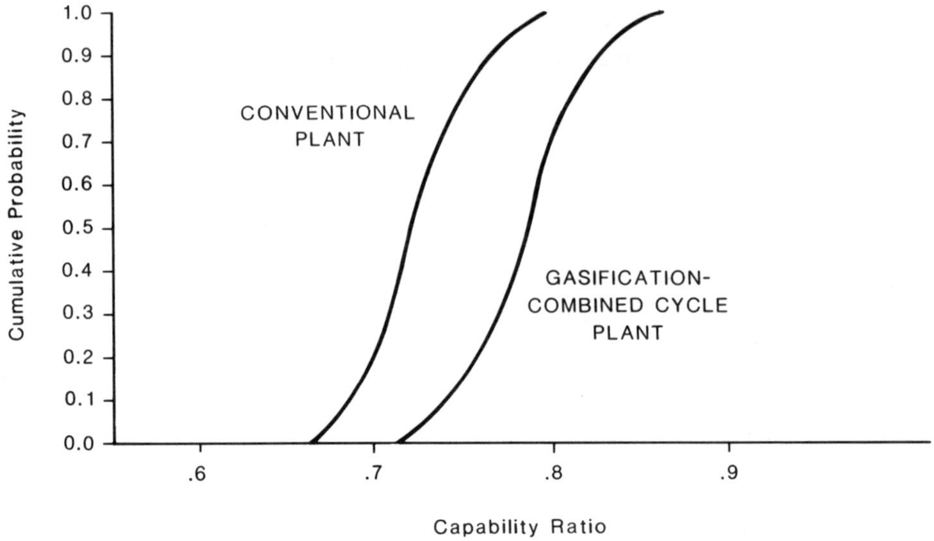

FIGURE 8.10. Cumulative Probability Distribution for Capability Ratios

a capability ratio of 0.81, and a heat rate of 8150, whereas the conventional coal plant could have a capital cost of $610 per kilowatt and a capability ratio of 0.74. Running the cost model with these numbers as inputs generates a cost associated with this scenario. A probability is associated with each scenario, obtained by multiplying the probabilities at each stage in the tree. The probability for the scenario just described is 0.25 × 0.55 × 0.25 × 0.50 × 0.58, or 0.01. The 243 cost and probability pairs that can be derived are combined to construct a probability distribution for the difference between total annual costs.

This procedure was used to develop probability distributions for the total annual cost of each technology and the difference between them. These distributions are illustrated in Figure 8.3. Figure 8.3a indicates that, based on the expert judgments incorporated in these calculations, the probability is 0.85 that the future integrated gasification-combined cycle plant will cost less than a current conventional coal plant. The expected cost difference is $41 per kilowatt per year (6.7 mills per kilowatt per hour). This difference is also apparent from Figure 8.3 (b and c). Figure 8.3c shows clearly that the expected costs of the gasifier are lower and the uncertainty (width of the probability density function) is broader than for the conventional plant.

It is preferable to display the probability distributions both as density (frequency) functions and as cumulative distributions. The density function (Figure 8.3c), which is the more familiar form, provides direct insight. However, probabilities can be read directly from the vertical axis of the cumulative distribution (Figure 8.3b).

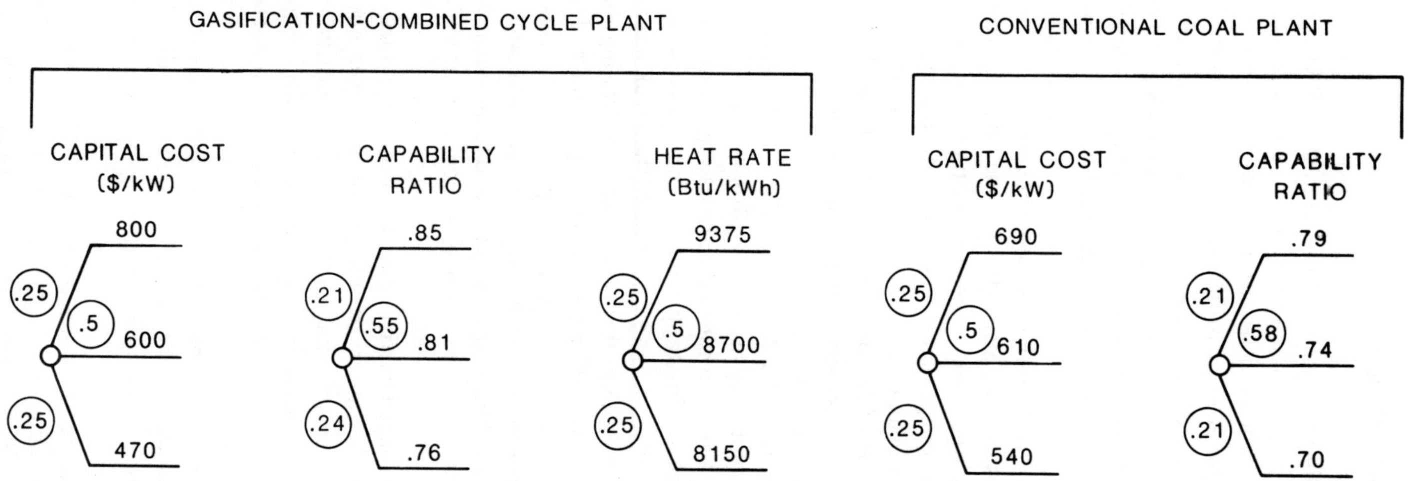

FIGURE 8.11. Probability Tree Used to Calculate the Probability Distribution on the Annual Cost Difference Between the Gasification-Combined Cycle and the Conventional Coal Plants. (Each circled number indicates the probability associated with the particular segment of the scenario.)

SUMMARY AND CRITIQUE

The probability distributions resulting from the EPRI case studies are easily interpreted and contain much more information than do single-point cost estimates. The probability distribution provides the decision maker with a display of the whole range of possible costs and indicates the likelihood of each. The distribution is a means of representing literally hundreds of outcomes in a single picture. The methodology goes beyond the sensitivity studies with which engineers are more familiar. The sensitivity analysis normally performed overlooks or postpones consideration of the likelihood and reasonable magnitude of variations from single-point estimates. Furthermore, these analyses often fail to account for joint variations or correlations.

A further benefit is that the methodology is self-documenting. Together, the tabulations of data and results, the definition of terms, brief computing routines, minutes of meetings and interviews, and presentation material all provide good decision documentation. In many organizations, including the EPRI, the documentation of decisions in an explainable and traceable form is valuable. The documentation strengthens confidence in management and minimizes nonconstructive controversy.

Although this chapter has dealt principally with the technical aspects of the methodology, human dimensions are also major determinants of its successful application. Participation in the analysis by the decision maker and experts is a crucial element of this approach. The analysis is doomed to failure if the analyst attempts to set probabilities rather than seek information from pertinent experts. The analyst's proper role is one of integrating and organizing information rather than evaluating or contributing technical data.

Valid participation requires a managed approach. Success depends on participants understanding their role, providing separate and independent estimates consistent with defined ground rules, and reviewing results. Internal review is necessary to correct errors, resolve ambiguities, and build confidence that the analysis is fair.

Yet, even when managed participation has been developed, experts may remain unconvinced of the validity of opinion concerning competing alternatives. Ultimately, the analysis may simply elevate uncertainties in cost-performance estimates to uncertainties about the judgment or motivations of the experts. The vagaries inherent in subjective judgment cannot be eliminated by this methodology, or any other for that matter. Peer-style review of experts' judgment (expressed as probability distributions) can be assisted by recording the issues considered when encoding probability distributions. This record can also be useful in replicating or extending the judgments as conditions change with new events.

The analysis presented here needs to be extended to provide decision makers with additional data to aid in making R & D choices. In particular, the competition between technologies in the marketplace needs to be modeled and important market uncertainties represented. Further work also must be done to include in the comparison such "intangible" factors as environmental acceptability, licensability, and the compatibility of new alternatives with existing personnel skills.

The approach generated in this study will surely see further development and application. Ultimately it will be applied beyond the R & D environment to the market itself, where utility planners will consider uncertainty explicitly in their choices for new power plants.

REFERENCES

Balson, William E., and Stephen M. Barrager, *"Uncertainty Methods in Comparing Power Plants,"* Final report prepared by Decision Focus Incorporated for the Electric Power Research Institute, EPRI FFAS-1048 (April 1979).

Brown, R.V., A.S. Kahr, and C.R. Peterson, *Decision Analysis for the Manager* (New York: Holt, Rinehart & Winston, 1974).

Garver, L., "Effective Load Carrying Capability of Generating Units," *IEEE Transactions on Power Apparatus and Systems* (August 1966):910.

Gildersleeve, O.D., Jr., *Generating Unit Reliability Analysis*, Internal EPRI memo, June 23, 1978.

Hampton, J.M., P.G. Moore, and H. Thomas, "Subjective Probability and Its Measurement," *Journal of the Royal Statistical Society* 136 (1973): 21–42.

Howard, R.A., "Decision Analysis: Applied Decision Theory," In *Proceedings of the Fourth International Conference on Operations Research* (New York: John Wiley & Sons, 1966), pp. 55–71.

Howard, R.A., "The Foundations of Decision Analysis," *IEEE Transactions on Systems, Science, and Cybernetics* SSC-4, no. 3 (September 1968): 1–9.

North, Warner, "A Tutorial Introduction to Decision Theory," *IEEE Transactions on Systems, Science, and Cybernetics* SSC-4, no. 3 (September 1968).

Poole, D., "Fossil Plant Performance and Reliability—A Program of Power Plant Improvement," *Proceedings of the Fifth Annual Reliability Engineering Conference for the Electric Power Industry*, Portland, OR, April 17, 1978.

Spetzler, C., and C.A.S. Stael von Holstein, "Probability Encoding in Decision Analysis," *Management Science* 22 (November 1975).

Tversky, A., and D. Kahneman, "Judgement Under Uncertainty: Heuristics and Biases," *Science* 185 (1974): 1124–31.

von Holstein, C.A.S. Stael, *Assessment and Evaluation of Subjective Probability Distributions* (Stockholm: The Economic Research Institute at the Stockholm School of Economics, 1970).

Winkler, R.L., and A.G. Murphy, "Experiments in the Laboratory and the Real World." *Organizational Behavior and Human Performance* 10 (1973): 252–70.

IV
Policy Implications

9

Toward Improved R & D Policy

George S. Tolley, James H. Hodge, and Mark A. Grenchik

Many who believe that research and development (R & D) is enormously beneficial may think the estimate that one third or more of our per capita income growth is due to R & D activity constitutes conclusive evidence that it is indeed beneficial, and that this is sufficient evidence for formulating policies. A conclusion might be that there is no need to indulge in what may seem to be the conjectural pastime of worrying more specifically about what the effects of R & D are on the economy or to be concerned unduly about the incentives to undertake R & D. Enthusiasts will tend to think that more R & D is better than less, and that this dictum extends to every kind of R & D.

Yet, we have seen several reasons to be concerned in more detail about R & D. First, pressure and change characterize the complex array of legal, administrative, and institutional arrangements within which R & D takes place. These arrangements profoundly affect private as well as government R & D; e.g., the nuances of the patent process are continually changing, the ability of a firm to monopolize its innovation varies with the administration in office, etc. The Economic Recovery Act of 1981, calling for faster depreciation of R & D assets, an increase in the deduction permitted for contributions of newly manufactured research equipment to universities, and a tax credit for R & D expenditure, is among the more recent social decisions designed to promote more R & D. One of the more important questions of our time is what the effects of such decisions are on society.

Second, many desiderata are served by the funds for which R & D competes, and protections given to inventors after the R & D is completed are by no means costless. Company decision makers, the public at large, and others with interests in alternative uses for the dollars devoted to R & D and the returns to it all will, in one way or another, form opinions about the beneficial effects of R & D or lack of them. These opinions in the end will largely govern the support given to R & D as a whole and to the balance of activities within it.

Third, R & D managers must make choices at every turn about which kinds of activities to support. They must balance in some cases among whole scientific fields, in other cases among programs within fields, and in still others, among individual projects.

Fourth, and perhaps most important, consider basic facts which characterize the R & D industry as well as the growth of productivity in the U.S. since the 1940s. In a recent book, Scherer summarizes the relevant statistics: "The growth rate of private business sector labor productivity, which averaged 3.1 percent per annum between 1947 and 1968, fell in stages since then and in 1977 to 1981 barely exceeded zero. Concurrently, real (i.e., GNP deflator-adjusted) company-financed industrial research and development (R & D) abruptly stopped growing in 1970 and, after a two-year hiatus, resumed its growth at a much slower rate, at least until recently" (Scherer, 1984, p. 286).

Assuming that there is a causal relationship between the rate of growth of R & D investment and that of labor productivity, it seems reasonable to blame at least part of the decline in real productivity on the shortfall in R & D growth. The motivation to study R & D policy seems all the greater in light of the fact that total economic performance may be at stake.

Scherer hypothesizes that most of the industries leading the postwar technological boom have entered some sort of maturity phase. Acceptance of the maturity phase hypothesis would mean, among other things, that across-the-board tax credits and subsidies in the U.S. in order to stimulate more industrial R & D would not be justified. As Scherer puts it, "When the well is drying up, investing in high-speed buckets is not apt to provide a lasting solution" (Scherer, 1984, p. 268). Rather, contributing to the stock of new scientific and technological concepts through more basic research is advised.

This discussion raises the policy issue of choosing among basic, applied and development research, all under the heading of R & D. Scherer remarks that lately the U.S. appears to have followed the wrong policies if the goal was to raise total productivity. He notes that "Industrial outlays for basic research barely increased in current dollar terms between 1968–74" and in real terms, they decreased (Scherer, 1984, p. 268).

These considerations point to the need for a coherent framework in which detailed analysis of specific R & D policies can be undertaken and for a catalogue of questions relevant to the evaluation of any specific R & D effort and the public policy that affects it.

R & D BENEFITS

Granted that there is an underlying need to know something about the effects of R & D activities, the first question is, Can any inquiry be reliable enough to contribute usefully to the decision-making process? Typically, the contemplation of this question brings to mind the idea of trying to assess the contribution of very basic advances, such as discovery of the law of gravity. Although an assessment of the effects of knowing the law of gravity might in fact be tractable, it is not the kind of assessment relevant to most R & D decisions. The results of most R & D activity are far less imponderable.

The example of even something as large scale as development of an electric automobile better illustrates the nature and tractability of more typical R & D evaluation problems. An innovation has beneficial effects if it can produce the same output while saving on inputs. In particular, an important part of the beneficial effects of an electric automobile will be in travel costs, most specifically, savings in fuel costs. These savings are estimable, at least to the round order of magnitude needed to make R & D decisions leading to development of such an automobile. The total savings will depend on the savings per mile and on the number of miles electric cars are driven. At the extreme, if no one uses electric cars, there will be no savings. Since these cars will be used only if they successfully compete with other forms of transportation, the benefits from R & D activity to develop an electric automobile will be importantly determined by the effects of the R & D in reducing the cost of producing it. Indeed, many prototype electric automobiles exist at the present time, with such factors as weight, battery life, and performance characteristics making them too expensive to compete effectively with automobiles powered by internal combustion engines. Using the model developed by Tolley and Townsend in Chapter 6, the cost reduction made possible by R & D can be used to estimate the likely penetration of the electric automobile into the total market for automobiles, which will influence the total miles of use of electric cars. The benefits of electric vehicle R & D thus depend on quantities that can be easily measured.

Comparisons of the beneficial effects of R & D to its costs will give aid in deciding how much of the nation's income to devote to the development of the electric automobile. Even more important for some purposes, the approach is needed in deciding which particular kinds of R & D activity on the electric automobile to support in view of their likely contribution to market penetration.

The example of the electric automobile suggests, as a starting point, that an innovation that lowers the cost of producing a good will generate a benefit approximately equal to the cost savings per good multiplied by the number of goods sold. Welfare has been increased because more output can now be produced with fewer resources. The resources saved can be spent to produce other goods. The basic logic remains the same if the approach is extended to take account of changes in total size of market, quality considerations, and indeed broader social goals.

The example suggests that the purpose of most R & D activity is to increase the output of goods and services, the value of which is not overly difficult to measure. It would be a disservice to throw consideration of these basic benefits out the window in face of the existence of extremely important but less obviously tractable consequences such as lives saved, more adequate national defense, or adequacy of foreign policy. Clearly, the evaluation of any R & D policy depends on many different factors, not the least of which is the increase in goods and services. Another temptation is to make blind assertions about what unforeseen spinoffs will be. It is hoped that the electric car example and the more thorough benefit estimations presented in Chapter 6 show that realistic analysis is tractable. Still another temptation is to suppose that since the success of any R & D activity is subject to uncertainty, one must give up hope of trying to choose activities making the largest contributions to pay off expectations. Although uncertainty introduces complications, they are certainly not insurmountable. On the contrary, Schulze and Cummings in Chapter 7 present a framework that deals with uncertainty in a straightforward and accurate manner.

R & D poses difficulties in valuation and uncertainty that are different only in degrees from other kinds of activities. The issue becomes not whether to evaluate R & D, but how to proceed in view of its unique characteristics. Beyond effects estimable in dollar terms, serious estimates of nondollar effects can and should be developed and arrayed for use in decision making.

Difficult to quantify benefits, spinoffs, and the likelihood of technical success are grist for the analyst wishing to contribute to the improvement of R & D. If one believes that better decisions can be made by objectively weighing consequences, the conclusion follows that these considerations need to be systematized and used intensively in the policy process.

THE LACK OF CAPTURABILITY OF RETURNS

Given a framework for deciding how much R & D it is worthwhile to undertake, the question becomes, Do we currently have too much, too little, or approximately the most desirable amount of production and application of new ideas? The primary argument usually given in support of the idea that not enough R & D is undertaken is that the person or business researching and developing does not receive sufficient benefits from an innovation and therefore underinvests in R & D activity. As soon as a new device or idea is known to a wide audience, others are able to imitate it freely or at low cost, reducing the benefits to the original inventor.

One way in which the private marketplace alleviates these problems is through mergers. The new, larger company is often in a better position to capture the benefits of an innovation and exploit the new knowledge. However, as Telser points out, there are still numerous problems. The innovation is not as widely produced as would be socially acceptable, and although the new firm may have a better chance at capturing the benefits, competition still poses a major threat. Moreover, the costs of merger can be prohibitively high, so that in most instances this is not a viable possibility.

The situation has been described as one in which inventors cannot claim property rights to their invention. Since few of the benefits are in the form of profits to the inventors, they do not undertake all projects whose total benefits are expected to exceed their costs.

THE PATENT SYSTEM

To remedy this situation, devices such as patent and trade secret laws have been developed that are designed to give inventors more of the returns flowing from their inventions. However, a problem with patents is that the owner of a patent has a degree of monopoly control over its use. The patent owner, acting as a monopolist may constrain output to keep the price people are willing to pay for the invention high and thus to increase his returns. The results are that the invention is employed less than it would be under competitive market conditions and that society does not benefit as much from the invention as it could. Thus emerges a fundamental trade-off in patent law. Because a patent allows a patent holder to act as a monopolist and so raise the expected return from innovative activity, it encourages R & D. On the other hand, the patent holder acting in self-interest will not have incentives for the device to be used as widely as would be most beneficial.

THE INCENTIVE TO INVEST TOO SOON

Another less recognized problem introduced by patents is associated with timing. To obtain maximum returns, a new process or product should be adopted at the point in time at which the net benefits (gross benefits minus the R & D costs of producing the innovation) are the greatest in today's dollars. The size of these net benefits may vary over time for several reasons. An example is a new product that will only be useful in a market that has not yet fully developed. Thus, the introduction of the innovation should be delayed until marketing structures, complementary products, and the like are developed to take advantage of it. As another example, the costs of the R & D for a project may vary over time. It may thus be most economical to carry out the R & D in stages over a period of time rather than adopt a crash program of development with more immediate results. Another possibility is that the costs of doing the R & D may decrease over time.

Even though benefits might be greatest from an R & D tempo that is less than maximum, the patent system provides incentives to researchers and sponsors of research to be the first to complete research and thereby secure the patent rights to it. This is because the person to obtain the rights gets all of the benefits and his competitors get none. This incentive is a competitive research situation inducing inventors to produce an invention and secure the patent rights as soon as there is any positive return at all, rather than to wait until the time that the return to society would be greatest.

THE TERM RIGIDITY OF PATENTS

Conceptually, there is some term of patent unique to each invention, that will just compensate the inventor, minimizing cost to society for use of the invention. This idea is at odds with the one 17-year term we now have, which is applicable to all patents. Although there are practical difficulties in finetuning the patent system for each invention, it should be possible to delineate broad classes. In each case, the term of patent right would depend on the costs of patent development and commercialization and on prices the patent owner can charge as determined by the nature of the demand for the final product.

WHAT IS PATENTABLE?

New knowledge can range from abstract ideas of wide applicability to something as highly specific as a well-defined mechanical device. To be patentable, an idea must be definite and definable in physical terms, which rules out many contributions to knowledge of the most important kind, particularly since more abstract contributions have wide applicability in a possibly diverse set of innovations. The connection between basic contributions of this kind and the returns to the originator are especially loose, often consisting of glory or recognition and professional promotion in various institutions. The incentives for such institutions to reward according to ultimate social product may be tenuous despite the best intentions.

A case can be made that it would be fruitful to broaden the definition of what is patentable and to take special measures to encourage basic research, the net returns to which can be enormous even though long deferred because it is typically inexpensive.

PATENTS AND THE COMPLEXITIES OF INFORMATION

The foregoing discussion of patents is based on economic incentives as they operate in a world of relatively great certainty. Other issues surrounding patents arise in relation to ambiguity about what the future holds. The risks inherent in a world of uncertainty are seen to be less, however, when it is noted that one does not have to commercially market an innovation when it is patented. Rather, at the time of patenting, the requirement is to show that one has a physically workable idea that could conceivably be commercialized. Edmund Kitch (1979) has visualized this process as one in which the taking of a patent is equivalent to the staking out of a claim for research activity. Once this claim has been established, the research and introduction of the invention can proceed at the most propitious rate. The gold rush analogy may be apt: Once the claim to the mine (research area) is established, further resources need not be wasted in hurried exploratory activity. In this regard, a patent system may encourage rather than deter the efficient timing of research and commercialization.

However, there is still an incentive to perform research at too early a time to obtain the patent or the right to perform further research. How serious this problem is depends on what percentage of the resources needed to produce and commercialize an invention must be spent on obtaining a patent. If the amount is small, then the problem is not serious and the patent system may be very efficient from a timing point of view. On the other hand, if a great deal of resources must be spent before a researcher is able to acquire the patent, then the timing problem is potentially serious.

A benefit often overlooked in the patent system is the fact that patented information is public. First, it lets people know who is doing what. Consequently, it helps prevent the duplication of research efforts. Second, the flow of information helps inventors take advantage of each other's work. Two inventors working on complementary projects have the information necessary to exchange their knowledge through cross-licensing agreements or the like.

TRADE SECRET LAWS

Institutions other than patent law affect the amount of R & D activity undertaken. Similar to patents, common law provides protection of trade secrets from theft, with a party being subject to prosecution for stealing production procedures that have been kept secret. An advantage of not patenting a process and instead trusting in trade secret laws is that one does not have to make the nature of the invention public. Even though a patented invention is fully protected, it is sometimes easy for a party to copy the invention with enough minor modifications to circumvent the patent. The success of such attempts to "invent around" an existing patent (and hence the incentive to resort to trade secrecy protection) depends upon the courts' attitudes toward patent law enforcement.

Whether it is more advantageous to rely on the trade secret laws or to take out a patent depends on the nature of the process or product being protected. Items such as machines, which are easily copied, are usually patented. However, for recipes and other processes that cannot be so easily unraveled by competitors, the trade secrecy option may offer the most protection. The classic example of this is the recipe for Coca-Cola, which is not patented (Watters 1978) but is instead kept locked up, presumably in the company safe.

PATENT INFRINGEMENT AND THE COURTS

Another consideration with regard to patent and trade secret laws is how they are enforced. Just as it is difficult to prove that a secret has actually been stolen from a company or inventor, it is difficult to defend a patent.

A patent holder sues a person for using the invention without consent. In response, the defendant files a countersuit in which the patent holder is charged with obtaining the patent fraudulently and employing it in violation of antitrust laws. The courts can encourage investment in R & D by consistently upholding the patent holder's right to his or her invention under all except the most blatant breaches of antitrust law. On the other hand, the courts can discourage R & D by consistently judging against patent holders.

Opinions have been expressed that the courts are so imbued with an antitrust mentality that they consistently judge against the patent holder on antitrust grounds. According to this view, the courts are excessive in their prosecution of patent holders and are having a severe effect on the quality of research which is being undertaken.

R & D AND BUSINESS REGULATION

Other facets of the government's relationship to business can have adverse effects on R & D activity. The connection between antitrust policy and private research is, again, a conduit for these effects. Price fixing allegations and policies toward allowed rates charged for licensing reduce the returns to innovations, thus discouraging R & D.

The 1980 report of The Committee for Economic Development details several ways in which government regulation can have a negative impact on R & D activity. Since regulated firms must use resources to comply with mandated standards, funds are diverted from R & D of new products and processes. Second, regulation increases the waiting time for returns on investment and hence discourages investment in new technologies. An example would be the long delays involved in developing drugs to cure diseases such as cancer. Third, many regulations may increase uncertainty in the return of R & D investments and hence reduce the incentive to innovate simply because regulation standards are usually open-ended and subject to change (CED, 1980, pp. 43–45).

One recent development in business formations in the U.S. seems to have avoided any interferences by the Justice Department, and so may have significant implications where the future of R & D in the private sector is concerned. Microelectronics and Computer Technology Corporation (MCC) of Austin, Texas, was formed in 1983 and "is a private sector joint research and development venture created to help maintain U.S. technological preeminence and international competitiveness in microelectronics and computers" (MCC literature, 1985). The firm is owned by 21 American microelectronic and computer companies each of which has representatives on a governing board of directors. Once research is conducted at MCC, MCC holds title to all resulting knowledge and patents and will license them to MCC shareholders participating in the firm's technology programs. Furthermore, the company literature indicates that "MCC technologies will be licensed to other companies, including smaller companies, on reasonable terms, up to three years after their availability to participating companies. Participants will receive about 70% of royalty income. The remainder will be used to finance further MCC research" [MCC, 1985]. Such a model for private sector R & D seems very promising and, should it pass the test of time where antitrust matters are concerned, may prove to be a viable means for promoting R & D in a more efficient manner.

Possible future policy implications arising from the existence of firms such as MCC would include a different structure of patents than the one in place today and hence, different incentives for private firms to engage in R & D activities. These and related issues would need to be considered before any progress in promoting better R & D activities in the near future can be made.

TAX TREATMENT OF R & D

Although certain government policies have undesirable effects on R & D, there exist others that at least in part, counteract them. For example, the federal government gives special treatment to R & D by permitting, beginning in 1954, the expensing of R & D investments for corporate income tax purposes. This encourages more R & D relative to other kinds of corporate investment.

Two major issues in the design of R & D tax incentives are "availability of the incentives to firms in various tax circumstances and the ability of firms to finance their R & D expenditures" (Lalonde, 1983, pp. 25–26). The standard tax related solution to the financing problem is for the government to provide assistance in the form of tax write-offs and tax credits. However, one of the chief problems with current government tax incentive policies is that new firms which have no tax liability and which are not profitable during early years cannot take advantage of these tax benefits. Hence, the larger, more established firm is favored over the smaller, newly established one with regard to R & D assistance even though the smaller firm is usually in particular need of R & D funds rather than the larger one. The Canadian government has proposed a way to get around this problem through the use of R & D financing contracts between individual investors and the firm conducting R & D activities. In effect, the small firm would be "allowed to renounce its unused credits and deductions and permit outside investors to claim an incentive" (Lalonde, 1983, p. 26).

A vehicle designed to circumvent the problems of predictability and risk facing investors is the tax credit for joint R & D ventures. Bozeman and Link argue that not only does this proposal encourage more R & D, but it is also conducive to a more competitive industrial environment. Because of the obvious possible violations of antitrust law which may stem from joint venture R & D, Bozeman and Link state that firms will want to take care to avoid such accusations. "One way to indemnify against the threat of antitrust action," they point out, "is for the firm to tilt the joint venture activity toward basic research" which is more acceptable under antitrust law than other kinds of R & D (Bozeman and Link, 1983, p. 117). The implication here is that not only will more basic research be stimulated, but competitive environments of industries will have been enhanced.

Other R & D tax incentives that have been recommended by the Committee for Economic Development would allow externally acquired patents and intangible technology to be subject to accelerated depreciation over a 10-year period or their demonstrated life, whichever is shorter. The reasoning is that the effective life of a patent often terminates long before the end of its legal life of 17 years due to product obsolescence or inflation.

FOR AND AGAINST GOVERNMENT SPONSORSHIP OF R & D

Cases in which a general patent system does not adequately promote certain types of R & D occur when, despite patent protection, an inventor is not sufficiently rewarded for an invention that produces benefits in the national interest that exceed those reflected in market incentives. Weapons development provides an example. A related case is that of technologies that have both civilian and military uses, such as nuclear power.

Space exploration is another example of this kind. There are reasons to expect health and energy to belong to this underprovided category as well, along with basic research in general. The arguments for some specific intervention in R & D are strong, but this does not say that past government expenditures have always been administered in the right doses or to the highest value areas. The questions raised here are concerned with both the effect of a policy such as weapons development on the national economy and the effect on international relations and stability.

A fundamental problem calling into question government sponsorship of R & D is that of designing a satisfactory incentive system to ensure that government policies will, in fact, reflect the national interest. Whereas the benefits of government sponsorship are evident in cases of the free market's failure, both economic costs and national interest must be considered in any assessment of the role of such sponsorship.

Furthermore, a problem intrinsic to the funding of government sponsored R & D is raised by Bozeman and Link. In the choice faced by policy makers between government sponsorship of R & D and tax incentives, longevity and stability of tax incentives are argued to have an advantage over direct government R & D expenditure since the former do not require budget review. Those government decisions which lead to more and better R & D activities would seem to be the preferred ones. If one assumes that a policy characterized by longevity and stability is conducive to more and better R & D, the disadvantages of direct government sponsorship of R & D become apparent.

Yet, as Bozeman and Link point out, neither are tax incentives for R & D costless. Such incentives may be viewed as indirect or future tax liabilities since the revenue which would have been generated in the absence of the incentives have had to come from some other source in order for the government to finance its expenditures. Allocating tax liabilities between current and future periods is certainly an issue which policy makers will want to consider, especially in light of possible effects on overall investment in human and non-human capital. Moreover, policy makers may be interested in the question of what different results in the level of social welfare would be expected if funds were appropriated for direct assistance in R & D programs rather than if tax incentives were distributed.

Given that there is a positive role for government sponsorship of R & D activities, policy makers are confronted immediately by three basic questions. First, To what extent should the government engage directly in R & D? Second, How well do current social decisions reflect this desired extent? Third, If the present decisions are less than socially optimal, how can better government sponsorship of R & D be facilitated?

A full response to the first question would require among other things, a careful statement about just what is the national interest. Such a statement, presumably, would reflect the social preference ordering of public goods established by a nation. These no doubt would include an effective national defense, energy independence, and perhaps, as suggested by Scherer, a greater public commitment toward basic research—all goods which are enjoyed by everyone but which no one individually has an incentive to provide.

One way in which to attack the second question with regard to the U.S. is to consider the current trends in direct government sponsorship of R & D activities. These trends consist of increased defense R & D, reduced civilian expenditures, and a reorientation of civilian R & D from development applied research to basic research. Furthermore with regard to basic research, the Reagan administration has favored hard sciences on the grounds that these "are more likely to contribute eventually to the nation's economic performance or to other goals such as national security" (CBO, 1984, p. 7).

Among the major policy issues outlined by the Congressional Budget Office in its report on R & D funding for the proposed fiscal year 1985 budget are those involving national defense, nuclear power, the space shuttle program, and national health care programs. The ability of the U.S. Department of Defense to use new and expanded budget authority efficiently merits special attention according to the CBO. The idea is that defense buildup might risk diverting qualified scientists and engineers from other activities in private industry. As the CBO points out, an increased weapons build-up, associated more with applied and development research than with basic research, could have profound effects with regard to the U.S. government's ability to foster more basic research.

The CBO report asserts that there is an imbalance between government funding nuclear R & D over other forms of energy. According to the government, this "could skew the rate at which different forms of energy become commercially available, a point that might be particularly relevant given serious economic problems currently confronting nuclear power plants" (CBO, 1984, p. 40).

Another policy issue regarding the U.S. Department of Energy is the trade-off between alternative energy technologies close to commercial use and many nuclear technologies "far from that stage" (CBO, 1984, p. 40). Policy makers will want to consider all relevant benefits and costs when deciding which R & D activities to fund and which not to fund.

How to deal with the possibility of a shortfall in revenue for R & D in the space shuttle and space station programs is a concern highlighted in the CBO report. "Growing competition from foreign space programs and from civilian space services in delivering payloads" are attributed as sources of this problem (CBO, 1984, p. 30). The CBO suggests greater commitment to international cooperation as one means of reducing the R & D costs of the U.S. space station system. The recent joint U.S.-European space shuttle mission is in the spirit of this recommendation. However, the trade-off is that internationalization of the space shuttle program "might compromise its potential military benefits," and hence, national security (CBO, 1984, p. 31).

As the CBO report notes, health R & D offers a means of cutting the costs of health care which are rising faster than the rate of inflation. However, this is at a cost itself since health care R & D is also becoming more expensive. Furthermore, there is the possibility that a successful R & D program may actually lead to higher health care costs "by increasing the quality of service provided by the health system and the number of patients it serves" (CBO, 1984, p. 54). Keeping track of trends such as these in relation to stated social objectives will assist future policy makers wanting to make constructive contributions toward a better R & D policy.

Finally, the third question merits special attention simply because of the government's role as a dominant player in the economy and hence its potential for encouraging as well as inhibiting more and better R & D. A priority among policy makers would appear to be the avoidance of policy whose implications lead to a decline in inventive activity.

Each of these three policy questions has been considered in much detail in a recent book and accompanying article by Richard R. Nelson of Yale University. Nelson suggests that instead of emulating the successes of other countries where the formulation and implementation of government sponsored R & D activities are concerned, U.S. policy makers would be wise to assess the cases in which sponsorship of R & D programs by the U.S. government has been a success. The cases in point to which Nelson refers include the development of the semiconductor and computers, new drugs, and technological progress in U.S. agriculture. What is remarkable about Nelson's findings is that the cases where government sponsorship of R & D activities has been successful do not pertain to any one category of R & D. Rather, they range from basic to the most applied research activities. Such findings underscore the point that formulation, implementation, and evaluation of government sponsorship of R & D activities are complex issues which require careful treatment by policy makers on a per case basis.

FORMS OF GOVERNMENT R & D

What issues have been raised where direct government sponsorship of R & D is concerned likewise are pertinent to direct government hire as well as cooperative agreements between public and private R & D. Direct government hire is used and appears eminently appropriate for weapons and related R & D involving defense and raising secrecy problems. Contracts and grants are a predominant form for research that is not secret and for which there is a desire to encourage R & D over and above what would take place in response to private incentives under the patent system. Cooperative agreements are helping to overcome the reluctance of business to participate in government R & D projects in which formerly patent returns were precluded if government sponsorship was involved. Prizes and special tax credits for specific kinds of R & D particularly in the public interest are relatively neglected and deserve further exploration.

THE RELATIONS BETWEEN PUBLIC AND PRIVATE R & D

Although cooperative agreements succeed in enlisting the participation of some private firms in government-sponsored R & D, those firms that do not succeed in participating (in a large endeavor, not all could conceivably participate) are discouraged from undertaking any R & D in the area of the sponsored research because of the government competition. Further modification of grant and contract procedures may be in order. Prizes and tax incentives do not share the problem, though they have their own. In some situations, the R & D would be undertaken anyway, and R & D that is not intended to be encouraged may inadvertently be eligible for government encouragement.

ENERGY R & D

Periodic concerns with regard to R & D have centered around energy. Recognition that foreign dependence on oil is the recurring primary problem and energy the secondary problem would almost certainly lead to a different emphasis in government-sponsored research related to energy. It should also be recognized that the increases in oil prices may be a more powerful incentive to energy R & D than explicit energy R & D programs. Devices in addition to direct government sponsorship of research now being emphasized include tax incentives for oil-saving R & D and raising the price of oil in importing nations above the world price. The latter strategy would discourage consumption as well as encourage R & D in line with the value to nations of reducing oil imports.

Additional problems related to energy R & D concern commitment to demonstration projects that fail because of overoptimism about costs to new technologies and the risks of developing a high-cost energy technology, e.g., oil shale, which would lead to large losses and pressures for subsidization should world oil prices fall in the future. Guarantees or other overt encouragements to high-cost technologies run the same danger.

CONCLUSION

In an era in which productivity change has shaped our lives and the belief in technology remains great, it is amazing how little we know about the relative importance of the various factors of R & D that act in different directions. Although almost certainly there are highly significant distortions in the kinds of R & D being undertaken, it is difficult at this time to say whether there is too much or too little R & D as a whole. Some suggestions for improvement can be made with considerable confidence, whereas others must be made more tentatively.

A few suggestions may be singled out as especially promising. A rethinking of the patent system would have merit. For instance, instead of a single fixed term for all patents, different classes of patents might be developed, providing for terms of, say, 3, 7, 17, and 30 years, depending on the type of invention. Legislation could be passed strengthening and clarifying protection against patent infringement as well as providing guarantees against regulation of pricing and licensing. A broader definition of what is patentable might be adopted. Provision could be made, at least in rare cases, for the government to buy out patent rights for an amount somewhat above what the inventor would earn, to make the use of the patent freely available. Strong assurances would be needed of adequate compensation in these cases, in order not to discourage R & D owing to fear of expropriation of patent rights.

A national policy toward R & D could be enunciated to provide a framework for government actions toward R & D extending beyond the patent system. A cornerstone of this policy would be a careful statement of what the national interest is in R & D, beyond providing a suitable, neutral incentive system for private R & D. In basic research preeminently, and in certain applied areas such as health and foreign energy dependence, a case can be made that there can be gains from promoting more and different R & D than would occur under private incentives as fostered by patents. The great challenge is to make government measures in these special cases truly effective. A range of policy instruments could include fuel tariffs, R & D tax incentives in special areas, and prizes. Attention should be given to avoiding government activities that through competition discourage private inventive activity. The result would be a different pattern of R & D policies than we have at present, with fewer expenditures in some areas and more in others, and with less emphasis on direct expenditures.

REFERENCES

Bozeman, Barry and Albert M. Link, 1983. *Investments in Technology: Corporate Strategies & Public Policy Alternatives,* New York: Praeger.

Committee for Economic Development, *Stimulating Technological Progress,* Washington, 1980.

Congress of the United States, Congressional Budget Office, *Research and Development Funding in the Proposed Fiscal Year 1985 Budget,* Washington, March, 1984.

Lalonde, Marc, 1983. *Research and Development Tax Policies.* Canada: Department of Finance.

Nelson, Richard R., 1982. *Government and Technical Progress: A Cross-Industry Analysis. New York: Pergamon Press.*

Nelson, Richard R., 1982. *Government and Technical Progress: A Cross-Industry Analysis.* New York: Pergamon Press.

Scherer, F. M., 1984. Innovation and Growth: Schumpterian Perspectives. Boston: MIT Press.

Watters, Pat, 1978. *Coca-Cola: An Illustrated History.* Garden City, NY: Doubleday.

Index

Administrative Office of the U. S. courts, 95, 98, 99
Agricultural research, 20–22
Analytical models
  energy, 18–20
  imperfect competition, 16–17
  life of a patent, 4, 30–32
  private and social returns, 10
  private incentives, 4, 28–30
  tax incentives, 4, 33–34
  timing of innovations, 11–14
Argonne National Laboratory, 106–108, 119
Arrow, K, J., 4, 11, 109
Art, and patent litigation, 96, 99, 100
Auction system, 89–92
Ayanian, R., 26

Balson, W. E., 154, 156, 157, 158, 159
Banner, D. W., 96, 100
Barrager, S. M., 154, 156, 157, 158, 159
Barzel, Y., 11, 16, 17, 50, 51, 70, 71, 89, 92
Baum, L., 96, 97, 99
Bayh-Dole bill, 115
Beck, R. L., 50, 62
Behrman, J. N., 91
Benefits, of R & D, 175–76
  see also Returns
Bhagwati, J., 50
Birch, J. J., 16
Bozeman, B., 181, 183
Brookhaven national synchrotron light source, 118
Brown, R. V., 150

Cheung, S. N. S., 30, 61
Clarke, E. H., 51
Clark Tax, 51
Coal gasification, 113, 154–69
Coal plants case study, 154–69
Coase, R. H., 9
Coca-Cola recipe, 180
Committee for Economic Development, 181, 182
Competition, imperfect, 4, 14–17
  analytical model, 16–17
Computer program, project evaluation, 131–36
Congressional Budget Office, 183, 184
Contracts, 60, 61
Cost and performance data, incorporating uncertainty into, 149–69
Cost reduction, 83–89, 125–37
Crowding out, 22

Dasgupta, P., 7, 11, 15, 16, 17, 28, 50
Davis, N. P., 110
Debreu, G., 15
Decision analysis, 150
Demsetz, H., 4
Direct estimation, of benefits and costs of R & D, 4, 23–26
Disclosure, patent, 54–55
DOE. *See* U. S. Department of Energy

Economic analysis, at early stages of development, 138–48
Economic Recovery Act (1981), 173
Electric Power Research Institute (EPRI), 149–69
Energy, 17–20, 102, 125, 185–86
  analytical model, 18–20
  federal funding for, 126–37
  federal policies on, 108–15, 184

see also National laboratories
solar, 140, 141–43, 144, 145, 146, 147, 148
Energy technologies, feasibility studies for, 139
Enforcement, patent, 4, 95–101, 180
Engel, R., 32
ERAB. *See* U. S. Energy Research Advisory Board
ERDA. *See* U. S. Energy Research and Development Administration
Evaluation, of R & D
framework for, 3–36
project, 125–37
Evenson, , 23
Expensing. *See* Tax incentives

Fethke, G., 16
Financing, of projects, 8
Firm, nature of, 8–9
Fossil fuel baseload generation technologies, 154–69

Garver, L., 163
Gasification combined cycle plant, 154–69
Gildersleeve, O. D., Jr., 163
Gordon, H. S., 50
Government regulation, 180–81
Government sponsorship, 3, 4, 35, 182–84, 185
see also National laboratories
Grabowski, H., 26, 27
Great Plains Coal Gasification Project, 113
Griliches, Z., 17, 23, 25, 50

Hampton, J. M., 153
Hardin, G., 50
HDR (hot dry rock) geothermal resources, 140–41, 144, 145–46, 147–48
Hilberry, N., 107
Hirshleifer, J., 24, 42
Hodge, J. A., 35, 36
Howard, R. A., 150

Imperfect competition. *See* Competition
Incentives
and patents, 12, 177
private, 3, 4, 27–30, 70
relation between social goals and, 4–22
Innovations, timing of, 3, 11–14, 70–93, 177–78
Internal rate of return (IRR) approach, 24, 25
Inventions, categories of, 42–43

Kahneman, D., 153
Kahr, A. S., 150
Kamien, M., 8, 10, 11, 15, 16, 28, 41, 70, 71
Kitch, E., 35, 50, 55, 62, 115, 179
Kitti, C., 11, 22, 32, 50, 51, 72
Knight, F. H., 9
Koenig, G., 96, 99
Krueger, A. O., 50

Laboratories. *See* National laboratories
Lalonde, M., 181
Langlois, R. N., 109, 110, 112
Laws. *See* Trade secret laws
Levin, R. C., 7, 9, 10
Licensing, 3, 32–33
and patents, 4, 6
Life, of patent. *See* Patent, life of
Link, A. M., 181, 182, 183
Litigation. *See* Patent enforcement
Logistic, 127
Loury, G. C., 11, 16, 28, 50

Machlup, F., 41
Mansfield, E., 22, 23, 24, 25, 27, 50
Market-Oriented Program Planning Study, 111
Market penetration, 127, 128, 132, 136
Market structures, 3, 16–17
*Markey, , 98
Moore, P. G., 153
Mueller, D., 26, 27

Murphy, A. G., 153
Muth, John F., 56

National laboratories, 102–21
Near-term civilian technologies, 112
Nelson, R. R., 8, 109, 110, 112
Nordhaus, W., 30, 41, 46, 47, 48, 51, 70, 71, 83
North, W., 150
Nuclear weapons development, 105, 110, 182, 184

Oil. *See* Energy
Optimal life, of patent. *See* Patent, life of
Optimal timing. *See* Timing

Pakes, A., 50
Passive solar home heating. *See* Solar energy
Patent(s)
  alternatives to, 56–63
  criterion for obtaining, 178–79
  effects on private incentives, 3, 27–30
  enforcement, 4, 95–101, 180
  federal policy on, 114–15
  and incentives, 12, 177
  and licensing, 4, 6
  life of, 4, 30–32, 41, 46, 48, 52, 53, 54, 64, 70–93, 178
  and resource allocation, 43–67
Peterson, C. R., 150
Policy, R & D, 173–86
Poole, D., 163
Portfolio analysis, 129–31
Posner, R. A., 46
Private incentives, 3, 4, 27–30, 70
Private R & D, problems in providing, 41–121
Private returns, 3, 4–10, 50
  and agriculture, 20
  analytical model, 10
  and energy, 17
Prizes, 59–61
Productivity, 174
Profit rates, definition of, 26, 27
Project evaluation approach, 125–69
Public R & D, problems in providing, 41–121

Rapoport, J., 23, 24, 25, 27
Rate of returns. *See* Returns
Regression analysis, 4, 26–27
Reinganum, J., 16
Research and development
  benefits of, 175–76
  direct estimation of benefits and costs, 4, 23–26
  evaluation of, 3–36
  national laboratories, 102–21
  policy, 173–86
  project evaluation approach to, 125–69
  resource allocation problem in, 41–67
  returns from, 3, 4–10, 17, 20, 22–27, 50, 176
  uncertainty, incorporating into cost and performance data, 149–69
Research contracts. *See* Contracts
Resource allocation, in R & D, 41–67
Returns, from R & D
  estimating, 4, 22–27, 176
  private, 3, 4–10, 17, 20, 50
  social, 3, 4–10, 17, 20
Reward structure. *See* Incentives
Romeo, A., 23, 24, 25, 27
Rose-Ackerman, S., 51
Ruttan, V., 20

Scherer, F. M., 4, 30, 51, 70, 71, 174, 183
Schmidt, W. E., 91
Schmookler, J., 17
Schumpeter, J. A., 9, 14, 15
Schwartz, , 70, 71
Schwarz, N., 8, 10, 11, 15, 16, 28, 41, 70, 71
Secrecy, 61–63
  see also Trade secret laws
Shankerman, M., 50

Social goals, relation between incentives and, 4–22
Social returns, 3, 4–10, 31
  and agriculture, 20
  analytical model, 10
  and energy, 17
Social value, of variable-life patent, 64–67
Solar energy, 140, 141–43, 144, 145, 146, 147, 148
Solar heat, project evaluation approach, 135
Space exploration, 182, 184
Spetzler, C., 153, 160
Srinivasan, T. N., 50
Stiglitz, J., 7, 11, 15, 16, 17, 50

Tax incentives, 3, 33–34, 181–82, 183
  analytical model, 4, 33–34
Telser, L., 16, 17, 177
Theory of Value, 15
Thomas, H., 153
Tideman, T. N., 51
timing of innovations, 3, 11–14, 70–93, 177–78
  analytical model, 11–14
Tolley, G. S., 17, 19, 35, 36, 136, 175
Townsend, S. B., 136, 175
Trade secret laws, 3, 4, 33, 177, 179–80
  see also Secrecy
Trombe Wall, 142, 145
Tullock, G., 51
Tversky, A., 153

Uncertainty, incorporating into cost and performance data, 149–69, 176
U. S. Atomic Energy Commission (AEC), 102
U. S. Department of Energy (DOE), 102, 103, 105, 107, 109, 111, 112, 115, 184
U. S. Energy Research Advisory Board (ERAB), 103, 104, 120
U. S. Energy Research and Development Administration (ERDA), 102, 105, 107, 111, 112
Usher, D., 50, 51
U. S. Office of Science and Technology Policy (OSTP), 103
U. S. Patent and Trademark Office, 97, 98, 99, 100

Variable-life ptaents, 58, 64–67
von Holstein, C. A. S., 153, 160

Wagner, S., 23, 24, 25, 27
Watters, P., 187
Weapons development, 105, 110, 182, 183
Weitzman, M. L., 58, 60
Williamson, O. E., 9
Willig, R. D., 43
Wilman, John, 17, 19
Winkler, R. L., 153
Wright, B. D., 6, 32, 42, 51, 57, 58, 61, 62, 65

Yu, B. T., 50